Markets and Economic Efficiency

Bruce W. Hamilton
Johns Hopkins University

Academx
Publishing Services

Markets and Economic Efficiency
Copyright © 2005 by Bruce W. Hamilton

Requests for permission to make copies of any part of the work should be mailed to:

Permissions Department
Academx Publishing Services, Inc.
P.O. Box 56527
Virginia Beach, VA 23456
http://www.academx.com

Printed in the United States of America

ISBN: 1-932768-28-9

TABLE OF CONTENTS

Chapter 1
Introduction

Economies, Resources, and Economic Efficiency

An **economy** is a set of institutions, laws, rules, and customs through which we transform a society's **resources** into **material goods and services** for consumers. Ultimately, we measure the success of an economy by its ability to deliver material goods and services to its consumers. For example, we naturally think of the economy of Chad as being less successful than the economy of the United States.

Since an economy's job is to transform resources into goods and services, it is not surprising that economies with richer endowments of resources frequently yield higher standards of living for their citizens than do economies which are poorly endowed. Chad is much poorer than the United States in part because its land is extremely unproductive, its labor force is unhealthy and poorly educated, and it is poorly endowed with physical capital -- plant and equipment, roads, telecommunications, etc.

But an economy's success at producing goods and services for its citizens depends upon more than the resources it has to work with; it also depends critically upon on the **efficiency** with which it transforms inputs into outputs. **Economic efficiency** is one of the central themes of this book. First we will define the concept of efficiency, and then we will ask what it looks like in terms we can relate to. Finally, we will ask how an economy's organization effects its efficiency.

An analogy will help us to see where we are going. Think of an economy as a car; it uses a resource (gasoline) to yield a product desired by a consumer (personal transportation). Our car can deliver more product (a longer trip) if it has more gasoline. But for a **given** amount of gasoline, it can deliver a longer trip if it is more efficient. Even a car with little gasoline can deliver a long trip if it is designed efficiently. And the same is true of economies. Some economies get 5 miles to the gallon, and some get 50. Japan,for example, is poorly endowed with natural resources and manages to produce a very high standard of living. Russia, on the other hand, is perhaps as well endowed with resources as any nation on earth. We can think of Russia as a 5 mpg economy; with such a poorly designed economy, even a huge stock of resources can not go far. And of course Chad has the worst of both worlds; a 5 mpg economy and very few resources.

If we compare standards of living over the world, it appears likely (though hard to measure and prove) that more of the world's poverty is caused by inefficiently organized economies than by a fundamental and unalterable poor endowment of resources. This is why the study of economic efficiency, and what sorts of institutions help to promote economic efficiency, is so important.

The Meaning of Economic Efficiency

Measuring the efficiency of an automobile is fairly straightforward; the greater the car's gas mileage, the greater its efficiency.[1] But economies produce many goods for many people, and we do not have a simple yardstick like gas mileage with which to measure and evaluate efficiency.

In some sense, we would like to say that an economy is more efficient if, for a given stock of resources, it delivers a higher standard of living to its people. But this is pretty vague. So we will use another definition, one that economists have found useful for over 100 years. This definition of efficiency is called **Pareto Optimality** after the 19th century Italian economist Wilfredo Pareto, who first articulated it in 1892:

● **Definition: Pareto Optimalty is a state of the world such that it is impossible to make any consumer better off without making another worse off.**

Before we explore the concept of Pareto optimality to see if it makes any sense, we have to define a couple of terms which are not clear.

First, what do we mean by a "state of the world?" This is simply a listing of all of the consumers in the world and what goods and services they consume. (Don't worry; we do not actually need to write down the list in order for the concept to be useful.)

Second, what do we mean by the notion of consumers being or becoming "better off?" To address this question, we use the concept of an indifference curve.[2] Recall that an indifference curve represents all of the combinations of goods which make a given consumer equally happy. Thus some particular consumer might be equally happy with any of the points along the curve II in Figure 1.1.

Whereas our consumer might be equally happy with all combinations of Gatorade and Flax which lie on curve II, he would be happier still at a point like α. And the point α also lies on an indifference curve; call it JJ. If our consumer is fortunate enough to have a combination of Gatorade and Flax that puts him on indifference curve JJ, he is "better off" than if he were at any point on II. A consumer becomes better off whenever he or she moves to a higher indifference curve.

---

[1] As many students know, it's not that straightforward, even with cars. One way to improve gas mileage, for example, is by reducing a car's size and weight. In the process, of course, we also reduce both passenger room and safety. Many people would not think of such design changes as improvements in efficiency.

[2] For students unfamiliar with indifference curves, refer to the appendix.

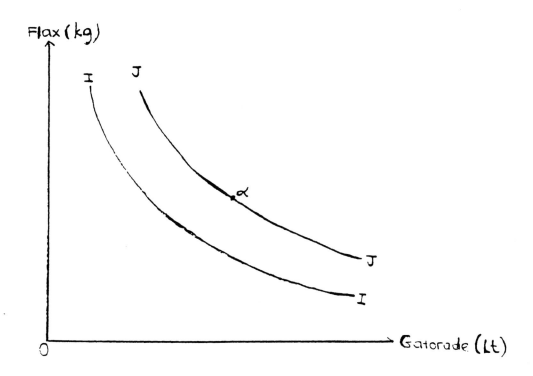

Fig 11.
(Indifference Curves)

The concept of indifference curves gives us a useful way to paraphrase the notion of Pareto optimality. Suppose we contemplate reshuffling society's resources, in hopes of moving one particular consumer to a higher indifference curve. At least in principle, there are a variety of ways we might make one consumer better off. Perhaps some factory is using its resources inefficiently; with the same resources, it can produce more Gatorade. We could give the newfound Gatorade to our target consumer, making him better off. Or maybe some factory is producing neither Gatorade nor Flax but some useless product like college textbooks. We could redirect this factory's resources to the production of either Gatorade or Flax, give the newfound Gatorade or Flax to our favorite consumer, and in the process make him better off. Notice that in both of these examples it was unnecessary to take Flax or Gatorade away from any other consumer in order to improve the lot of our target consumer; we were able to find a way to produce more Gatorade and/or Flax with the resources already at hand.

But finally, through diligent search, suppose we have found all of the malingering factories and all of the textbook factories.[3] There is still one more way to make our favorite consumer better off: Simply confiscate some Gatorade or Flax from another consumer and give it to our friend. Pareto optimality exists when confiscation is the **only possible** way to make one consumer better off.

At first glance, many people find this definition a bit strange; surely if we are in a state of the world from which we can't make anybody better off without hurting somebody else, that is bad news rather than some nirvana of perfect efficiency. But notice that the definition is completely consistent with that which you would apply to our automobile analogy. Once you have received your allocation of gasoline, there are two possible ways to take a longer trip: improve the efficiency of your car or steal gasoline from your neighbor. And when your car is as efficient as possible, the only remaining possibility is to steal from your neighbor (i.e., make your neighbor worse off).

Pareto optimality implies that all of the slack or waste has been eliminated from the system; thus if we have achieved Pareto optimality it is not possible to help a consumer by eliminating waste; there is simply no more waste to be found and eliminated.

Pareto optimality sometimes goes under the synonym of **economic efficiency**; another good phrase which captures its meaning is **absence of waste**. When something is being wasted, it is possible to get something for nothing; simply eliminate the waste and reap the rewards. Lack of Pareto optimality is simply a failure to eliminate waste.

Who's Rich and Who's Poor: What Economic Efficiency Ignores

---

[3]There are other possible sources of economic inefficiency; indeed, these will be the major focus of this book. But for the moment, to illustrate the meaning of efficiency, we will stick to these.

1.4

Economic efficiency is surely a good thing; who do you know that actually approves of waste? But it is important to keep in mind the fact that waste is the only evil that Pareto optimality addresses. In a Pareto inefficient economy (one with textbook factories or malingering Gatorade factories), it is at least possible to help the poor without hurting the rich; we can eliminate the waste and give the proceeds to the poor. But once the waste has been eliminated, there is only one possible remaining way to help the poor; follow the example of Robin Hood and take from the rich.

The world without Robin Hood might be Pareto optimal, and so might the world with Robin Hood. But after Robin Hood the rich are not so rich and the poor not so poor. When we are discussing economic efficiency, it is important always to remember that we are addressing only the evil of waste. Elimination of waste may or may not help to eliminate poverty. The notion of Pareto optimality is blind to this question. In effect, achievement of Pareto optimality means acquiring the biggest possible pie. But efficiency says nothing about who gets the pie.

Chapter 2
Efficiency Among Consumers

We will begin by ignoring an aspect of efficiency which may appear to be the centerpiece of the whole notion. We will ignore the whole question of efficiency in production.[1] For better or for worse, society's factories have produced some specific combination of Gatorade and Flax, and by some method each consumer has been given an allotment of G and F. For the moment we won't even say where the consumers got their Gatorade and Flax. By stripping away the issue of production, we can concentrate on one important portion of the Pareto optimality question:

● **When is it possible to make one consumer better off without hurting any others, simply by reshuffling a given stock of consumer goods?**

We can simplify the problem even more by dealing only with two consumers at a time, and with only two goods.[2] In Figure 2.1a we see that Blanche has 15.5 liters of Gatorade and 5.5 kg of Flax. Otto, in Figure 2.1b, has the same amount of each good. So between the two of them, there are 31 liters of Gatorade and 11 kg of Flax. We now pose the following question: Is there a way to re-allocate the stock of 31 liters of Gatorade and 11 kg of Flax so as to make Blanche better off without harming Otto?

A little reflection will reveal that we can't answer this question unless we know a bit about Blanche and Otto.

Suppose Blanche really likes Flax and is not particularly fond of Gatorade; Otto is her opposite. He loves Gatorade and has only a passing interest in Flax. Surely they will both be happier (on higher indifference curves) if Otto gives up some of his flax for some of Blanche's Gatorade. In particular, there is definitely a deal to be made which would leave Blanche better off and not hurt Otto. The original allocation of Gatorade and Flax was wasteful. Quite literally, all that Gatorade was wasted on Blanche, as was the Flax on Otto.

But now suppose that Blanche started out with 10 liters of Gatorade (to Otto's 21) and Otto started out with 3 kg of Flax (to Blanche's 8). Is it still possible to find a deal which helps at least one of them and does not hurt the other one? Intuitively, the answer ought to depend on the strength of Blanche's preference for Flax, and the strength of Otto's preference for Gatorade. It could be that at 21 liters Otto has lost some of his enthusiasm for Gatorade.

---

[1]We will return to the important topic of production efficiency in Chapter 3.

[2]Shortly we will show that everything we say about two consumers is also true when we recognize that there are more than two consumers in the world. Similarly, everything we say is true when we recognize that there are more than two goods.

It turns out that the added information we need about Blanche and Otto is precisely the information that is carried in their indifference curves. Once we know the shapes of their indifference curves we know the strength of their respective preferences for Flax and Gatorade. So let's return to the original problem (in which Blanche and Otto each have 15.5 liters of Gatorade and 5.5 kg of flax) and see how much more we can learn by using their indifference curves.

Blanche, as we recall, is a Flax lover; and Otto is the same to Gatorade. Our first task is to figure out how to draw indifference curves to reflect these preferences. We'll mark the original endowment (15.5 G; 5.5 F) as point i on Figures 2.2a and 2.2b. Blanche's love of Flax is represented by a relatively flat indifference curve at point i. This flatness means that she is willing to give up quite a bit of Gatorade to get one more unit of Flax. The two arms of the triangle beginning at i labelled ΔG and ΔF are of respective lengths 5 and 1. This tells us that, beginning at point i, Blanche is willing to give up 5 liters (out of her 15.5) of Gatorade to get 1 more unit of Flax.

From the same starting point, i, Otto is only willing to give up one unit of Gatorade for one unit of Flax. Gatorade is more desirable to Otto, and thus he is less willing to part with it in exchange for Flax.

- Exercise 2.1: On a sheet of graph paper, draw a pair of axes, and label the vertical axis x_1 and the horizontal x_2. Pick a point depicting a positive amount of both x_1 and x_2.
  i. Draw an indifference curve through this point which shows that the consumer has a relatively strong desire for x_1. (He should be willing to give up a lot of x_2 in order to gain a little x_1.)
  ii. Now trace along this indifference curve in a "northwesterly" direction, giving the consumer more x_1 and less x_2. As you move in this direction, what happens to the consumer's relative desire for x_1?

If you drew your indifference curve with the "right" curvature, it became steeper as it approached the x_1 axis. And the steeper the curve, the more x_1 our consumer is willing to give up in order to get more x_2. Even an x_1 lover can eventually get so much x_1 that x_2 starts to look good.

Notice in Exercise 2.1 that the indifference curves are indeed **curves**; for both Otto and Blanche, the indifference curve gets steeper as it gets closer to the y axis. When Otto finds himself near the y axis, with lots of Flax and not much Gatorade, his relative craving for Gatorade is even stronger than when he has a relatively abundant stock of Gatorade; thus his indifference curve is even steeper (remember that a steep indifference curve reflects a strong desire for the good on the x axis). Even Blanche, when she becomes sufficiently Gatorade-deprived, has the steeper indifference curve of one who is reluctant to part with more Gatorade.

Mutually Beneficial Trades

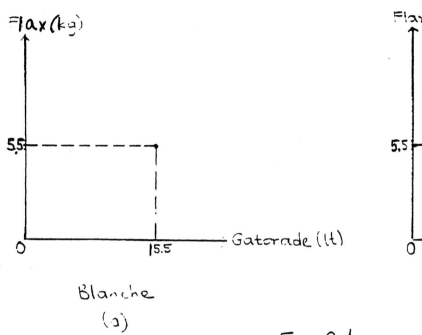

Blanche

(a)

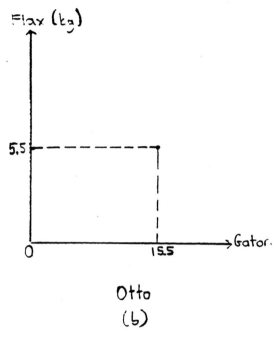

Otto

(b)

Fig. 2.1

So long as opportunities remain for our two consumers to trade to their mutual benefit, the condition of economic efficiency has not been achieved. Let's see what such a state of the world looks like when we use indifference curves. Figure 2.3 reproduces the indifference curves of Figure 2.2, and as in Figure 2.2, both consumers begin life at **i**. Blanche now offers a **deal**, or trade, to Otto. In particular, she proposes to give up a specific portion of her Gatorade, labeled ΔG in Figure 2.3a,[3] in exchange for a specific portion, ΔF, of Otto's Flax. The deal she proposes leaves her on the same indifference curve that she was on at point **i**, so she does not care whether Otto accepts her deal or not.

We now plot the same trade on Otto's graph, to see whether he will find it acceptable. The same ΔG which Blanche gives up is **added** to Otto's stock (if he accepts the trade, that is). So, whereas Blanche moves to the left by the amount ΔG, Otto moves to the right ΔG. Similarly, Blanche's proposed deal will increase her holding of Flax, moving her up ΔF in Figure 2.3a. This increase comes out of Otto's flax stock, so he moves down ΔF. Notice that Otto's Δ's are exactly equal to Blanche's, except that Blanche's positive Δ's become negative Δ's for Otto, and vice versa. That's what makes them trades.

In general, we can depict a proposed trade by a move to the **left** and **up** for one consumer, and an **equal** move to the **right** and **down** for the other consumer. So from any starting point we can sketch out a deal in a pair of graphs like Figures 2.3a and 2.3b. And after sketching out the deal itself, we can see whether the consumers will like it.

As it turns out, the specific deal proposed by Blanche in Figure 2.3a is very attractive to Otto. Blanche's deal moves Otto from point **i** in Figure 2.3b to point **ii**. As we can see, Otto moves to a higher indifference curve; thus he accepts Blanche's offer.

All of this proves that the initial allocation, at which Blanche and Otto are both at point i, is not economically efficient; we have found a way to make one consumer better off without making any other consumer worse off. (We know that Blanche is not worse off, and as no other consumers are involved in the trade, they are not worse off either.)

Before moving on, it is important to develop these notions a little more fully; we will do that through the following exercises. The easiest way to do the exercises is to trace or copy Figure 2.3 and work from your copy.

● Exercise 2.2: In the trade which Blanche proposed above, Otto moved to a higher indifference curve but Blanche did not. If Blanche had been a tougher negotiator, she could have formulated a proposal which would have made her better off but left Otto no better off than before. Draw a trade (a ΔF and a ΔG for Blanche which are precisely offset by opposite values of ΔF and a ΔG for Otto) in which Blanche is the only one who

---

[3]We'll have to remember that for Blanche ΔG is negative; that is, she is proposing to give it up.

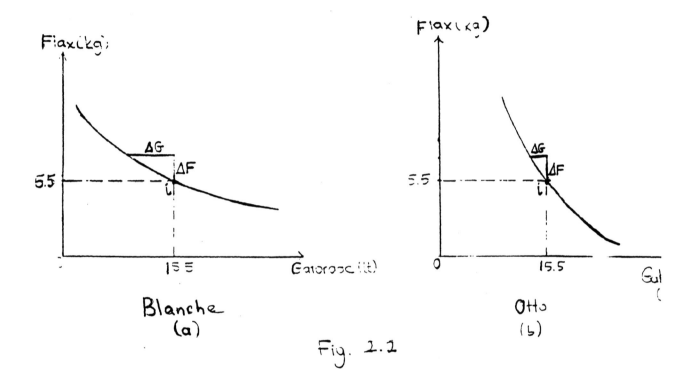

Blanche
(a)

Otto
(b)

Fig. 2.1

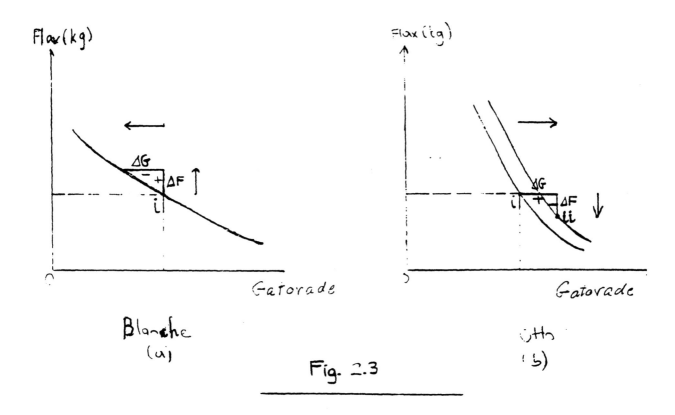

Fig. 2.3

gains from the trade. (But check to make sure that Otto will accept the trade. Also check to make sure it really is a **trade**; Blanche's gain is Otto's loss and *vice versa*.)

- Exercise 2.3: Again, start both consumers at point **i**, and devise a trade which moves **both** of them to higher indifference curves.

- Exercise 2.4: Once again start both consumers at point **i**. Now suppose that Blanche proposes a trade in which she gives some of her Flax to Otto in exchange for some of his Gatorade. Is it possible to carry out such a trade without hurting at least one of the consumers?

- Exercise 2.5: The trade which we described in the text (Blanche gets ΔF from Otto, and in exchange Otto gets ΔG from Blanche) left Blanche indifferent and Otto better off. And as we discussed, this was possible because of the shapes of the two consumers' indifference curves at point **i**. Your task is to assign Otto a new personality, which you do by re-drawing his indifference curve (Recall that he has a whole set of indifference curves; for this exercise, however, you only need to draw one of them).

i. First, give Otto an indifference curve (a new personality) which would leave him just indifferent to Blache's $\Delta G;\Delta F$ proposal from Figure 2.3a.
ii. Next, give Otto an indifference curve that would cause him to reject Blanche's $\Delta G;\Delta F$ proposal. In redrawing Otto's indifference curves, in what way have you transformed his personality? (Have you made him more of a Flax lover, more of a Gatorade lover, or what?)

Return now to Figure 2.3. We can see intuitively that Blanche's proposed deal $\Delta G;\Delta F$ makes Otto better off without hurting her because at point **i** where both consumers are starting, Blanche's indifference curve is flatter than Otto's. (In Exercise 2.5 you went through two stages of flattening Otto's indifference curve through **i**. In 2.5i, Otto's indifference curve took on the same slope as Blanche's; in 2.5ii, Otto's became flatter than Blanche's.)

In order to gain more insight into the problem, we now need to be mathematically specific about the meaning of the indifference curve's slope. Recalling that the slope is equal to "the rise over the run," we can express the slope of Blanche's indifference curve at point **i** as $\Delta F/\Delta G$, which is $1/(-5) = -.2$. By contrast, at point **i**, the slope of Otto's indifference curve is $(-2)/2 = -1$.

The slope of a consumer's indifference curve precisely expresses the terms under which he or she is willing to exchange one good for another. Blanche is willing to exchange .4 Flax for 1 Gatorade; Otto is willing to exchange 1 for 1.[4]

---

[4]Since indifference curves are truly curved, it is not literally correct to say that the slope of Blanche's indifference curve "at point i" is $\Delta F/\Delta G$. The slope continually changes as we move along the curve. $\Delta F/\Delta G$ is the average value of the slope

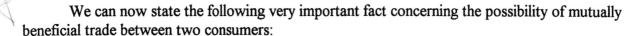

We can now state the following very important fact concerning the possibility of mutually beneficial trade between two consumers:

- Fact 2.1: If two consumers are currently at points **i** and **ii** (on their respective indifference curves), it is possible to find a trade which helps one of them without hurting the other only if the slopes of their respective indifference curves at **i** and **ii** are different. However, if the slopes of the indifference curves at **i** and **ii** are the same, then it is impossible to find a trade which helps one without harming the other.

Fact 2.1 is of central importance in this book; if you understand it thoroughly, much of the rest of the book will readily make sense; if you do not understand it, the rest of the book will make no sense at all. And perhaps the best way to understand it is to try to prove that it is wrong:

- Exercise 2.6: Turn to Figure 2.4, which depicts the starting point of Fact 2.1; Consumer **A** has the consumption combination, or bundle, labeled **i** in Figure 2.4a; Consumer **B** has the bundle labeled **ii** in Figure 2.4b. Copy 2.4a and 2.4b onto separate sheets of paper which are thin enough to see through.

i. Draw an indifference curve (anything that's downward sloping and properly curved) through **i** on Figure 2.4a. Line up this graph with Figure 2.4b by placing point **i directly** beneath point **ii** in Figure 2.4b, and then trace the same indifference curve onto Figure 2.4b (and so that the axes of the two graphs point the same way). Now try to find a trade which makes Consumer A better off without making B worse off. If you drew your indifference curves correctly, you will find that it is impossible to devise such a trade. The reason is that you have drawn the slope of **A**'s indifference curve at **i** equal to the slope of **B**'s indifference curve at **ii**.

ii. Now give Consumer **B** a personality transformation; rotate his indifference curve through **ii** so as to make it flatter. Verify that it now is possible to find a trade which makes one of the consumers better off without hurting the other one.

Fact 2.1 gives us a description of one important component of economic efficiency:

- Corollary to Fact 2.1: The following must be true if we are in a state of economic efficiency or Pareto optimality: The slope of every consumer's indifference curve, measured at his or her actual consumption bundle, must be the same as that for all other consumers.

In Exercise 2.6i, you were asked to depict the facts as described in the Corollary to Fact

---

over the interval from i to ii. Students concerned about this technical point should think of the trades we describe in this book as being quite small; that way the average slope over the interval is almost the same thing as the slope at the point i.

2.1; at points **i** and **ii** respectively, you drew the slopes of the two consumers' indifference curves the same (that's what the tracing should have done). And in 2.6i we found no inefficiency; it was impossible to improve the lot of one consumer without harming the other. In 2.6ii, the starting point was inefficient; there was a way to do better, and it would have been wasteful for the consumers to stay at points **i, ii**.

Fact 2.1 and its Corollary state that there is economic waste so long as there are two consumers anywhere in the world whose indifference curves at their points of consumption (i.e., points like **i** and **ii** above) are different. If two such consumers exist it is possible to make at least one of them better off (and probably both) without increasing production or finding and using more resources. They can be made better off simply by letting them trade the goods they already have. If we fail to exploit such an opportunity, we are wasting some of the world's resources.

The Economy's First Task: Efficient Distribution of Goods

We stated above that Fact 2.1 is very important. It is important because it helps us to understand one of the crucial tasks we would like an economy to perform. Assuming we want our economy to minimize waste, we can now give our economy the following assignment:

● Assignment 2.1: To the extent possible, distribute the world's goods and services in such a way that all consumers' indifference curves' slopes (measured at the point of actual consumption) are the same.

The assignment looks absolutely overwhelming. Suppose you try to carry out Assignment 2.1 just among students in your class. It would seem necessary to interview all of your classmates, to propose trades with all of them, and if a trade is made repeat the process to see if the first round of trading opened up new trading opportunities. And carrying out all of these trades among your classmates is just a tiny beginning; there are over 5 billion people in the world, and that's a lot of interviewing.

Hoping you are suitably impressed with the enormity of the task, we now ask how the Assignment is approached by a market economy.

Consumers in a Market Economy

{In this section we will discuss the basics of the theory of consumer behavior in a market economy, culminating in the tangency between a budget constraint and an indifference curve. Students completely familiar with this concept can skip to ___; students with some familiarity should read this section. Students who are uneasy about budget constraints and indifference curves should turn to the Appendix and then return to this section.}

In terms of material goods, a consumer's objective is to get to the highest indifference curve possible. Indifference curves are like contour lines on a topographic map, and a consumer can be thought of as a mountain climber. He doesn't care where he is on any one contour line; all

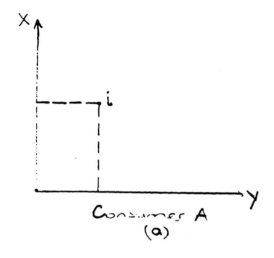

Consumer A
(a)

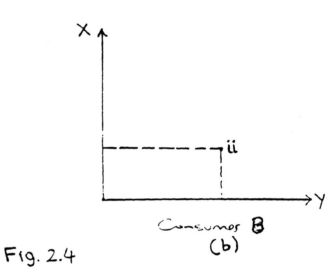

Consumer B
(b)

Fig. 2.4

he cares about is getting on the highest possible contour line. He can go as high as his budget will take him.

As discussed in the Appendix, we use the **budget constraint** to delineate all of the combinations of goods that a consumer can afford. Return to Blanche, who consumes only Flax and Gatorade. When we last met her we did not say **how** she got that original allotment of Flax and Gatorade; it evidently just appeared on her doorstep. But now we'll put Blanche in a market economy and give her a specified amount of income (later in the book we'll tell you where her income comes from). Now instead of finding Flax and Gatorade on her doorstep, she uses her income to buy it. The first step in figuring out how much she'll buy is to figure out how much she can afford. And to answer that we need to know the prices of Flax and Gatorade.

For the moment, we'll simply make up values for the prices of Flax and Gatorade (as with Blanche's income, later in the book we will tell you where these prices come from in a market economy.) We will call the price of Flax P_F and the price of Gatorade P_G. Blanche's budget constraint is shown in Figure 2.5a. Its vertical intercept is Y/P_F; if she spends her entire income on Flax she can afford Y/P_F. The horizontal intercept is Y/P_G; if she spends all her income on Gatorade she can afford Y/P_G. Finally, the slope of the budget constraint is $-P_G/P_F$, minus the ratio of the two prices.[5]

Blanche wants to get on the highest possible indifference curve but can only afford points on the triangle below her budget constraint. Whereas her indifference curve labelled 4 would be nice (and other indifference curves higher than 4 would be nicer still), she doesn't have enough income to reach 4. The highest one she can reach (i.e., afford) is 3.[6] Blanche chooses the only point on Indifference Curve 3 that she can afford, which we have labeled *.

For our purposes, the crucial feature of the point Blanche chooses, point *, is that it is **tangent** to the budget constraint. We know this (tangency) must be true of *; if it were not tangent it would have to cut the budget constraint, like ** on Indifference curve 2. The very fact that curve 2 cuts the budget constraint ensures that there is another higher indifference curve that touches the budget constraint. And the very fact that curve 3 is tangent to the budget constraint

---

[5]If you are not clear on the interpretation of the slope and the intercepts of the budget constraint, turn to the Appendix, pp.____. Also, as suggested in the Appendix, make up some numbers, such as Y = $100, P_F = $2/kg, P_G = $4/liter. Then plot all the combinations that Blanche can afford, and check to see that the intercepts and slope are what they should be.

[6]Don't be fooled by the numbering of these indifference curves; they are designated with numbers just for convenience. Blanche has countless indifference curves (not shown) between curves 3 and 4, just as there are a countless number of contours on a map. The map may only show contours for 1000 and 2000 feet, but on the mountain itself there is a contour at 1056.73 feet.

ensures that none of Blanche's higher indifference curves can touch the budget constraint.

Now we know that Blanche's chosen point, *, lies at a point on an indifference curve which is tangent to the budget constraint. From this we know that her point * **has the same slope as the budget constraint**. Now it's time to return to Otto.

Like Blanche, Otto receives some income (from a source to be specified later). He may receive more or less than Blanche; we needn't worry about that. And like Blanche, he buys Gatorade at price P_G and Flax at price P_F. His budget constraint is drawn in Figure 2.5b. Like Blanche's, the slope of his budget constraint is $-P_G/P_F$. The best point he can afford is labelled ☺. And just like * for Blanche, Otto's indifference curve at ☺ has a slope of $-P_G/P_F$.

At this point something truly remarkable has happened: Otto and Blanche, by the mere fact of facing the same price for Flax, and the same price for Gatorade, necessarily end up at points on their respective indifference curves with identical slopes. Both * and ☺ lie on indifference curves with slopes equal to $-P_G/P_F$.[7]

Therefore, Otto and Blanche do not need to interview one another to see whether they can strike a mutually beneficial bargain. Blanche and Otto do not even need to know of one another's existence; each can rest assured that, if the other does exist, Flax and Gatorade are allocated efficiently between them.

What is true for Otto and Blanche is true for all pairs of consumers, so long as prices do not vary from one consumer to another. Furthermore, what is true for Flax and Gatorade is true for all pairs of goods. Blanche and Otto need not bargain over Flax and Gatorade, or automobiles and shoes, or anything else which is bought and sold in the market economy. This brings us to the second crucial fact in this Chapter:

• Fact 2.2: So long as all consumers face the same prices when they purchase goods, the goods will be allocated among consumers efficiently. That is, there will be no possible way to re-allocate the goods among consumers, making one consumer better off, except by making at least one other consumer worse off.

This is an astonishing and remarkable fact. Without anybody trying to do so, the institutions of the market economy tend to bring about a completely waste-free allocation of goods among consumers.

Of course, there is a big "IF," which we will discuss later: The remarkable conclusion only follows IF all consumers face the same prices. If Blanche can get her Flax at a better price than

---

[7]To repeat a point we have made before, the indifference curves are truly curved; when we say that the slopes of Blanche's and Otto's indifference curves are identical, this statement is true only at the points of consumption, * and ☺, for Blanche and Otto.

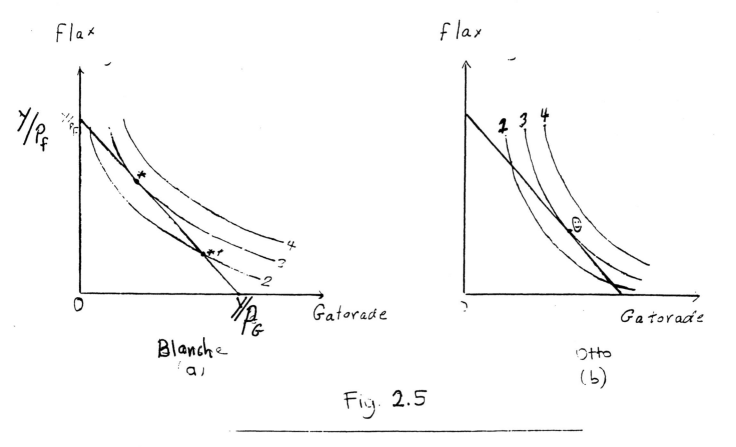

Fig. 2.5

Otto, her budget constraint will have a different slope from Otto's, as will her indifference curve at the point of her consumption. After both do their shopping there's still room for a trade, because they didn't face the same prices. We will return to this big "IF" several times later in this book. But for the moment stick with the assumption that all consumers do face the same prices.

The price mechanism allocates most of the Gatorade to the Gatorade lovers and most of the Flax to the Flax lovers, for the simple reason that, when faced with the choice and the price, the Gatorade lovers will leave most of the Flax to the Flax lovers. And to repeat a point we made above, the consumers of the world never even have to meet one another in order to bring about this result.

- Exercise 2.7: Imagine that you have just walked out of a grocery store after shopping; the groceries are still in your shopping cart. A fellow grocer approaches you and suggests that you both look through both grocery carts to see if you might want to swap some groceries. You know nothing about this fellow-shopper except that his indifference curves slope downward and are bowed in toward the origin. Explain to your fellow grocer why he is wastign his time.

- Exercise 2.8: In Alaska, both Flax and Gatorade cost twice as much as in the Lower 48. An Alaskan just arrived in San Francisco and for some reason brought his stock of Gatorade and Flax with him. You, on the other hand, just stocked up in San Francisco. Do you think you and the Alaskan might be able to strike a mutually beneficial trade? Why or Why not? Hint: Study the slopes of the budget constraints.

But It Doesn't Really Work That Way

According to Fact 2.2 above, all potential waste among consumers is eliminated by the "fact" that every consumer faces the same prices as every other consumer. But simple observation tells us that prices of individual commodities vary from store to store, from city to city, from country to country, and even by time of day. Does this mean that Fact 2.2 is just an abstraction with no applicability to the real world? And for that matter, is there any reason to believe that there is any tendency for a given commodity to sell at the same price in all times and places? We will explore both of these questions briefly here, and return to them several times later in the book.

Arbitrage and Comparison Shopping

Suppose that Gatorade sells at a much higher price in City A than City B. This price "spread" creates an opportunity for an entrepreneur to make a profit by buying in City B and selling in A. Making money from a price spread such as this is called **arbitrage**. Since we can assume the world is full of people who would like to make a profit, it follows that the world is full of entrepreneurs who are seeking out these **arbitrage opportunities**.

Whereas arbitrageurs make their money from a price spread (buy cheap and sell dear), their own profit-seeking actions tend to eliminate the price spread. If many arbitrageurs buy Gatorade in City B and sell it in City A, eventually A will run low on Gatorade, and the price there will rise. And B, newly awash in arbitrageur-supplied Gatorade, will see the price fall. Arbitrage is a powerful force which tends to eliminate price spreads, and as a side effect enhances the efficiency with which goods are allocated to consumers.

On a much less grand scale, comparison shopping accomplishes the same thing as arbitrage. If there are two gasoline stations, one charging $1.05 and one charging $1.10, consumers are much more likely to buy from the one charging $1.05. Eventually the one charging $1.10 is likely to be forced to reduce his price.

Often, however, price spreads are not reduced or eliminated by arbitrage or comparison shopping. It is instructive to inquire why arbitrage does not work in these circumstances. We will explore a few instances below.

Time-of-Day Price Variation

Telephone calls are cheaper at night than in daytime. And movies are frequently cheaper mid-day than at night. Is this a failure of the equal-price principle that is required to ensure efficiency? Interestingly, we can see the answer to this question by asking whether these time-of-day price spreads create arbitrage or comparison shopping opportunities.

Look first at movie tickets. Suppose matinee tickets sell for $1 and evening tickets sell for $5. I know that 100 people in my apartment complex are planning to go to the movie this Saturday night. I buy 100 Saturday matinee tickets and offer them to my neighbors for $3. They are not interested; they want to go at night. In the eyes of these consumers matinee and night tickets are simply **not the same commodity**. The afternoon and evening movie tickets are not identical in the sense that two bottles of Gatorade are identical. Therefore the premise of equal prices, underlying Fact 2.2, is not violated by this example.

It is clear that the same can be said of telephone pricing. Stock brokers and bankers are not willing to buy night-time phone calls from an arbitrageur, nor are they prepared to comparison shop and make their calls at night. Comparison shopping forces similar prices between AT&T and Sprint, but not between day and night calls.

Geographic Price Variation

Oranges are cheaper in Florida than in Alaska; does this violate the equal-prices premise underlying Fact 2.2? Again, ask whether an arbitrageur could make money, or whether consumers have an incentive to comparison shop.

In particular, imagine an arbitrageur who goes to an Alaskan who pays $15/lb for oranges and says, "I'll sell you oranges for $12/pound. Of course, the oranges I agree to sell to you are in

Florida." The Alaskan does not accept this offer; an orange in Florida is not the same thing as an orange in Alaska.

Students who have travelled in foreign countries know that the prices of some familiar goods vary from country to country. Some of this variation is driven by cost differences, like the Alaska Orange example above. But some international price variation is brought about by government policies such as tariffs and other import restrictions or sales taxes. Thus for example, the price of gasoline in most European countries is approximately 4 times what it is in the United States, because these countries levy a huge gasoline sales tax.

Why don't arbitrageurs make money on the spread between the European and American prices of gasoline (and in the process eliminate the spread)? The answer is pretty clear: In this particular setting, arbitrage goes under the name of "smuggling," and European customs officers prevent arbitrageurs from carrying out their work. When price spreads of this sort exist, they do indeed lead to an inefficient allocation of the world's goods among consumers.

- Exercise 2.9: Divide the array of consumer goods into two: G (for Gasoline), and E (for Everything Else). The price of E is $1 in both the United States and France. But the price of G is $1 in the United States and $5 in France. Ignore the fact that it is costly to ship gasoline between the U.S. and France (suppose you can fax it). Using indifference curves, sketch out a possible mutually beneficial transaction between an American and a Frenchman.

Exercise 2.9 reveals a concept which we will explore more thoroughly in Chapter 10: When governments levy taxes, the efficiency of allocation of goods is damaged.

- Exercise 2.10: Each year The Economist gives a list of Big Mac prices for various countries (all converted into dollars at the official exchange rate). Below is their "Hamburger Standard" for 1994:

Country	Price	Country	Price	Country	Price
USA	2.30	Denmark	3.85	Mexico	2.41
Argentina	3.60	France	3.17	Poland	1.40
Australia	2.84	Germany	2.69	Portugal	2.53
Belgium	3.10	Greece	2.47	Russia	1.66
Brazil	1.58	Holland	2.85	Singapore	1.90
Britain	2.65	Hong Kong	1.19	S. Korea	2.84
Canada	2.06	Hungary	1.66	Spain	2.50
Chile	2.28	Italy	2.77	Sweden	3.20
China	1.03	Japan	3.77	Switz.	3.96
Czech Rep	1.71	Malaysia	1.40	Taiwan	2.35

i.   Does the international "spread" in Big Mac prices strike you as "large" or "small?"

ii.   Do you think that either arbitrage or comparison shopping tend to equalize Big Mac prices across countries?

iii. Can you think of any other economic forces which might tend to equalize Big Mac prices across countries?

iv.   Do you think that the price variation represented in this table reflects a failure of economic efficiency, or is it just that Burger Kings in different countries are "different goods?"

But There are not Just Two Commodities

In all of our graphs there were only two commodities; we pretended for example that Blanche and Otto spent their entire incomes on Flax and Gatorade. How do we deal with the obvious fact that we choose not among two, but among literally thousands of commodities?

In fact, we restricted our examples to two commodities for only one reason: there are only two dimensions on a piece of paper. A graph on a sheet of paper has only x and y coordinates, and thus we cannot physically draw either indifference curves or budget constraints depicting three or more goods. We can depict these concepts using fairly straightforward algebra, and in advanced economics courses that is what we do. But until you get to those advanced treatments, we ask you to accept the following as an act of faith:

●   Everything that we have stated regarding economies with two commodties carries over directly, with no change in the important conclusions, to three or more commodities.

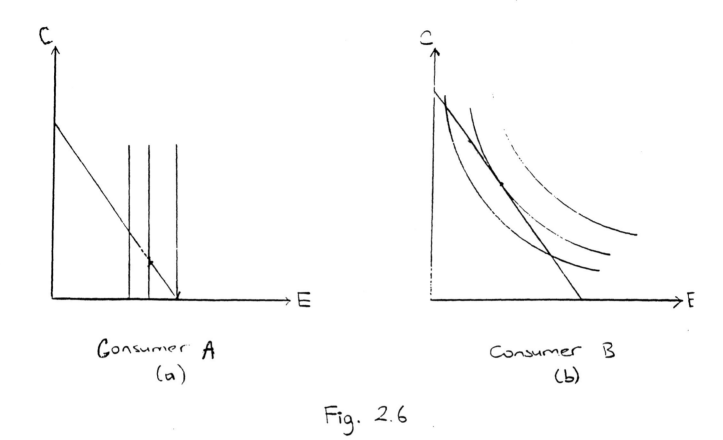

Consumer A
(a)

Consumer B
(b)

Fig. 2.6

To keep our thinking straight it is frequently useful to perform the mental exercise we used in Exercise 2.9 above: If we are particularly interested in one commodity, say Gasoline, then we specify the commodities as being Gasoline on the one hand and Everything Else on the other. This is a useful trick that we will employ several times in this book.

What if There is Some Commodity that I do not Cosume at All?

The two commodities are cigarettes (C) and Everything Else (E) Two consumers' budget constraints and highest attainable indifference curves are shown below, in Figures 2.6a and 2.6b.

- Exercise 2.10: One of the consumers in Figure 2.6 enjoys smoking; the other is adamantly opposed to smoking. Figure out which consumer is the non-smoker and verify that the indifference curve is drawn correctly.

- Exercise 2.11: Trace the indifference curves from Figure 2.x, and highlight the points of consumption that both consumers choose. But do not draw in the budget constraints.
  i. Is there a way for these two consumers to trade so as to make one better off without hurting the other? Therefore, is the current allocation of C and E between the two consumers efficient?
  ii. At the points of consumption, are the slopes of the two consumers' indifference curves the same?

In this case, when C and E are allocated efficiently between the two consumers the slopes of their indifference curves are not equal (contrary to the assertion of Fact 2.1). But it remains true that the commodities are allocated efficiently so long as both consumers face the same prices. Thus the more important of the two highlighted Facts of this chapter is unchanged when a consumer consumes none of one of the available goods. For the remainder of the book we will assume that each consumer consumes some of all (both) goods. But it is important to remember that all of the important facts remain true even when consumers do not consume all of the goods.

Conclusion

In this chapter we have seen three important things:

- A given total stock of goods is distributed efficiently among consumers **only** if, at the point of actual consumption, all consumers' indifference curves have the same slope.[8]

If this condition is violated, then it is possible to redistribute society's goods in such a way

---

[8]Recall that this statement needs to be modified, though not in an important way, if some consumers do not consume all of the available goods.

as to make at least one consumer better off without harming anybody else. And if such a possibility exists, it is wasteful to leave the opportunity unexploited.

- So long as all consumers face the same prices for the various goods produced by the economy, their own selfish optimizing behavior will lead them to points of equal slope on their respective indifference curves.

So long as all budget constraints have the same slope (that is; so long as all consumers face the same prices), the desire of consumers to get on the highest possible indifference curve ensures efficiency in the allocaton of goods to consumers. Thus the mere fact (if indeed it is a fact) that all consumers face the same prices is enough to ensure that consumer goods are distributed in a completely waste-free (efficient) manner.

- Arbitrage and comparison shopping are powerful forces which tend to ensure that all consumers face the same prices for all goods.

If different consumers do face different prices for the same good, this creates an opportunity for an arbitrageur to make money on the "spread" between the high and low prices. The very act of making money on the spread tends to eliminate the spread itself.

Collectively, these three facts tell us that in a market economy with prices, there are potent forces constantly at work which tend to eliminate any waste in the allocation of goods to consumers. It would be foolish to claim that all waste among consumers is eliminated, even in the most smoothly operating market economy. Nevertheless, the forces at work through the price system do a remarkable job of fostering economic efficiency.

A Note Before Moving On

In virtually all of the remaining chapters of this book, we will use the analytical tools developed in Chapter 2. We will repeatedly see trade triangles of the type introduced in Figure 2.2 and 2.3 and lines whose slope is a price ratio, like the budget constraints of Figure 2.5. We will see effiiciency when slopes are equal and waste or inefficiency when they are not. We will see many instances of prices tending to equalize these important slopes, and in the process fostering economic efficiency. But we will also see many instances in which prices fail to equalize important slopes, and thus foster inefficiency and waste.

In some sense, much of the remainder of the book is little more than a repitition of Chapter 2, applied to different settings. Therefore, you will find it **much** easier to understand the rest of the book if you take the time to thoroughly understand Chapter 2.

Chapter 3
Production

In Chapter 2, society's stock of Gatorade and Flax was just "there." We did not say anything about where it came from or who produced it.

But in reality consumer goods are produced by people using resources, and they can be produced either efficiently or inefficiently. In this chapter we will begin to explore the question of efficient resource use.   As in Chapter 2, we will again keep the problem focused by pretending that society produces only two goods. For a change of pace, the two goods will be Corn and Wheat. And to streamline the problem still further, for the moment we will assume that both Corn and Wheat are produced with only one resource: Land.

The specific concern of this Chapter is: **How much Corn, and how much Wheat, will society produce?**

The first thing to do in addressing this question is to see what our options are; what combinations of Corn and Wheat **can** be produced, given the land and the rainfall in the various regions of the country? In order to answer this question we must build up the **Production Possibilities curve**, a curve showing all of the combinations of Corn and Wheat which could possibly be produced, given the distribution of land and rainfall in the nation.

Table 3.1 gives the maximum amount of Corn, and the maximum amount of Wheat, that each of 10 States (A through J) in the United States can produce. For example, if all land in State A is planted to Corn, it will yield 100 bushels; if instead the same state is planted in Wheat, the yield will be 50 bushels.

Table 3.1
Maximum Corn and Wheat
Production for Ten States[1]

State	Corn	Wheat	Corn/Wheat $(-\Delta C/\Delta W)$
A	100	50	2.00
B	35	30	1.17
C	15	80	0.19
D	90	90	1.00
E	250	100	2.50
F	50	100	0.50
G	200	40	5.00
H	3	60	0.05
I	400	60	6.67
J	175	60	2.92
TOTAL	1318	670	

For each state the Corn-column entry gives the total Corn that could be grown in that state if the state grew nothing but corn; the Wheat-column entry shows the same thing for wheat. The TOTAL entry for Corn (1318) shows the amount of Corn that could be grown in the country if every State were planted just in Corn. If the etire country were planted in Wheat the total yield would be 670.

●   ☆Exercise 3.1[2]: Making a Production Possibilities Curve (first try). Make a graph with

---

[1]The numbers are made up. We could make up numbers for all 50 States but it would get very tedious and we would not learn any more than we will from 10 States. So we will assume that these ten States make up the entire nation.

[2]The easiest way to do Exercise 3.1 and most of the succeeding exercises in this chapter is to use a spreadsheet. Begin by entering the data from Table 3.1 onto a spreadsheet, and then ask the computer to perform the various arithmetical and graphical operations which are called for in

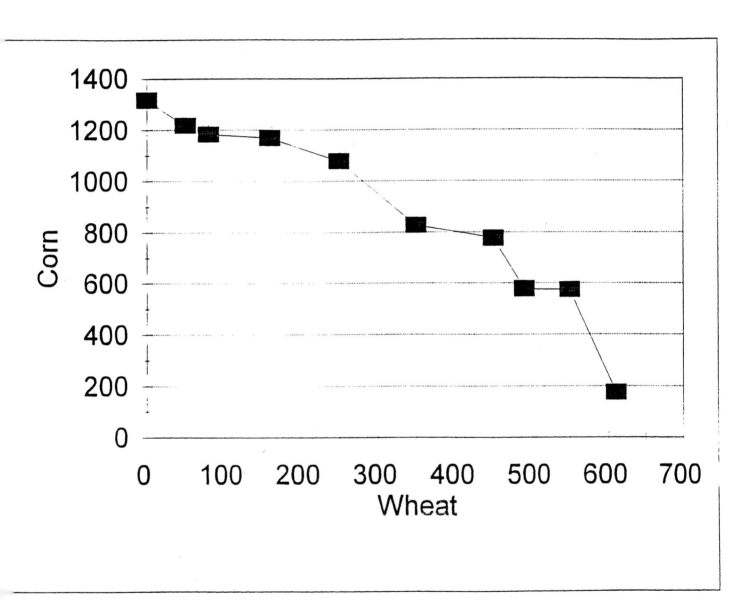

Figure 3.1a
"Production Possibilities"
(States Assigned Alphabetically)

Corn on the y axis and Wheat on the x axis. The Corn axis must run from 0 to at least 1400 and Wheat from 0 to 700. Begin by assigning all of the States to Corn production (indicate the point (0,1318) on the graph). Next plot the nation's total output of Corn and Wheat if you pull state A out of Corn production and put it in Wheat production. (You should get (50,1218) on your graph). Now, one at a time, add the other states to wheat production on the graph. (In step 2, states A and B are producing Wheat; in Step 3, A, B, and C are producing Wheat, etc).

All of the combinations of Corn and Wheat production you have depicted on the graph are possible; no State's capability is being used twice or assigned a production "quota" that it cannot achieve. So what you have constructed **could** be a production possibilities curve, though it certainly does not look like the production possibilities curves you have seen in other textbooks. And there is a reason for the strange shape you got; when assigning States to Corn and Wheat production, we shouldn't just pick them at random, or in alphabetical order. It would make more sense to assign the best Wheat producing States to Wheat and the best Corn producing States to Corn, to the extent this is possible. Let's try again and see if we can expand the production possibilities by moving States from Corn to Wheat production in some order other than alphabetical.

- ☆Exercise 3.2: Getting the Production Possibilities Curve Right. For each State the final column entry gives the ratio of possible corn production to possible wheat production. State A, for example, is able to produce twice as much Corn as Wheat; State H, on the other hand, can only produce 1/20 as much corn as wheat. Re-order the States in the table, beginning with the state with the lowest Corn/Wheat ratio (State H) and ending with the state with the highest ratio (State I). On the same graph you used for Exercise 3.1, perform the same exercise: First move State H from Corn to Wheat production, then move the next one on your list (leaving H in Wheat), and so on. Finally, when all of the other States have been already assigned to Wheat production, move State I (Iowa) into Wheat production.

Clearly it would be wasteful for society if we ended up on the "production possibilities curve" you drew in Exercise 3.1. For any point on the curve from 3.1 (except the ends) it is possible to produce more of both Corn and Wheat, simply by changing the assignments given to the various states.

The curve from Exercise 3.2 s indeed the production possibilities curve; there is no better way of ranking the states than the one you employed in Exercise 3.2.

Why is it that we get the true production possibilities curve when we rank states according to their ratios of maximum Corn production to maximum Wheat production?

---

the next several exercises. All exercises which can fruitfully be done on a spreadsheet are indicated by a ☆.

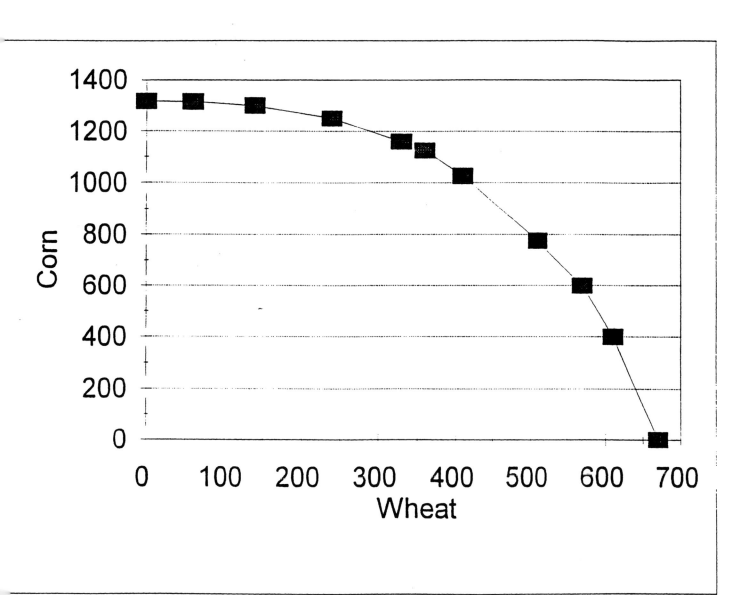

Figure 3.1b
Production Possibilities
(States Assigned Efficiently)

The answer is that this ratio tells us the **cost**, measured in **lost Corn production**, of taking each state out of Corn production and putting it in Wheat production. More specifically, this ratio is the amount of Corn production which will be lost **per bushel of added Wheat production** if the indicated state is shifted from Corn to Wheat. When State A moves from Corn production to Wheat production we lose two bushels of Corn per gained bushel of Wheat. By contrast, when State H is shifted, we lose only .05 bushels of Corn per gained bushel of Wheat. It would be wasteful to have State H in Corn production and State A in wheat production at the same time.

- Exercise 3.3: Suppose State A is currently assigned to Wheat Production, and State F is assigned to Corn production. Calculate what will happen to the nation's Corn, and Wheat, production, if we switch A to Corn and F to Wheat.

Notice that we have given the Corn/Wheat column an alternative label: $-\Delta C/\Delta W$. The reason for the extra label is this: If (for example) State A is moved from Corn production to Wheat production, the ratio in this column tells us how much the nation's Corn production will fall **per unit** increase in Wheat production.

To restate the basic point: If we are currently producing nothing but Corn, the **cheapest** way to acquire some Wheat production is to take H out of Corn production and put it in Wheat production. If after moving H into Wheat production, we still want more, the next cheapest source of wheat is State C; a bushel of Wheat from State C costs .19 bushels of foregone Corn production.

- ☆Exercise 3.4: Again using the data from Table 3.1, create a "production possibilities curve, moving states from Corn to Wheat in precisely the opposite order from what you used in Exercise 3.2. (Move State I first). Just as the rule followed in Exercise 3.2 represented the best possible order in which to allocate states, the order in 3.3 represents the worst possible order. Try to explain what is so inefficient about the rule you followed in this exercise.

- ☆Exercise 3.5: Create a table like Table 3.1, in which all states have the same number in the Corn/Wheat column. If you want, you can make the states literally identical (same Corn, same Wheat, same Corn/Wheat), or you can make some states better at both Corn and Wheat than other states. What does the production possibilities curve look like? Does this make sense?

- ☆Exercise 3.6:
i. Try to make up numbers for a table like Table 3.1 which yield a production possibilities curve which is bowed in toward the origin; even if you move States from Corn to Wheat production in the best possible order, the resulting curve is bowed in. Is such an outcome possible? Why or why not?
ii. Make a table like Table 3.1, using whatever values you want for Corn and Wheat. (As

you will need this table for later exercises in this chapter, create four blank columns to the right of the (-ΔC/ΔW) column.) Generate the production possibilities curve implied by your data. Regardless of the original data you chose (the Corn and Wheat possibilities for the individual states) the curve should be bowed out.

• Fact 3.1: Production possibilities curves are always bowed out from the origin.[3]

• The Reason for Fact 3.1: In any economy, resources differ from one another; some are natural "specialists" at producing one good; some at another. This fact alone is sufficient to cause the production possibilities curve to be bowed out.

Fact 3.1 is a true fact because it is always possible to form a table like Table 3.1, in which we rank the "states" or more generally the bundles of inputs according to the cost of shifting the state from Corn to Wheat production. From such a list we can always construct the production possibilities curve. Starting from a point where all of the resources are devoted to the production of one good, begin by hypothetically shifting one "bundle" of resources, and then another, into the production of the other good. If at every step we shift the cheapest remaining bundle (in the sense we defied cheap above) this process will necessarily yield a bowed out production possibilities curve.

We employed the fiction that the production of Corn and Wheat require only land because that fiction makes it much easier to see why the production possibilities curve is bowed out (and yes, it is worth knowing; this is an important fact). In Chapter 5 we will examine production which requires not only land but also labor and capital. Though we will not be able to prove it, Fact 3.1 will continue to be true in that more realistic setting.

The True Meaning of Cost

Any time we shift resources from Corn to Wheat production, we sacrifice Corn production; **this lost Corn production is the true cost of increasing Wheat production.** Somewhere, somebody must give up some Corn consumption if Wheat production is to be increased.

---

[3]This is not quite a true fact; there are two circumstances under which production possibilities curves might be bowed in. Neither of these circumstances arises in basic economics; they are dealt with only in fairly advanced treatments. And neither need concern readers here. But for completeness, the two possible causes of an inward-bowed production possibilities curve are:
(i) significant diseconomies of scale in the production of one or more of the commodities, and
(ii) a negative externality which the production of one commodity inflicts upon the output of the other. Unless you intend to do advanced work in economics, forget that you ever read this footnote.

We tend to think of the cost of Wheat production (or the production of any other good) as the **cost of the land, labor, and capital** required to produce it, or as the **price that merchants charge** for it. But as consumers, our ultimate concern should be, if Wheat production is increases, by how much will Corn production fall? For if we use more of our land to produce Wheat, the true cost is that we will have less Corn to eat.

In later chapters in this book, we will explore some important relationships between the price of a good and the true cost of producing it.

What Will be Produced?

We now know what combinations of Corn and Wheat **can** be produced, given society's resources. The next question is: Which point on the production possibilities curve will actually be selected; what combination of Corn and Wheat will be produced? Of course, it is not possible to know what will actually be produced until we know two things:
(1) Who decides how society's resources will be used, and
(2) What forces influence their decisions? For example, if the government controls the resources, it might arbitrarily decide that the economy will produce only Corn.

In this book we concentrate on the allocation process in **market economies**, in which economic decisions are made by individual consumers and entrepreneurs. Therefore, it is tme to introduce the next force at work in the economy: **profit maximization**. We assume that there are entrepreneurs in our midst whose objective is to make as much profit as they can.

For the present we will assume that there is just one entrepreneur. The residents of our 10 States rent their land to this entrepreneur. We will not worry just yet about how much rent they charge for their land; we'll just call it R. The entrepreneur grows Corn and Wheat, and sells it to the residents of the States (the very people from whom he rented the land).

At this point in the analysis we will not ask what determines the prices that the entrepreneur can charge for Corn and Wheat. We will discuss the forces which influence prices in Chapter 4. At present, we will simply make up prices and see how they influence the entrepreneur's actions. We'll call the price of Corn P_c and the price of Wheat P_w. The entrepreneur's profit is the proceeds from selling Corn and Wheat, less the rent he has to pay for the land. We can write this as an equation:

$$\Pi = P_c \cdot C + P_w \cdot W - R \tag{1}$$

This simply says that the entrepreneur's profit, which we call Π, is equal to total revenue ($P_c \cdot C$, the revenue from selling Corn, plus $P_w \cdot W$, the revenue from selling Wheat) less the rent the entrepreneur must pay to the residents of the States. The entrepreneur's objective in life is to make Π as big as possible.

Remember, our entrepreneur has rented all of society's resources; he has the ability to produce any combination of Corn and Wheat that is on the production possibilities curve. So the question is: What point on the production possibilities curve yields the greatest Π?

We will approach this question somewhat the same way as we did the consumer's highest-indifference-curve problem from Chapter 2: We will construct a series of "level curves" along which Π is constant, and we will then look for the highest level curve that touches the production possibilities curve. Let's begin with the level curves.

- Exercise 3.7 (Equal-profit lines): Let's assume that P_w = $1/bu and that P_c = $2/bu. The rent, R, that the entrepreneur has to pay is $1000. Draw a graph with Corn on the vertical axis and Wheat on the horizontal. Plot all of the combinations of Corn and Wheat production that yield $1000 in profit. HINT: Start with the end-points; that is, calculate how much Corn the entrepreneur must grow in order to get $1000 in profit (after paying R, remember) assuming he just grows Corn. Then do the same assuming he just grows Wheat. Now try to fill in the points in between. If you have trouble, proceed as follows: Begin at the all-Corn point you already plotted. Reduce Corn production by one bushel. Figure out how much added Wheat production you need to keep profit at $1000. Repeat this process until you reach the all-Wheat point you plotted above. When you connect these dots, what does the graph look like? (It should be a straight line sloping downward.) Can you explain why it looks this way?

In exercise 3.7 you plotted all of the combinations of Corn and Wheat production, sold at the indicated prices, that yield $1000 in profit. We don't know whether it is possible for the entrepreneur to actually earn this $1000, because we don't know whether the equal-profit line you drew touches the production possibilities curve. To learn this we will have to show both the equal-profit line and the production possibilities curve on the same graph. In Figure 3.1, we show the $1000 equal-profit line from Exercise 3.7 and the production possibilities curve from Exercise 3.2 on the same graph.[4] We see that indeed it is possible for our entrepreneur to earn $1000 in profit, for example by producing 725 Corn and 550 Wheat, or by producing 1000 Corn and no Wheat.

- Exercise 3.8: On the graph you used for Exercise 3.7, first sketch the production possibilities curve (it should look like Figure 3.1). Now, on the same graph, draw a new equal-profit line showing all of the combinations which would yield $2000 in profit. Is it possible for the entrepreneur to earn $2000 in profit? Explain. Is it possible for the entrepreneur to earn $10,000?

Your second equal-profit line should be parallel to the first one. And there is an important

---

[4]The production possibilities curve in this graph is the one you should have gotten in exercise 3.2, and the equal-profit line is what you should have gotten in Exercise 3.7. Check to see that yours look like this.

reason for this: The slope of each equal-profit line is $-P_w/P_c$. This fact will turn out to be very important later; let's try to see why it's true.

Imagine sliding down the equal-profit line. A slide down the line represents a decline in Corn production and an increase in Wheat production. Such a "slide" is depicted in Figure 3.2; the entrepreneur began at * and ended at **. Corn production fell by ΔC, and proceeds from the sale of Corn fell by $\Delta C \cdot P_c$. Wheat production rose by ΔW and Wheat revenue rose by $\Delta W \cdot P_w$. But since the "slide" from * to ** was along an equal-profit line, it must be the case that the loss of Corn revenue is exactly offset by the gain in Wheat revenue. In other words the change in Corn revenue plus the change in Wheat revenue must be 0, if the line itself is truly an equal-profit line. So let's write it as an equation:

$$\Delta C \cdot P_C + \Delta W \cdot P_W = 0 \tag{2}$$

(Recall that Corn production declined, so ΔC is negative)

This equation just says that total profit from Corn plus Wheat does not change when we slide along the equal-profit line. Now, unfortunately, we have to perform a little bit of algebra. We'll take it in steps. First, add $(-\Delta C \cdot P_c)$ to both sides of Equation (3.2):

$$\Delta W \cdot P_W = -\Delta C \cdot P_C \tag{3}$$

Next divide both sides of equation (3) by P_c. Now divide both sides of this new equation by ΔW. You should end up with (3.4):

$$\frac{\Delta C}{\Delta W} = -\frac{P_W}{P_C} \tag{4}$$

Remember now that (3.4) is really the same "sentence" as (3.2); we just rearranged it. And (3.2) is a description of a slide down an equal-profit line. So (3.4) also describes a slide down the equal-profit line; les't see what it says.

The left-hand side of (3.4) is the standard expression for the slope of a line; quite literally, the left-hand side refers to the rise over the run. This slope is negative; the move from * to ** was brought about by a negative ΔC and a positive ΔW. Equation (3.4) tells us that the slope of the equal-profit line is minus the ratio of the goods' prices.[5]

---

[5]Notice that the algebra and the logic (as well as the answer) are the same as for the consumer's budget constraint. If a consumer has a budget to be allocated between Corn and Wheat, the slope of his budget constraint is $-P_w/P_c$. The algebra of Equations (3.2) to (3.4) is

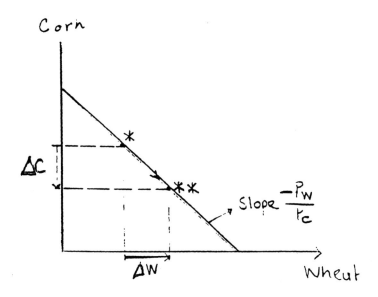

Fig. 3.2

Since the slope of each equal-profit line is the same ($-P_w/P_c$) we now know that our entreprenneur's map of equal-profit contours is a series of parallel lines (with slope $-P_w/P_c$), just like the lines you drew in Exercise 3.8. Higher lines represent higher profit. The entrepreneur's objective is to get to the highest possible line.

We depict the entrepreneur's decision in Figure 3.3. Once again this shows the production possibilities curve from Table 3.1, and a whole map of equal-profit contours based on the numbers we used in Exercses 3.7 and 3.8. The entrepreneur maximizes profit at ☺ on the graph. This is the highest equal-profit line that still touches the production possibilities curve.

A Messy Detail About the Production Possibilities Curve

When you drew the production possibilities curve you may have drawn straight lines connecting your plotted dots, like the piecewise linear depiction in Figure 3.4. But you will notice that we have always drawn it smooth, like the curve in Figure 3.3. The curve (Figure 3.3) is probably a better depiction of reality, and that's what we will continue to use in this book. In this section we will try to reconcile the smooth curvature with the way you constructed the production possibilities curve in Exercise 3.2. (If you are not disturbed by the curvature, you can just skip the rest of this section.)

Any State in the Table could be subdivided into Counties and we could make a table of Counties using the same format as Table 3.1. The Counties in State D might have Corn/Wheat ratios ranging from 0.80 to 1.20. If we were to use this information we could fill in more points on the production possibilities curve. And each County, in turn, could be subdivided into square miles (known in the agricultural community as Sections). Each time we divide the land more finely we obtain a better approximation to the true shape of the production possibilities curve. This process will generally lead to a smooth production possibilities curve, as you can see by carrying out Exercise 3.9:

● ☆Exercise 3.9: The Production Possibilities Curve for State D. We know from Table 3.1 that State D is able to produce 90 Corn or 90 Wheat. Divide State D into 10 Counties (Counties 1 through 10) and make a table like Table 3.1. Make up numbers for Corn and Wheat for each County, taking care to do the following: (i) When you add up all of the Counties' Corn entries, be sure they sum to 90. (ii) When you add up all of the Counties' Wheat entries, be sure they add up to 90. (iii) Make sure that each County's Corn/Wheat ratio is between 0.80 and 1.20. Now trace out the production possibilities curve just as you did for Exercise 3.2. You should have gotten the familiar bowed-out shape.

Exercise 3.9 gives a more microscopic view of one segment of the Nation's production possibilities curve. You see that the segment is bowed out. If we were to divide a County into

---

exactly the same as that in the Appendix, where we discuss the shapes of budget constraints.

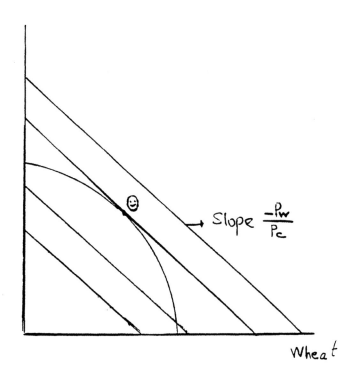

Corn

Slope $\dfrac{-P_w}{P_c}$

Wheat

Fig. 3.3

Figure 3.4

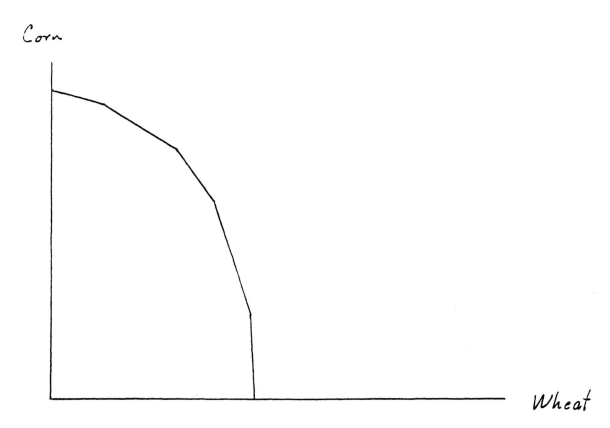

Corn

Wheat

square miles, we would see that each County's production possibilities curve is bowed out as well. If each little segment of the production possibilities curve is bowed out, no matter how microscopically we look at it, then the whole curve must be smoothly bowed out as we have drawn it.

But remember what you learned in Exercise 3.5: If all of the Counties in the State are identical to one another, that State's production possibilities curve is a straight line. The curvature of the production possibilities curve arises because different resources have different capabilities.

What Combination of Goods is Produced?

Just before our side-trip to explore the curvature of the production possibilities curve, we discovered that a profit-maximizing entrepreneur will select the point on the production possibilities curve which is tangent to an equal-profit line. (This is depicted in Figure 3.3.) With this fact in mind, and also remembering that the slope of the equal-profit line is $-P_w/P_c$, we can learn some interesting things about how the quantities of Corn and Wheat supplied by entrepreneurs change as their prices change.

(In Exercises 3.10 - 3.15, you are asked to find specific values either for Wheat or P_w. However, we have not given specific enough information on the shape of the production possibilities curve for you to give precise answers.[6] You should be able to give good approximations, though.)

●   Exercise 3.10: In Exercise 3.7 we began to construct a family of equal-profit lines, based on the "information" that $P_w = \$1$ and $P_c = \$2$. In succeeding Exercises we determined the quantities of Corn and Wheat that would be produced at these prices. Now we're going to start over: Set $P_w = \$2$ (leave $P_c = \$2$). Construct a new family of equal-profit lines and find the point where one of these is tangent to the production possibilities curve. (This should not be nearly as hard as it was the first time. Now you know that the slope of the equal-profit line is $-P_w/P_c$. So all you have to do is calculate this ratio (it's equal to -1) and start drawing parallel lines of slope -1.) When P_w went up (from \$1 to \$2), what happened to the amount of Wheat supplied by the entrepreneur? What happened to the amount of Corn produced?

In Exercise 3.10, we experimetally raised the price of Wheat. The entrepreneur responded to this by increasing his output of Wheat (the higher price means that Wheat farming is now more profitable). But notice that the only way to increase Wheat production is to cut Corn production (since we were on the production possibilities curve, there is no other way to produce more Wheat).

●   Exercise 3.11: Leave $P_w = \$2$, and raise P_c to \$4. Draw the new equal-profit lines and

---

[6]In particular, we haven't broken our States down into Counties, Sections, acres, etc.

find the profit-maximizing combination of Corn and Wheat production. If you did it right, you should be right back at ☺, the profit-maximizing point when P_w = $1 and P_c = $2). Why do you get the same answer you did in Exercise 3.x?

The Supply Curve

The supply curve for any commodity is a graphical answer to the following question: **Holding the price of the other good fixed, how much of a specific good will be supplyed for various values of that good's price?**

Translating into the specific examples used in the Exercises of this Chapter, holding P_c fixed at $2/bu, how much Wheat is produced for various values of P_w? We have already answered this question for two values of P_w; $1 in Figure 3.3 and $2 in Exercise 3.10. These two points are plotted in Figure 3.5. Depending on our degree of patience, we could repeat Exercise 3.10 many times, with different values of P_w, and in the process plot as many points as we want on the supply curve for Wheat. We're going to do just a little bit of this in Exercise 3.12:

● Exercise 3.12: If the price of wheat were 0, it seems pretty obvious that a profit maximizing entrepreneur would grow no Wheat. Draw an equal-profit line which shows this. Now gradually raise P_w until you find the **highest** value of P_w at which the entrepreneur will still grow no Wheat. This is the P_w intercept for the supply curve which we began to plot in Figure 3.5.

● Exercise 3.13: If the price of Wheat is high enough, our entrepreneur will produce no Corn. Find the lowest price of Wheat you can, such that the entrepreneur will still produce no Corn. This is another point on the supply curve; what is it?

The Supply Curve Moves When the Other Price Changes

Look at the definition of the supply curve given above: the first phrase is "holding the price of the other good fixed." There is a different supply curve of Wheat for every price of Corn. Everything we did in Exercises 3.11 - 3.13 was based on an assumption that P_c = $2. But if P_c = $1, all of our answers in Exercises 3.11 - 3.13 change. And this of course means a different supply curve for Wheat.

● Exercise 3.14: In Exercise 3.12 above you found the highest P_w for which the entrepreneur would not be willing to grow any Wheat. But you found this assuming P_c = $2. Now answer the same question (the highest P_w at which he still won't grow Wheat, assuming P_c = $1.

● Exercise 3.15: (Now we'll find the other end of the new supply curve). Assuming P_c = $1 (as in Exercise 3.14 above) find the lowest P_w at which the entrepreneur will still produce

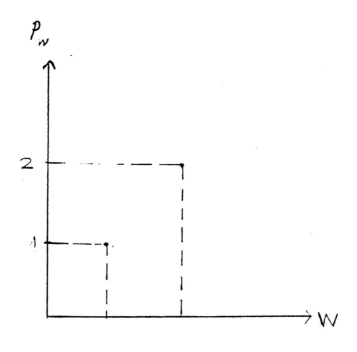

Fig. 3,5

all Wheat and no Corn. This is the other end of the new supply curve. Plot both of these points (the one from Exercises 3.14 and 3.15) on the same graph you used to draw your first supply curve.

Supply and Margial Cost

The supply curve of Wheat answers the following question (holding the price of Corn fixed, remember): for any give value of P_w, how much Wheat will be supplied? We can learn more about this by looking once again at Figure 3.3, which depicts the profit maximizing combination of Corn and Wheat. For a specific P_w (and P_c), we simply find the slope of the family of equal-profit lines and then find a point of tangency with the production possibilities curve. The point we find gives the profit maximizing supply of Wheat (as well as Corn). The crucial feature is the tangency between the production possibilities curve and the equal-profit line. We described this tangency in equations 3.2 - 3.4. We will now write equation 3.4 in a slightly different form:

$$\frac{P_C(-\Delta C)}{\Delta W} = P_W \tag{5}$$

First, check to see that equation 3.5 is really the same thing as equation 3.4; we just multiplied both sides by $-P_c$. Now we can give a very important name to the terms on the left hand side of equation 3.5: it is **marginal cost.**

- Definition 3.1: **Marginal Cost** is the value of alternative output sacrificed for a small increase in the production of a specified good.[7]

- ☆Exercise 3.16: Exploring Marginal Cost. Make your own copy of Table 3.1 from the book. As you will need them for later exercises, make four blank columns to the right of the one labelled $(-\Delta C/\Delta W)$. Fix $P_c = \$2$, as in Exercises 3.10. Label the first of your new columns "Value of Lost Corn." In this column calculate the value of Corn production lost if the State is switched from Corn to Wheat production. (The first State in your Table should be H; if it is taken out of Corn production, the nation's corn production falls by 30 bu; at \$2/bu, the value of lost Corn production is \$60. Do this exercise for the remaining States.) In the next column, for each State calculate the value of lost Corn production **per bushel of increased Wheat production.** You get this by dividing the "Value of Lost Corn" entry by the "Wheat" entry. For State H, you divide \$60 by 300, getting \$0.20.

---

[7]This definition probably looks strange to students who are familiar with marginal cost curves constructed from a firm's total cost of labor and capital. But bear with us. We will see later in the book that the two approaches to marginal cost usually come to the same thing. And when they don't come to the same thing, something is wrong with the other way of thinking of marginal cost. The one we use here is right.

You can label this column "Marginal Cost."

What is the meaning of the $0.20 for State H in your table? Checking through your calculations, you can see that it means the following: If we switch State H out of Corn production and into Wheat production, we lose $0.20 worth of Corn production per bushel of increased Wheat production.

Now it is useful to think of our entrepreeur's profit-maximizing decision in terms of a comparison of price and marginal cost. The entrepreneur could approach his profit-maximization problem by repeatedly asking the following question: Should I increase Wheat production a little bit? In particular, suppose I decide to produce one more bushel of Wheat; will my profit go up or down?

Of course, if he does increase Wheat production by one bushel, he will get some good news and some bad news.
Good News: He gets to sell the "new" bushel of Wheat for P_w.
Bad News: He has to cut back on Corn production and therefore has less to sell; his Corn receipts fall. By how much do Corn receipts fall? **Corn receipts fall by MC.** By the calculations you did in Exercise 3.16 above, if the entrepreneur withdraws just enough State-H land from Corn production to increase Wheat production by one bushel, his Corn receipts will fall by $0.20.

Profit Maximizer's Rule to Live By: Increase Wheat production by a little bit **if P_w is greater than MC.**

- ☆Exercise 3.17: Once more turn to the table you began preparing in Exercise 3.16. Leave P_c = $2, and set P_w = $1. First calculate the profit the entrepreeur will make if he plants the whole coutry in Corn. Now shift one State at a time over to Wheat production, and after each shift, calculate the entrepreneur's profit. Put the answer in the next Column of your table, and label the column Π (for profit). (When the whole country is in Corn, Π = $2x1318 - $1000 = $1636. When you shift State H into Wheat, Corn revenue falls by $6 and Wheat revenue increases by $60, so Π rises to $1690 (1636 + 60 - 6). (Remember, each time you add a Statc to Wheat production, the previously shifted ones should remain in Wheat production.) Which is the last State that the entrepreneur would want to shift into Wheat production? What happens to profit if he continues to shift more States into Wheat production?

From the above exercise, you should notice that it is profitable to shift States into Wheat production so long as Marginal Cost is less than P_w. When Marginal Cost is greater than P_w shifting a State into Wheat production reduces profit. When Marginal Cost equals P_w, profit doesn't change; it doesn't matter whether the State is in Corn or Wheat.

Here's a simple restatement of the Profiit Maximixer's Rule to Live By: Increase Wheat

Production up to the point where

$$P = MC$$

A profit maximizer increases Wheat production up to the point where the good news from icreasing Wheat productio (P) is just equal to (no longer greater than) the bad news (MC).

As a final set of Exercises in this chapter, we will plot a **Marginal Cost Curve**, and show that it is the entrepreneur's **Supply Curve.**

- ☆Exercise 3.18: Make one more column in your table; label it Total W. In this column we will write down the nation's total Wheat production, assuming that the "current" state plus all of those above it are in Wheat production. Thus for example, the entry for State H is 60. The next State on your list should be State C; when its 80 is added to national Wheat production, the total jumps to 1000. Now prepare a graph. On the x axis plot Total W, from the column you just prepared. On the y axis plot MC. You should get an upward sloping curve; this is the Marginal Cost curve.

- Exercise 3.19: On the graph you just prepared, draw a horizontal line starting from $1 on the y axis. Label it P_w. This line depicts $P_w = \$1$. Work across this line to see where it hits the MC curve (this represents the level of Wheat output where P = MC). At this level of Wheat output, what was the last State moved into Wheat production? Is this the profit maximizing last state to move into Wheat production?

In Exercise 3.18 you plotted MC against the total amount of Wheat produced; the more Wheat production the higher is marginal cost, because all of the low-cost States are already in Wheat production. I Exercise 3.19 we saw that this MC curve also serves as the Supply curve; once we have costructed the MC curve, we can immediately use it to find the profit-maximizing level of output for any given value of P. We just draw a horiizotal line at the value of P we are innterested in, and see where it intersects the MC curve.

Conclusion

This has been a long and difficult chapter. We'll try to isolate the high points here.

- The production possibilities curve shows all of the combinations of goods which can be produced, given the society's stock of resources. Since resources differ in their ability to produce different goods, the production possibilities curve is bowed out from the origin.

- The profit maximizing mix of goods occurs at the point on the production possibilities curve whose slope is equal to (minus) the ratio of the output prices. (Though this point seems tedious, it will turn out to be very important.)

- The Marginal Cost (MC) of producing a good is the cost of increasing that good's output by a small step. The proper measure of marginal cost is the value of the alterative output sacrificed by taking this small step.

- It is possible to construct a MC curve; a plot of MC agaist the total amount of the good produced. This MC curve is identical to the Supply curve. For any given price of the good, we can use it to read off the quantity of the good which will be produced under profit maximization.

- Profit is maximized at that quantity where Price equals Marginal Cost; the good news from expanding output equals the bad news.

Chapter 4
Consumers Meet Producers

In the first section of Chapter 2, consumers were just somehow "endowed" with bundles of consumer goods; we did not say anything about where the goods came from. Not only did we fail to talk about how the goods were produced; we did not even mention how the consumers might have gotten the goods in the first place. Later in the Chapter, we gave the consumers some income (but didn't say how they earned it) and they acquired their consumer goods by buying them (but we didn't say how the goods were produced or who sold them).

In Chapter 3, an entrepreneur produced goods and offered them for sale. But we never asked whether there were any consumers who wanted to buy the goods offered by the entrepreneur.

In this Chapter, producer and consumer will meet for the first time. As in Chapter 2, we will pursue three different questions:

- Question 4.1: Can we describe the difference between an economically efficient, and an economically inefficient, combination of goods produced?

- Question 4.2: In a market economy, what combination of goods **will** actually be produced?

- Question 4.3: Is the combination of goods produced in a market economy efficient or inefficient?

Economically Efficient Production

In Chapter 2 we found a set of conditions under which it is impossible to re-allocate a **given** stock of goods among consumers in such a way as to make at least one of them better off without harming anybody else. We saw that any given stock of goods is allocated among consumers efficiently if consumers are at points of equal slope on their respective indifference curves. When this condition is satisfied, there are no more mutually advantageous "deals" to be struck.

In that chapter, the only "tool" available for helping consumers was the reshuffling of a given stock of goods.

Finally we saw that this efficient allocation of a given stock of goods tends to be achieved if all consumers face the same prices as one another.

But from Chapter 3 we know that society has many options (limited by the production possibilities curve) regarding what combination of goods to produce. This means that the bundle of goods available for consumers to enjoy is not just given by nature; the mix is **determined** by the actions of producers.

So now we have to ask a new question: Under what circumstances is it possible to make one consumer better off without harming any other consumer, **by channging the mix of goods that are produced and made available to consumers?**

To take an obvious and extreme example, suppose all consumers love Wheat and have no taste for Corn at all, while the entrepreneur produces nothing but Corn. Clearly, we could make all consumers better off by replanting the whole nation in Wheat.

To explore the question further, turn to Figure 4.1. In Figure 4.1a we draw society's production possibilities and indicate the current mix of production by *. In Figure 4.1b we draw the current consumption bundle, #, of one consumer in the society, along with his indifference curve through that point. And we now ask the following question: By moving along the production possibilities curve, is there a way to make this consumer better off without harming any other consumer? First, study the movement along the production possibilities curve, from * to **. Wheat production falls by ΔW; the total Wheat available to consumers will decline by this amount. On the other hand, the resources freed up by cutting Wheat production are now available for increased Corn production; Corn output rises by ΔC, and this ΔC is available for the benefit of consumers.

Let's suppose that one particular consumer (namely our old fried Otto, depicted in Figure 4.1b) reduces his own Wheat consumption by the entire production loss, ΔW. We show this by transferring ΔW to Figure 4.1b (the loss begins at #, Otto's consumption point before any of this began). We already know that no other consumer need be harmed by the shift of production from * to **; Otto has reduced his Wheat consumption enough that nobody else has to.

Thanks to Otto's sacrifice, there are enough freed-up resources to produce a additional ΔC of Corn; suppose we give all of this newfound Corn to Otto. On the graph we depict this by transferring ΔC from Figure 4.1a to 4.1b; as a result of his loss of Wheat and his gained Corn, Otto moves to ##. Given the way that we drew the graph (that is, the shapes of the production possibility and indifference curves) Otto is better off at the end of this process than he was at the beginning.

We have certainly found a way to make one consumer better off by moving along the production possibilities curve. Was any other consumer made worse off? The answer is No; no other consumer's bundle of consumption goods changed at all. The entire reduction in Wheat production was "covered" by Otto's reduced Wheat consumption; other consumers did not have to cut back on Wheat consumption at all. And since Otto took all of the new Corn production, nobody else's consumption of Corn needed to change either.

The starting point, (*,#, and whatever the other consumers were getting) was wasteful

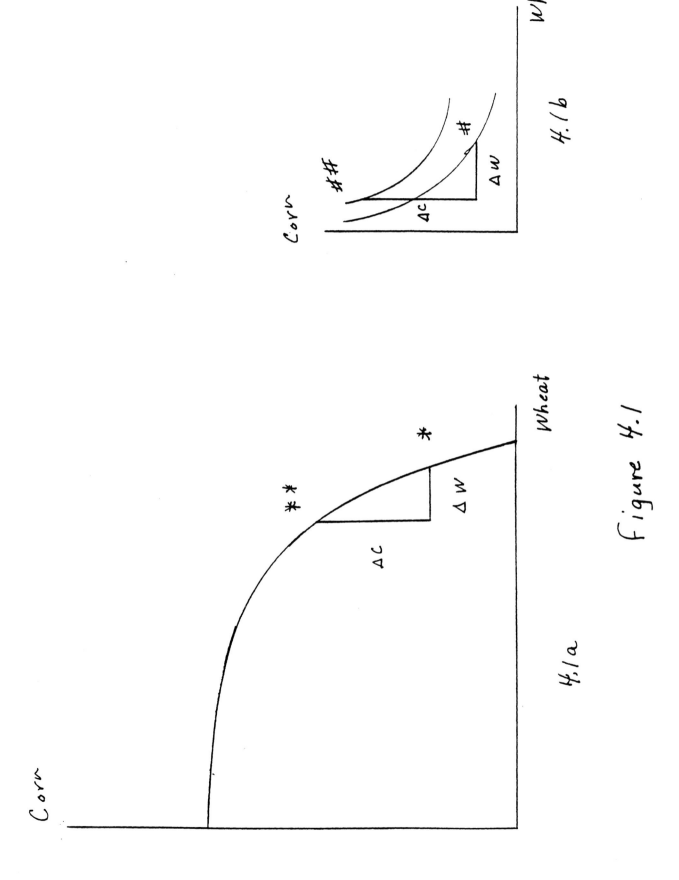

Figure 4.1

(not efficient); from that starting point we have found a way to make one consumer better off without harming any other consumer. An economy which is efficient (not wasteful) will not rest at (*,#).

Notice that we have not said anything about whether entrepreneurs would be interested in moving from * to **. All we have said is that if society is at the (*,#) starting point, it is physically possible to reshuffle resources so as to improve one consumer without harming anny others.

Also notice that we are using "trade triangles" of the sort we introduced in Chapter 2, but that they look a little different here. In Chapter 2, two consumers were trading a **given** stock of the goods; when we depicted a gain for Otto, we had to depict an identical loss for Blanche. Thus Otto's trade triangle was a flipped-over version of Blanche's. But here an increase in Corn **production** is an **increase** in Otto's corn consumption. Thus we represent the "deal" simply by transferring the same trade triangle from Figure 4.1a to 4.1b.

- Exercise 4.1: Make your own copy of Figure 4.1, highlighting the points * and #. Starting from * and #, now contemplate a **cut** in Corn production, with the freed-up resources devoted to Wheat production. Sketch out such a move from *. Transfer the move to Otto, and ask whether he is made better off or worse off.

- Exercise 4.2: Still working with your sketch of Figure 4.1, give Otto a new personality. In particular, give him an indifference curve through # such that he is just indifferent to the proposed move to ##. (But don't violate the basic rules governing the shapes of indifference curves: make sure that it is downward sloping and bowed in toward the origin.

- Exercise 4.3: Give Otto a final personality transplant; give him an indifference curve such that he would prefer staying at # to moving to ##.

- Exercise 4.4: Restore Otto's original personality (the indifference curve from Figure 4.1b). Now we'll change the makeup of society's resources; as a result of a shift in global weather patterns, the nation's ability to grow Wheat has increased and its ability to grow Corn has decreased. Draw a new production possibilities curve (still let it pass through *) reflecting the new weather pattern. See if you can draw this new production possibilities curve in such a way that, beginning at (*,#, and wherever the other consumers are), efficiency is improved by increasing Wheat production (and therefore Otto's Wheat consumption).

- Exercise 4.5: If Otto has the indifference curve through # that you drew in Exercise 4.2, then sliding along the production possibilities curve cannot make him better off without making another consumer worse off. What is the crucial difference between this graph and the ones you drew in Exercise 4.1, 4.3, ad 4.4?

- Fact 4.1: If the slope of the production possibilities curve (at the current point of production) is equal to the slope of each consumer's indifference curve (at the point of consumption) then the combination of goods produced is economically effiicient (not wasteful).

We saw in Exercises 4.1 - 4.5 that a move along the production possibilities curve can make Otto better off without harming any other consumer only if the slope of his indifference curve through his current consumption point (#) has a different slope from the production possibilities curve at the current point of production (*). If the slopes are the same there is no way to make him better off (except by making somebody else worse off).

What's true for Otto is true for everybody else. If any consumer is in a position like Otto's in Exercise 4.1, 4.3, or 4.4, then a gain which harms nobody is waiting to happen. When **all** consumers are like Otto in Exercise 4.2 (which we now depict in Figure 4.2), then there are no more gains to be had by sliding along the production possibilities curve.

Fact 4.1 is true for a fairly straightforward reason: The slope of the production possibilities curve is the **rate** at which it is physically **possible** to "transform" Wheat into Corn, or vice versa.[1] A small move "up" the production possibilities curve costs ΔW and yields ΔC; the slope is the gain in Corn per unit of lost Wheat. The slope of the indifference curve conveys somewhat similar information; it is the **rate** at which a consumer is **willing** to "transform" Wheat consumption into Corn consumption (or vise versa). Suppose our resources are able to "transform" one bushel of Wheat into two bushels of Corn but consumers are willing to "transform" one bushel of Wheat into just one bushel of Corn (as in Figure 4.1). Then this move along the production possibilities curve leaves us with an extra bushel of Corn that can be used to make somebody better off.

What Combination of Goods Will be Produced and Consumed in a Market Economy

For any **given prices** of Corn and Wheat, we know (from Chapter 3) what mix the economy will produce; it is that combination where the slope of the production possibilities curve is equal to (minus) the ratio of the goods' prices. Such a situation is depicted in Figure 4.3; recall that the straight line has slope $-P_w/P_c$; it is the equal-profit line. (Bear in mind that P_w and P_c are just made-up numbers; they have been determined by the textbook author, not by the economy.)

Now, for these same made-up prices, we need to see whether the nation's consumers wish to purchase the combination that was produced. So far, we do't kow that entrepreneurs can actually **sell** C^* at P_c and W^* at P_w. To address this question, we need to return to the study of consumers.

---

[1] Of course the economy cannot perform the alchemy of physically transforming Corn into Wheat. The "transformation" we refer to entails a decision to pull resources out of Wheat production and redirect them to Corn production.

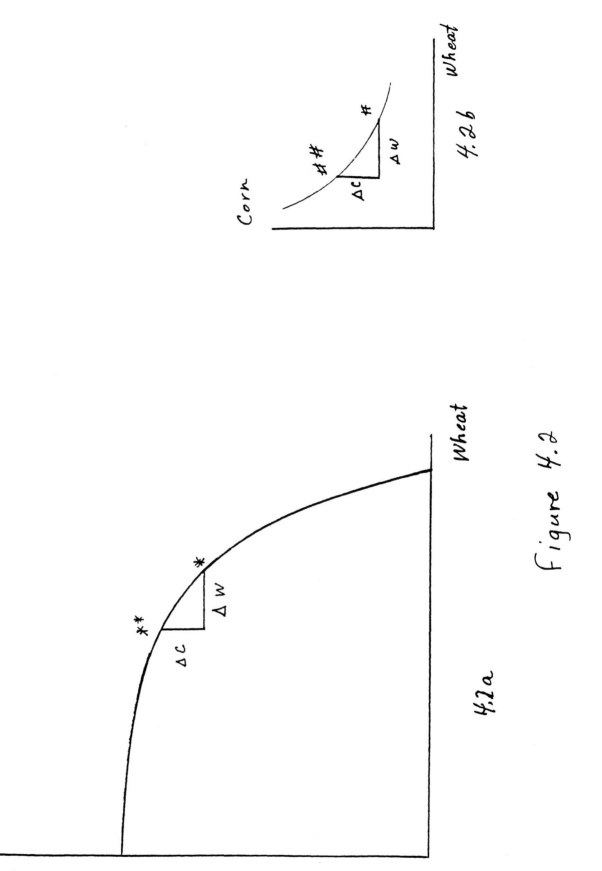

Corn

Wheat

4.2a

Corn

Wheat

4.2b

Figure 4.2

In order to know how much of these goods consumers will want to purchase and consume we need to know their incomes, the prices and the shapes of their indifference curves. (Remember, we learned in Chapter 2 that the mix of goods demanded by a consumer is a function of income and prices, which determine the shape of the budget constraint, and consumer preferences. So far we know prices (we made them up), but we do not know anything about the consumers' incomes or about their indifference curves.

Where Does Income Come From?

We consumers earn income from only two sources:
(i) by selling resources including labor to entrepreneurs, or
(ii) by being an entrepreneur and earning a profit.

Ultimately, the sale of resources to etrepreneurs, and profit earned by entrepreneurs, are the sole sources of income in any society. For most of us the main resource we sell is labor. Some of us also sell the services of land (that is, rent land out). Some of us (for example stockholders) rent out the right to use physical capital.[2] And some earn income by lending and earning interest. This lending is really an act of making resources available to entrepreneurs, in exchange for an interest payment.

Some of us also receive Social Security or other **transfers**, generally from the goverment. These transfers really represent income earned by somebody else. In the case of Social Security, for example, workers pay Social Security taxes (out of their labor income) which are then paid back to Social Security recipients. The income comes from selling labor to entrepreneurs; the Social Securiity System intervenes in such a way that the person who earns the income and the person who gets to spend it are not the same.

Aggregate Income

Take a look again at Figure 4.3, showing the Nation's production possibilities curve and (for a specific set of prices) a tangent equal-profit line. The equation for this line appeared as (3.1) in Chapter 3; we'll re-arrange it just a little bit and rewrite it here:

$$\Pi + R = P_C \cdot C + P_W \cdot W \qquad (1)$$

Notice that equation (4.1) looks a lot like a budget costraint. First, look at the left hand side: if this were a normal consumer's budget constraint, we would have Y (income) instead of Π+R (the entrepreneur's profit plus the rent he has to pay to owners of the resources). But in

---

[2]The stockholder example may eed a bit of explanation: The owner of Gemeral Motors shares actually owns a (very small) share of the plant and equipment of GM. Dividends represent GM's (the entrepreneur's) payment for the right to use the plant and equipment to manufacture cars. Stockholders, just like laborers or landlords, sell resources to entrepreneurs.

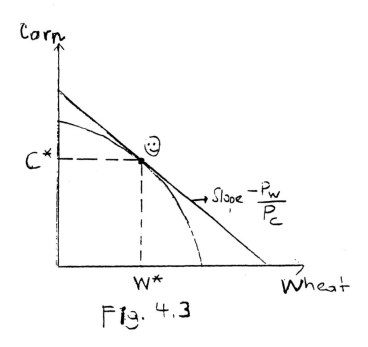

Fig. 4.3

fact, Π+R is the **total income earned by all consumers in the nation**. It is the entrepreneurial income Π plus the income the rest of us earn by selling our resources to the entrepreneur.[3]

Now look at the right hand side. If this were a budget constraint, we would interpret the right hand side as the consumer's total expenditure on Corn and Wheat. Here we interpret it as **total proceeds from the sale of consumer goods.**[4]

This gives us a whole new (and important) interpretation for equation (4.1). The left-hand side is the aggregate income earned by producing and selling the nation's consumer goods, and the right hand side is the total proceeds from selling these goods. What is the meaning of the fact that these two things are equal?

- Fact 4.2: The total income earned in the act of producing and selling a given volume of consumer goods is precisely sufficient to purchase that same volume of goods.

To see intuitively why Fact 4.2 is true, think of the following specific example. An entrepreneur produces and sells $1000 of consumer goods. He pays $600 iin wages and rent, and keeps the remaining $400 as profit. Thus the total income earned is $1000, just enough to buy the $1000 worth of goods that were produced. When we add up all of the similar stories for all of the nation's entreprneeurs, workers, and landlords, we get a picture like Figure 4.3 and an accounting relationship like equation 4.1.

- Fact 4.2: An equal-profit line of the sort drawn in Figure 4.3 represents the nation's aggregate budget costraint.

Figure 4.4 reproduces the production possibilities curve and equal-profit line of Figure 4.3. Notice that on the same graph we could draw an individual consumer's budget constraint (that is, the axes are Corn and Wheat; the right set of axes for a budget constraint). No one consumer can afford to the nation's entire output of Corn and Wheat, so we would expect this budget constraint to be pretty small compared to the production possibilities curve. We've drawn

---

[3]In Chapter 3, the only resourcc was land. But that was just to keep the explanation of profit maximization easy. Nothing important changes when we recognize that the entrepreneur has to pay not oly rent but also wages, dividends, and interest. If you want, you can think of **R** in equation 4.1 as representing not only Rent but also wages, interest and dividends.

[4]In Chapter 3 we pretended that there was only one entrepreneur in the economy, because that way it was easier to see what was meant by profit maximizationn. But we need not stick with this unrealistic fiction. It is fine to interpret the left hand sdie of (4.1) as the sum of all entrepreneurs' profits plus payments to landlords, workers, and so on. And we can think of the right hand side of (4.1) as all of the revenue earned by all of the nation's entrepreneurs from selling Corn and Wheat. (On the other hand, if you prefer, you can continue to think of only one entrepreneur.

such a budget constraint and called it **a**. Notice that its slope is the same as that of the equal-profit line; for both, as you already know, the slope is $-P_3/P_c$.

The budget constraint labelled **a** in Figure 4.4 belongs to our friend Blanche, from Chapter 2. Otto, as it happens, earns the same amount of income as Blanche. So his budget constraint is identical to hers.

If Blanche and Otto were to pool their incomes (for example, if they were to get married) their pooled budget constraint would have the same slope as **a** but be twice as far from the origin (due to twice as much income). We've drawn this as "budget constrait **b** in Figure 4.4.[5]

Now we can continue to add other consumers to the "Blanche and Otto Family;" the more consumers we add the greater will be their combined income and the higher will be the combined budget constraint. Fact 4.2 states that if we continue this exercise until we have combined the incomes of all of the consumers in the economy, the aggregate budget constraint will pass through the combination of goods actually produced. Aggregate income is exactly sufficient to buy these goods back from the entrepreneurs who are selling them.

What Will Consumers Demand?

For a **given** set of prices P_w and P_c, we now know what will be produced (shown as * in Figure 4.4) and what consumers can afford given their budget constraints. In aggregate they can afford any combination of goods which lies on the aggregate budget constraint, labelled II in Figure 4.4. But given these prices (which we just picked out of thin air, remember) we still don't know what combination of Corn and Wheat consumers will want to **purchase**. The only thing we know for sure is that all consumers will select points on their own budget constraints. We can't know more about any consumer without knowing the shapes of his own indifference curves.

Whatever we know about one consumer's chosen consumption bundle, we know for the other consumers as well. All consumers will choose points on their budget constraints, but that's all we know. So with this very modest information let's return to Figure 4.4. It is certainly possible that when we add up all of the consumption bundles chosen by the various consumers, we'll get a point like #.

But something is clearly wrong with this picture. Entrepreneurs produce *, hoping to sell it to consumers at the prices given (P_w and P_c respectively). Consumers (entrepreneurs, workers, and land owners alike) contribute their resources to the production of *, earn income in the process, and then try to buy back the consumer goods which they collectively produced. The problem is, at the prices we picked, the bundle which entrepreneurs produced is not the bundle

---

[5]The mere act of drawing the aggregate of Blanche's and Otto's budget constraints does not imply that they are in any way connected with one another; they may never have met. We are simply asking how much the two of them can afford in aggregate.

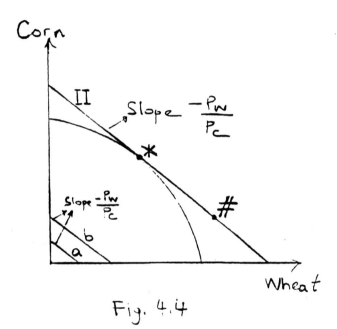

Fig. 4.4

that consumers want to purchase. That is what happens when textbook authors pick the prices of goods.

- Fact 4.3: Collectively, consumers think that they can afford many combinations of goods which in fact cannot even be produced. Furthermore, of all the points that consumers think they can afford, generally only one can actually be produced.

To see that this is right, conduct the following mental experiment: Suppose that every consumer in the country resolved to purchase nothing but grapes for the next year. Aggregate national personal income in the United States in 1994 was $_____, and the price of grapes in a supermarket in Baltimore was $1.00/pound. Simple arithmetic tells us that under the assumptions we're making here, total demand for grapes would be about _____ pounds. (Actual grape production in 1994 was approximately _____). Needless to say, the United States is not able to produce _____ pounds of grapes.

- Exercise 4.6: (In this Exercise we will roughly sketch the price line and production possibilities curve from the grape example above.) The two goods are Grapes and Everything Else (E). We'll designate Everything Else as dollars' worth of other consumption; thus $P_E = \$1$. And we know that $P_G = \$1$. In 1994 Americans purchased ___ E (National personal income less expenditure on Grapes), and _____ pounds of Grapes.

i.   First, draw an aggregate budget constraint which passes through the actual 1994 point of consumption (Put E on the vertical axis and G on the horizontal). If you drew it right, the consumption point should be almost at the vertical axis, depicting the fact that Americans bought a lot more E than G.

ii.   Now draw a production possilities curve tangent to the actual 1994 point of consumption. Note the point consumers would "like" to buy if they spent all of their incomes on grapes, and then note the maximum number of grapes which can be produced.

iii. On the same graph, and to scale, try now to draw the budget constraint of an individual consumer, whose income is $50,000. If you have your units right, this individual budget constraint should be so small on the graph that it is invisible (unless you used a huge piece of graph paper).

iv.   Now suppose that not all consumers want to live on only grapes next year. Only the consumer you drew in (iii) plans to switch to all grapes. When this one consumer tries to switch to all grapes, will the economy be forced into an impossible position like the one depicted in Figure 4.4 and the graph you drew in (i) of this exercise?

Fact 4.3 occurs because the production possiibilities curve is truly curved, but consumers cannot see this curvature. All they see are their budget constraints, which are straight lines.

Equilibrium

Figure 4.4 does not describe a stable situation. Entrepreneurs hope to sell more Corn than consumers want to buy, and consumers want to buy more Wheat than entrepreneurs produce. The obvious solution to this dilemma is to reduce P_c and raise P_w.[6]

It's not hard to see why economic forces would tend to move prices in the direction we have indicated above. Consumers are not buying all of the Corn that entrepreneurs want to sell; it's piling up on shelves and cutting the price seems like a sensible thing to do. Wheat, on the other hand, is sold out by noon with consumers hoping for more. Entrepreneurs would surely take advantage of this shortage by raising the price of Wheat.

- Exercise 4.7: Make a fairly accurate copy of Figure 4.4 on your own paper (you will probably be best off making it considerably bigger than in the book). Now assume that P_c has just fallen by 50% (presumably because entrepreneurs couldn't sell their whole stock at the original price).
  i. Draw the new equal-profit line through the point * (the combination that was produced before P_c fell by 50%). Is * still the profit maximizing production combination?
  ii. Draw the equal-profit line you need to indicate the new profit maximizing production combination.
  iii. After the change you depicted, do consumers still think they can afford # from Figure 4.4?
  iv. Redo all of Exercise 4.7i-iii under the following new assumption: Instead of a 50% decline in P_c, assume that P_w doubled (from where it was in Figure 4.4). How do your answers compare with those you got the first time through the problem (that is, when you assumed P_c fell by 50%)?

Exercise 4.7 shows what happens to production when P_c falls or P_w rises. Furthermore, it tells us **something** (though not everything) about what happens to desired consumption. Production moves from * to **. Desired consumption (or **Demand**, as it is called) shifts from # to somewhere on the new aggregate budget constraint.

On the chance you got it wrong in Exercise 4.7, Figure 4.5 shows what your answer should have looked like. As you probably already saw when you did Exercise 4.7, production shifts "up" the production possibilities curve, to **. And demand must lie somewhere on the new aggregate budget constraint. It is certainly plausible (though not certain) that a budget constraint change of the type depicted would cause consumers to increase demand for Corn and cut demand for Wheat (after all, the price of Corn went down relative to the price of Wheat). So it is reasonable to anticipate that the economic forces unleashed by the price change will move the

---

[6]Actually, since the actions of both consumers and entrepreneurs are determined only by the **ratio** of P_w to P_c, it does not matter whether P_w rises, P_c falls, or both.

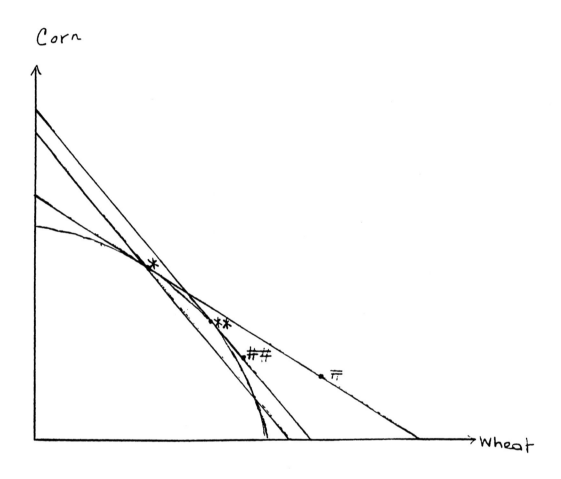

Fig. 4.5

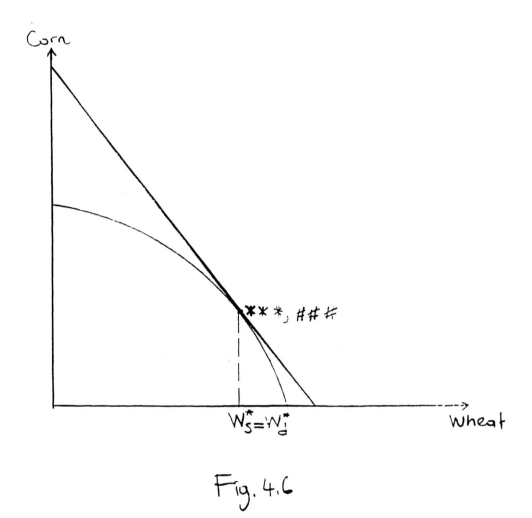

Fig. 4.6

combination demanded to a point like ##.

The reduction in P_c (or the increase in P_w, or both; it doesn't matter) moves the economy from (*,#) to (**,##). As you can see, the gap between the supply of, and demand for both Corn and Wheat has shrunk. Consumers still want more Wheat than is produced and less Corn than is produced, but the discrepancy between what is produced and what is demanded has shrunk.

More Wheat is demanded by consumers than supplied by entrepreneurs and more Corn is supplied by entrepreneurs than is demanded by consumers, so there is still pressure for P_w to rise and/or P_c to fall. This pressure o prices continues until the economy arrives at a position like that depicted in Figure 4.6. Here P_w has risen enough to completely eliminate the gap between Wheat supplied and demanded. Has the rise in P_w also eliminated the gap between supply and demand for Corn?

- Exercise 4.8: Draw a production possibilities curve and a tangent equal-profit line (assume you have been told the prices of the two goods so you can do this). On the graph indicate the combination of goods supplied by entrepreneurs with an **s** (for supply). Now pick a point on the aggregate budget constraint (have you already drawn it?), not the same as **s**; label this point **d** (for demand). When you did this, was it possible to pick a point such that:
i.   consumers demand more of both Corn and Wheat than is supplied;
ii. supply of Wheat is equal to demand, but supply of Corn is not equal to demand;
iii. demand for **both** Corn and Wheat is less than supply?

You should see from Exercise 4.8 that there are only three possible situations for the economy to be in:
i.   A "disequilibrium" set of prices which cause the demand for Corn to exceed the supply, and the demand for Wheat to fall short of supply;
ii. A "disequilibrium" set of prices which cause the demand for Wheat to exceed the supply, and the demand for Corn to fall short of supply;
iii. An "equilibrium" set of prices which cause demand and supply of both Corn and Wheat to be equal to one another.

We refer to the first two possibilities as "disequilibrium" because, whenever the economy is in condition (i) or (ii) there will be pressure for prices to change. And as we saw above, this price pressure tends to move the economy from a position like (i) or (ii) to a position like (iii). There is always pressure tending to move an economy toward condition (iii) above, and we gave a graphical depiction of this resting place, or equilibrium, in Figure 4.6:

A Cautioary Note About Equilibrium

In the next section of this chapter, as well as in other chapters of this book, we will discuss the properties of the equilibrium depicted in Figure 4.6. But students should be aware that economic equilibrium does not always look like Figure 4.6. Sometimes an economy is subject to other forces, which we will discuss later in the book, which tend to force an economy away from the (s=d) position of Figure 4.6. For example, equilibrium does not look like Figure 4.6 when one of the industries (Corn or Wheat) is a monopoly (we will discuss equilibrium with monopoly in Chapter 9). As we will show in Chapter 6, the equilibrium of Figure 4.6 is a **perfectly competitive** equilibrium, in which every entrepreneur is so insignificant that by himself he cannot change the price of a good.

The equilibrium of Figure 4.6 will also be disturbed if there are taxes (Chapter 10) or a phenomenon known as "externalities" (Chapter 11).

To repeat, the equilibrium of Figure 4.6 tends to arise only under a rather idealized set of conditions. We will analyze this ideal through Chapter 8, and in the subsequent Chapters we will look at things that go wrong with the ideal.

Is Equilibrium Efficient?

We know that an (ideal) economy is always pushed toward an equilibrium which looks like Figure 4.6; the combination of goods supplied is that point which is a tangency between an equal-profit line and the production possibilities curve, the combination demanded is the same point (though as we have seen this occurs only after the forces of price adjustment have done their work).

We also know what an economically efficient (Pareto optimal) mix of production and consumption looks like: Efficiency occurs when at the point of supply the slope of the production possibilities curve is identical to the slopes of all consumers' indifference curves at their points of consumption.

Economic efficiency is a state of the world in which it is impossible to make a consumer better off w/o making another worse off.

The time has come to ask whether the market forces we have discussed in this chapter tend to bring about an efficient mix of production and consumption.

• Exercise 4.9: (An equilibrium with two consumers). First, draw a production possibilities curve for Corn and Wheat, and then draw a tangent equal-profit line and show the combination of goods supplied (by now, this should be pretty easy). Next, on two separate graphs, draw budget constraints for Blache and Otto, assuming that they are the only consumers in the economy. (Since they are the only consumers in the economy, between them they get all of the Π and all of the R.) For both Blanche and Otto, draw an indifference curve tangent to the budget constraint, and indicate the amount of Corn and Wheat that each of them demands. Then, on the equal-profit line you drew above, plot the total demand (from both Blanche and Otto) for Corn and Wheat.

When you transferred total demand from the Blanche and Otto graphs to the production possibilities curve, you should have found that total demands lie somewhere on the equal-profit

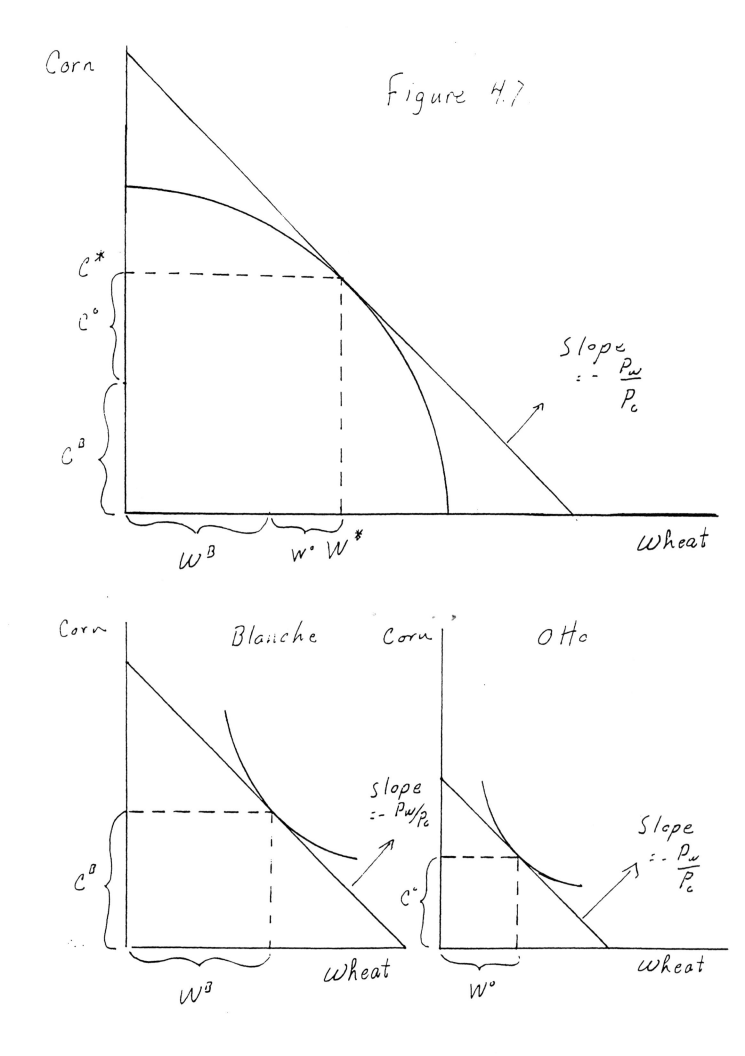

Figure 4.7

line; this is because you should have drawn the two budget constraints so that they add up to the equal-profit line. But unless you were incredibly lucky, your plotted total-goods demanded combination was not the same as the combination of goods supplied You drew a disequilibrium, from which there is pressure for prices to change.

- Exercise 4.10: Do just what you did in Exercise 4.9, except this time draw an equilibrium. [The easiest way to draw this is as follows: (i) Draw the production possibilities curve and a tagent line. (ii) Draw two budget constraints (on two different graphs) with the same slope as your tangent line above, making sure that the y-intercepts of these two budget constraints add up to the y-intercept of the equal-profit tangent line. (iii) On the production possibilities curve, plot the amount of Corn actually produced, and divide that amount however you want between Blanche and Otto. Plot this amount of Corn respectively on Blanche's and Otto's budget constraints. (This will automatically ensure that Otto's plus Blanche's Wheat consumption, as read from the budget constraints, add up to the total Wheat production you found above. Check it out if you don't believe us.) (iv) For both Blanche and Otto, draw an indifference curve tangent to the consumption point you just assigned to them.[7]]

After carrying out Exercise 4.10 you should have a set of graphs that looks like Figure 4.7 below. Like Figure 4.6 above, it is a depiction of equilibrium, but it is more detailed in that it shows individual budget constraints and indifference curves. Note that it truly is an equilibrium; total supply equals total demand, and there is no tendency for either price to change.

Is Equilibrium Efficient?

Looking at Figure 4.7, we can ask whether it depicts an efficient, or a inefficient (wasteful) allocation of the nation's resources. And we explore this question the same way we did in Chapter 2; ask whether there are any possible trades which will make one consumer better off without harminng another.

We already know that it is impossible for these two consumers to trade **with one another** so as to help one without harming the other; we discovered in Chapter 2 that so long as all (in this case both) consumers face the same prices, they will choose points on their indifference curves with identical slopes.

Now we have to see whether it is possible to improve the lot of one consumer without

---

[7]As we will emphasize in Exercise 4.11, it is "cheating" to draw the indifference curves after you have assigned consumption bundles to the two consumers. You "should" do it by drawing the indifference curves first, and then finding prices and incomes which cause supply to be equal to demand. But this "right" way of doing it is very hard, and the shortcut we recommend here does indeed give you a graphical representation of an equilibrium. And the purpose of the exercise is to get such a representation so we can study it.

harming another by changing the combination of goods produced. From earlier in this chapter we kow that such a move along the production possibilities curve **sometimes** can improve the lot of one consumer without harming any other. (See Exercises 4.1 and 4.2) This is possible **only** when the slope of the production possibilities curve (at the point of production) is different from the slope of some consumer's indifference curve (at the point of consumption). When all of these slopes are identical, there is no way to "get something for nothing" by sliding along the production possibilities curve.

When we look at Figure 4.7, we see that **all** of the relevant slopes are identical: Blanche's indifference curve at d_b (b for Blanche) has the same slope as Otto's at d_o, and they are both identical to the slope of the production possibilities curve at **s**. The reason is that all three decision makers are "lining up" with the same prices. Blanche and Otto study the ratio P_w/P_c in deciding which goods to buy, and the entrepreneurs study the same ratio in deciding which goods to sell.

- Fact 4.4: In the ideal economy described in Chapters 2 - 4, even though **nobody** makes any effort to achieve economic efficiency, a consequence of the selfish efforts of consumers and entrepreneurs to do the best they can for themselves tends to bring about a completely Pareto optimal, or economically efficient, or waste-free, state of the world.

When one thinks of the possibilities for economic waste in the world -- production of oranges when consumers would rather have apples, delivery of oranges to apple lovers and vice versa, and so on countless times -- Fact 4.4 is a truly remarkable fact. The price system, which evolved without anybody formally "inventing" it, and which continues to function with very little maintenance, may well be the greatest labor saving device in the history of mankind. To see this, first do parts(i) - (iv) of Exercise 4.11. Then **at least think about** how you would do part (v):

- Exercise 4.11: Carefully draw a reasonable-looking production possibilities curve on a large piece of graph paper. The output produced by this economy is to be shared among 5 consumers; call them C1 - C5. Then do the following

i. For each of the 5 consumers draw a set of indifference curves (also do this on graph paper). Make the consumers different from one another, but be sure to obey the rules of indifference curves (make sure each consumer's indifference curves are downward sloping, bowed toward the origin, and do not cross one another).

ii. Pick a point on the production possibilities curve; as you know, this represets a combination produced. (Do not draw a price line; just pick a point).

iii. Distribute the output from (ii) above to the 5 consumers in any way you want to, but make sure that the total amount that you gave the 5 consumers is equal (in total) to the amount that was produced.

iv. Check to see whether the combination produced, along with the consumption bundles given to the various consumers, is wasteful. Unless you cheated, probably by drawing the indifference curves (step (i)) after you handed out the goods (step (iii)) or were incredibly lucky, the allocation of goods is wasteful. There are likely all kinds of gains that can be realized among consumers, and between consumers and the production possibilities curve.

v. (This is where it gets hard) **Without using a system of prices like we did throughout this chapter**, try to find a way to move from the wasteful outcome of steps (i) through (iii) to an outcome in which all waste has been eliminated.

If a benevolent planner were to try to allocate a society's resources without waste, he would face a task like step (v) above, only infinitely more difficult. Imagine trying to carry out step (v) but with the following added complications:

i. There are 250 million consumers (we'll give you a break and not ask you to eliminate waste worldwide; stick to the United States);

ii. You don't actually know the shapes of everybody's indifference curves, so you ether have to interview everybody (it will be a long interview) or somehow do without this information;

iii. There are not just two goods in the economy; there are thousands of different goods;

iv. Products are manufactured not just with land, but also with various categories of labor and capital. We need to be sure that the various inputs are not wastefully assigned to production tasks (to take a trite example, don't put lefties at shortstop).[8]

This is an utterly impossible task for a planner to carry out. But the remarkable conclusion from Fact 4.4 is that it is unnecessary to ask a planner to even try to carry out such an overwhelming task. All we have to do is to protect the integrity of the price system; selfish consumers and entrepreneurs will do the rest.

Conclusion

We began this chapter by characterizing an economically efficient point on the production possibilities curve; we discovered the following:

● Economic efficiency requires that the slope of the production possibilities curve (at the point of production) be identical to the slope of every consumer's indifference curve (at the point of consumption).

If this condition is violated, it is possible to make one consumer better off without harming any other consumer.

Next we characterized **equilibrium**; where the economy **will** end up, given the idealized set of forces outlined in this chapter. An equilibrium occurs when a given set of prices causes the quantity supplied to be equal to the quantity demanded for every good in the economy.

Finally, we compared the equilibrium with the economically efficient outcome and discovered that (under the ideal set of conditions analyzed in this chapter):

---

[8]We haven't explored this issue yet; iit is the subject of Chapter 5.

• An equilibrium has all of the properties of economic efficiency; the forces which drive an economy toward equilibrium perform another role at the same time; the forces of equilibration tend to eliminate all economic waste.

In the next three chapters, we will fill in some important details in this story. The subsequent chapters will discuss a long list of things that can go wrong between the ideal described in the first part of the book, on the one hand, and the actual working of a market economy, on the other.

Chapter 5
Firms that Produce One Output
and Hire a Mixture of Inputs

The firm we introduced in Chapter 3 rented land from consumers and then decided which parcels of land to devote to Corn, and which to Wheat. Students who have studied the theory of the firm in any standard Elements or Intermediate Theory book know that this is a pretty odd way of looking at firms. And presumably all students know that firms typically go about things in a manner almost completely opposite to what we described here: they specialize in producing one or a few goods, and decide what **combination** of inputs to hire in order to most profitably produce this good.

In this chapter, we will look at firms in this more traditional, and in some ways more sensible, way. We will see that all of the insights from Chapters 3 and 4 continue to be correct when we look at firms from this new perspective.

The One-Output Competitive Firm

Now we'll think of a firm which has already decided to specialize in the production of one particular product; having probably exhausted your tolerance for Corn and Wheat, we'll just call the good **x**. There are two inputs in the economy, labor (**l**) and capital (**k**).[1]

We will assume that there are many other firms which also hire **k** and **l** to produce **x**; that is, the industry is **competitive**. In a **competitive industry**, the presence of other identical firms forces each firm to charge the going price (or less) for its output; if he charges more his customers will buy from the competition. So our firm does not have a choice to make regarding the price he charges for his wares; he must look up the price in the newspaper and live with it.

In reality, of course, some firms do not face as much competitive discipline as others. Individual wheat farmers genuinely regard the price of wheat as beyond their control, like the weather. But automobile manufacturers, particularly before the wave of foreign competition which began in the late 1970s, had considerable discretion in the prices they set. Firms which do have some power to set the prices of their goods are called **imperfectly competitive**; we will study such firms in Chapter ___ .

---

[1]Of course, in reality, an entrepreneur has many more than two types of inputs to choose from; there are many categories of labor (differentiated by specific skills, for example), many categories of capital (tractors, airplanes, and buildings, for example), and many categories of land (the various States that we analyzed in Chapter 3, for example). We restrict ourselves to two inputs in the text because we want to carry out graphical analysis with the two inputs on the axes. Everything we say about a firm with two inputs would apply equally well to a firm with many different inputs. But we would have to use algebra rather than geometry to show it.

Since the firm has no control over the price of **x** or the prices of inputs (we'll let **w** (for wage) stand for the price of labor, and **r** (for (rental) stand for the price of **k**) it faces only three choices: the amounts of **k** and **l** to hire and the amount of **x** to produce.[2] Let's assume he's already decided to produce a given amount of **x** (we'll call it **x'**); now he has to decide what combination of **k** and **l** to use.

The first component of this decision is simply to make a list of all of the combinations of **k** and **l** that are capable of producing **x'**. Such a list can then be transformed into a graph, which might look something like Figure 5.1:

For our hypothetical firm, the curve drawn in Figure 5.1 depicts all of the combinations of **k** and **l** that are capable of producing **x'**. We refer to this curve as an **isoquant** (for "equal quantity" of output). Notice that it is downward sloping (you should be able to figure out why this makes sense) and bowed in toward the origin. In Exercise 5.1 we will think about why it's bowed in toward the origin.

- Exercise 5.1: Look at * on Figure 5.1, as compared with **. You see that, compared with **, * uses a lot of **k** and not so much **l**; we refer to * as a relatively **capital intensive** method of producing **x'**; think of it as an assembly line with the most advanced robotics. Point **, by contrast, uses more **l** and not so much **k**; it is more **labor intensive**.
- i. Beginning at *, draw amount of **extra k** that would be required (to keep **x** constant at **x'**, remember) if the entrepreneur were to reduce his labor force by 1.
- ii. Now beginning at ** (the more labor intensive production plan) ask the same question as in (i); how much more **k** would be required if the entrepreneur were to reduce his labor force by 1?
- iii. How would your answer to 5.1 (i) and (ii) change if the isoquant were a straight line?
- iv. How would your answer change if the isoquant were bowed out from the origin, like a production possibilities curve?

The bowed-in isoquant displays the following characteristic: The firm can more easily give up some of its labor (capital) if its current production plan is relatively labor (capital) intensive. When the firm has a lot of labor and relatively little capital, he can replace some of his plentiful labor with a relatively insignificant increment to capital. But at a point like *, labor is already used very sparingly, and it is harder to find a way to reduce it any further. That is why the isoquant gets steeper closer to the **y** axis.

The Cheapest Way to Produce x

---

[2]Actually, as we will see, he has only two choices. Surely, once he has decided how much **k** and **l** to hire, he directs these inputs to produce as much **x** as possible.

Isoquant

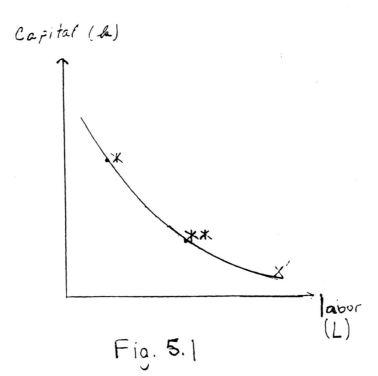

Capital (k)

labor (L)

Fig. 5.1

Now we know all of the possible ways to produce **x'**; it's time to find out which is the **cheapest** possible way. After all, if the firm intends to sell **x'** as part of a plan to maximize profit, the other part of the plan must be to produce **x'** as cheaply as possible.

Remember, in this chapter we are looking at cost from the perspective of the firm that specializes in producing **x**; he cares about the cost (to him) of **k** and **l**; he neither knows nor cares about the cost of producing **x** measured in the value of foregone **y** (**y** is the other good, produced by a different group of competitive firms).

The cost of any combination of **k** and **l** can be written as

$$C = w{\cdot}l + r{\cdot}k \tag{1}$$

where **C** is the cost that the firm incurs. **w·l** is the cost of labor (the wage rate times the amount of labor employed) and **r·k** is the cost of capital. Now (by a familiar method) we are going to use equation 5.1 to plot a family of **equal-cost lines**. An equal-cost line depicts all of the combinations of **k** and **l** that cost the same amount of money.

- Exercise 5.2: Assume that **w** = $5 (per hour) and **r** = $10 (per "machine"). Make a graph with **k** on the vertical axis and **l** on the horizontal.
 i. Draw all combinations of **k** and **l** that cost $1000.
 ii. Draw all combinations that cost $2000.
 iii. Draw an isoquant which is higher than (never touches) either of your equal cost lines.
 iv. Draw an equal-cost line which shows the cheapest possible way of producing the output represented by your isoquant, and give an approximate value for this cost.
 v. Draw another equal-cost line which shows more expensive ways of getting to the isoquant.

- Fact 5.1: The cheapest way of producing any given level of output (of a specific good) occurs at the point on the isoquant which is **tangent** to an equal-cost line.

This tangency represents the lowest equal cost line which touches the isoquant.

- Exercise 5.3: In exercise 5.2 you drew several equal-cost lines.
 i. Are they parallel? (If you say no, go back and check your work in Exercise 5.1.)
 ii. Calculate the slope (give a specific number).
 iii. Write an expression for this slope, relating it to **w** and **r**. [HINT: In terms of its algebraic layout, Equation (5.1) looks virtually identical to Equation 2.1 (the consumer's budget constraint from Chapter 2), and Equation 3.1 (the entrepreneur's equal-profit line from Chapter 3). For both of these equations we figured out how to relate the slope of the line to the prices.]
 iv. Returning to Exercise 5.2, raise the wage rate to $10 and draw one equal-cost line. How does this slope compare with that you got in Exercise 5.2? Given what you now know

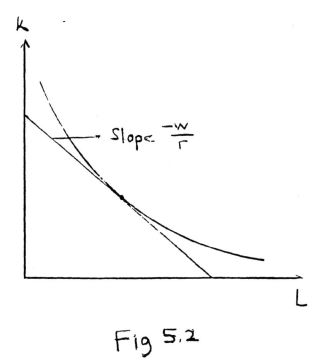

Fig 5.2

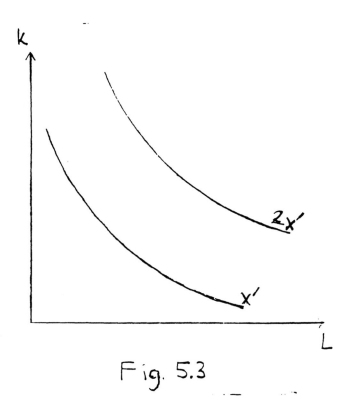

Fig. 5.3

about the slope of the equal-cost line and the prices of capital and labor, check to see whether your new equal-cost line turned out the way it should have.

We now know that a profit-maximizing one-output firm goes to a point on an isoquant which is tangent to an equal-cost line, and we know that this slope is equal to the ratio of the input prices. All of this is depicted in Figure 5.2.

A Whole Family of Isoquants

Figure 5.1 shows all of the combinations of **k** and **l** that are capable of producing a specific amount of output **x'**. (To indicate that **x'** is the amount of output produced by the various combinations on the isoquant, we've labeled the isoquant **x'**.) But what if the firm wanted to produce more **x**, say **2x'**? Surely the only way to do this is with more **k** and **l**. We have drawn such an isoquant in Figure 5.3, and labeled it **2x'**. We have drawn isoquant **2x'** in such a way that it takes exactly twice as much **k** and **l** to produce **2x'** as it does to produce **x'**. Both the labor intensive method and the capital intensive method are still available to produce **2x'**, and for both methods twice the output requires twice the original doses of **k** and **l**.

Economists refer to the type of isoquant configuration we drew in Figure 5.3 as **constant returns to scale**.[3] Although we frequently think of constant returns to scale as "typical," there are many instances in which this pattern does not actually hold. It could be that when a firm doubles its use of each input, it is able to more than double its output; we call this case **increasing returns to scale**. And there are some instances in which output cannot be doubled unless all of the inputs are more than doubled; we call this **decreasing returns to scale**.

● Exercise 5.4: Copy or trace Figure 5.3 onto your own paper. Figure out how to alter this picture, first to depict increasing returns to scale and then to depict decreasing returns to scale.

In most of this book we will simply deal with the "standard" case of constant returns to scale; we will try to let you know when outcomes would be significantly different under increasing or decreasing returns to scale.

Economically Efficient Allocation of Capital and Labor

Society has a limited stock of resources (capital and labor); this means that the limited stock of capital and labor must somehow be allocated among the various firms in the economy. We need to ask three questions:

---

[3]The name makes sense; if we increase the **scale** of a production process, by doubling all inputs, then under constant returns to scale the output doubles.

5.5

- First, what is an economically efficient allocation of labor and capital among different firms?
- Second, how do markets allocate labor and capital among firms?
- Third, do markets tend to allocate labor and capital efficiently? In this section, we turn to the first question.

In Figure 5.4a an **x** producing firm currently produces **x'**, using the labor; capital combination designated α. In Figure 5.4b, a **y** firm currently produces **y'**, using the input combination labeled β. By the method we have already employed several times, we will see whether it is possible for these two firms to trade inputs with one another and in the process make one consumer better off without making another one worse off.

- Exercise 5.5: (This should be familiar territory by now) Copy or trace Figure 5.4 onto your own paper. Cut **x**'s capital stock by a small amount and give it to **y**. Now take enough labor from **y** to keep the output of **x** constant at **x'**. What happened to the output of **y**?

You should know from previous work on consumers that it was possible to hold the output of **x** constant and at the same time increase the production of **y** (without taking resources from any of the other firms in the economy) only because at α and β, the initial points for both firms, the isoquants' slopes were different.

- Exercise 5.6: Draw a graph with the two consumer goods, **x** and **y** on the axes. Pick some point in this graph representing total national output of **x** and **y**. This is total national production when your **x** firm was at α (producing **x'**) and your **y** firm was at β (producing **y'**). (Presumably other firms were also producing **x** and **y** also, but your trade between the two firms whose isoquants you have drawn will not affect those other firms.) As a result of the reshuffling of **k** and **l** you did in Exercise 5.5, draw what happens to national output of **x** and **y**. Was the original point on the production possibilities curve?

From Exercise 5.6 you should see the following: Failure to allocate **inputs** in an economically efficient manner means that the economy is inside, rather than on, the production possibilities curve. Any time inputs are not allocated efficiently (as depicted in Figure 5.4), two firms can swap inputs in such a way as to increase the production of one good without diminishing the output of the other good.

- Fact 5.1: Inputs are allocated efficiently only when the slopes of all firms' isoquants (at the point of production) are identical. When this occurs (and only when this occurs) the economy is on its production possibilities curve.

Market Allocation of Capital and Labor

Will market forces tend to allocate inputs efficiently? Or to put the same question

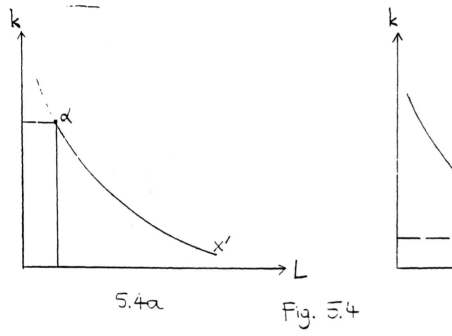

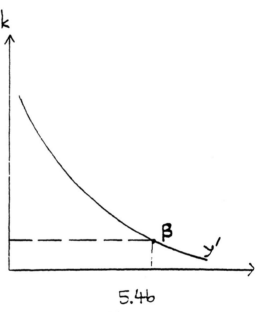

5.4a   Fig. 5.4   5.4b

differently, can we count on market forces to drive the economy toward the producton possibilities curve?

We have assembled all of the pieces required to answer this question very quickly. Entrepreneurs want to minimize cost; that is, they are constantly striving to be in a position like Figure 5.2. By working out Exercise 5.7, you can see what happens to resources when all firms try to minimize cost.

- Exercise 5.7: On one graph, draw an isoquant for the production of some good; then, on another graph (but with the units the same) draw an isoquant for another good. You can draw the isoquants however you want, so long as they obey the basic rules (downward sloping and bowed inward). Now make up numbers for the prices of your two inputs. On each of your isoquant graphs, draw the equal-cost line which depicts the cheapest possible way to produce the level of output indicated by your isoquant.
  i. Assuming each of your firms produces its output in the cheapest possible way, it is possible for them to swap inputs in such a way as to increase the output of one good without decreasing the output of the other good?
  ii. Would your answer to part (i) be different if you had drawn your isoquants differently (but still obeying the basic rules)?

- Fact 5.2: So long as all firms face the same prices (as one another) for their inputs, their own selfish desire to minimize their production cost tends to lead the economy to a point on (and not inside) the production possibilities curve.

Why Not Do it This Way in the First Place?

In this chapter, we have treated firms as specialists; each firm hires a group of inputs and uses them to produce a specific output. This is quite different from the firm we discussed in Chapter 3. In that chapter, remember, a single firm produced all of the goods consumed by the public. If the Chapter-5 view of firms is so much more realistic, why did we bother with the Chapter-3 fiction in the first place?

The answer is that we could look at the Chapter-3 firm and clearly see the true cost of producing one particular commodity. When the Chapter-3 firm produced a bit more corn, it was very evident that the true cost of that production was foregone wheat production. On the other hand, when we look at firms as we do in this chapter, it **appears** that the cost of increasing corn production is the cost of the extra labor and capital.

In reality, the extra labor and capital is costly because of the wheat it could have produced had it not been moved into corn production; the only reason that labor and capital are expensive is that they have **alternative uses**. When our society produces more corn, the true cost is what we really lose; wheat production.

Conclusion

In this chapter we began to think of firms as specialists; some firms produce one type of good and some produce another. We also introduced the notion that firms compete with one another in selling their wares; it is this competition which deprives any one firm of any power to manipulate the price of its goods.

Next we introduced the notion that firms hire inputs, and that they compete with one another for the services of these inputs. This competition for inputs causes inputs to be allocated among firms efficiently; that is, competition for inputs tends to force the economy onto (rather than inside) the production possibilities curve.

Chapter 6
The Allocation of Labor

Introduction

By now we can see that the economy's task is to allocate inputs among various productive activities, and to allocate the outputs which are produced to society's consumers. In a market economy, the instruments of this allocation are **prices**.

In Chapter 2, we simply picked arbitrary output prices and studied consumers' responses. We also "gave" our consumers arbitrary incomes to spend on the various consumer goods. We did not say where either the prices or incomes came from; we just made them up.

In Chapter 3 we continued with made-up prices, and studied the effect of these prices on entrepreneurs' decisions.

In Chapter 4 we began to observe how the economy itself determines prices; for the first time we saw the notion of **equilibrium**. And we made some progress toward seeing where incomes come from; we learned that the aggregate of all consumers' incomes is a price line which passes through the combination of goods produced; aggregate income is just sufficient to buy back all of the consumer goods which the economy produces. But we still said nothing about the forces which determine individual incomes.

In Chapter 5 we explicitly introduced separate **inputs**; labor and capital. But we fell back to the habits of Chapters 2 and 3; we made up numbers for the prices of these inputs. (We got something out of that exercise; we learned that so long as all entrepreneurs face the same prices for all inputs, the economy will tend to be on, rather than inside, the production possibilities curve.)

The time has come to see how the economy itself determines prices of inputs. The step from Chapter 5 to Chapters 6 and 7 is analogous to the step from Chapters 2 and 3 to Chapter 4; in the earlier chapters we pick prices and study the responses of consumers and producers; in the latter we study the economic forces which influence the prices themselves.

Labor and Leisure

As we emphasized in Chapter 4, consumers earn their income by selling inputs (mostly labor, for most of us) to entrepreneurs; this is how we earn the income with which we buy consumer goods. But virtually none of us work to our absolute physical limit. At some point the extra income is not worth it; we would rather have **leisure**. By going to work, we are giving up some of our leisure time in exchange for consumer goods.

Figure 6.1 gives a map of a consumer's indifference curves between leisure and "consumption." Consumption is simply dollars' worth of expenditure on consumer goods.[1] Just like Corn and Wheat, the consumer likes both leisure and consumption; his indifference curves slope downward and are bowed in toward the origin for the same reasons we articulated in Chapter 2. And as in Chapter 2, the consumer's objective is to get on the highest indifference possible.[2]

The consumer will go to the highest indifference curve he can afford, just as in Chapter 2. In Chapter 2 we gave the consumer some income, out of which he bought the goods. We defined what the consumer wants (the indifference curves) and what the consumer can afford (the budget constraint). We then simply asked, among all the combinations that the consumer can afford, what is the most desirable combination? We will use exactly the same method here.

Of course, consumers do not buy leisure and consumption out of a fixed income; instead, they sell part of their fixed leisure endowment. The act of going to work is the act of selling (potential) leisure in exchange for a wage. We need to explore this notion and see what the consumer's budget constraint looks like.

- Exercise 6.1: Draw a graph with **C** (consumption) on the vertical axis and **l** (leisure) on the horizontal. The vertical axis will represent **daily** consumption, and the horizontal **daily** leisure. The highest value on your horizontal axis should be 24 hours (the length of the day). The maximum value on the vertical axis needs to be about $5000

i. Your consumer receives $10/day in interest or dividends; he gets this without even working (and therefore we usually refer to it as **unearned income**). On your graph plot the amount of **C** and **l** your consumer obtains if he doesn't work at all.

ii. Next, incorporate the fact that your consumer has an opportunity to work for $10/hour. First, plot the amount of consumption he could afford if he worked 24 hours per day (don't forget the $10/day he receives without working).

iii. Now fill in the amount of consumption he can afford if he works 1, 2, 3, etc. hours per day. When you connect the dots, you have drawn the budget constraint facing this consumer; he can afford any consumption/leisure combination on the line you drew.

iv. What is the slope of the budget constraint?

v. Re-do steps (i) - (iv) with a wage rate of $20. Does the new budget constraint make sense?

vi. Write down an equation for the budget constraint. You should be able to use this

---

[1]Collapsing all other goods (besides leisure) into one commodity does not change any of the analysis, so long as we don't allow the prices of these goods to change during our analysis of leisure.

[2]Notice that the indifference curve stops at 24 hours (per day) of leisure. Since the day has only 24 hours in it, it would be nonsensical to ask the consumer what quantity of consumer goods he would require to go along with 36 hours per day of leisure.

Consumption (C)

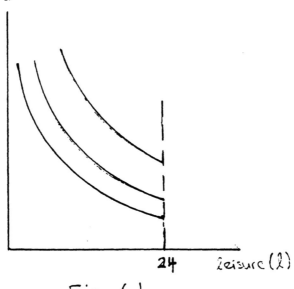

24   leisure (ℓ)

Fig. 6.1

6.3

euqation to do steps iii and iv without "filling in the dots."

In the first part of Exercise 6.1, you should have gotten a budget constraint with a slope of -10; in the second the slope should be -20. Note that in each instance the slope is equal to minus the wage rate. See if you can figure out why this makes sense (by how much does consumption rise if your consumer gives up one more hour of leisure?).[3]

Figure 6.2 reproduces the budget constraints you should have gotten in Exercise 6.1 above; see how you did. We have also drawn indifference curves tangent to each of the budget constraints. Point * is the consumer's best consumption-leisure choice if w = $10/hour; ** is the best choice if w = $20/hour.

- Exercise 6.2: Turn to Figure 6.2, first looking at the case where w = $10/hour. Note that the amount of leisure chosen is 16.5 hours per day.
i. What happened to the other 7.5 hours per day?
ii. When the wage rises to $20/hour, does the amount of **labor supplied** by the consumer rise or fall? (Note that the amount of labor supplied is the length of the day (24 hours) minus the amount of leisure taken by the consumer.)
iii. In (ii) above you should have found that labor supply rose (from 7.5 to 8 hours per day) when the wage rose from $10 to $20 per hour. Is it possible to draw a set of indifference curves, without violating the basic rules of indifference curves (downward sloping, bowed inward, and no touching or crossing of other curves), which would lead to the opposite conclusion; namely that a rise in the wage rate leads to a reduction in labor supply? (Remember, a reduction in labor supply is identical to an increase in leisure demand.)
iv. On the graph you drew for Exercise 6.1, draw the budget constraint for a worker facing a $10/hour wage (as in part (ii) of that exercise) but now give you consumer $30 of interest or dividend income. Would you expect this added interest or dividend income to increase or decrease the amount of labor supplied by the worker?

As in the case of two consumer goods, the consumer seeks out a point of tangency between the budget constraint and an indifference curve. That is, the consumer trades in leisure for goods (by moving along the budget constraint) up to the point where the indifference curve has a slope of **-w**.

- Exercise 6.3: Our consumer has to choose between two different job offers. Job Offer (i) pays $10 per hour and he gets to work at home. Job Offer (ii) pays $12 per hour but he has to pay $10 per day to commute to work and park. Which offer should he accept?

---

[3]Technically, the slope of the budget constraint is -w/p, where p is the price of consumer goods. Thus as always the slope of the budget constraint is equal to a price **ratio**. But since we are measuring consumption as dollars' worth of consumption, the price of consumption is automatically $1. So -w/p and -w are the same thing.

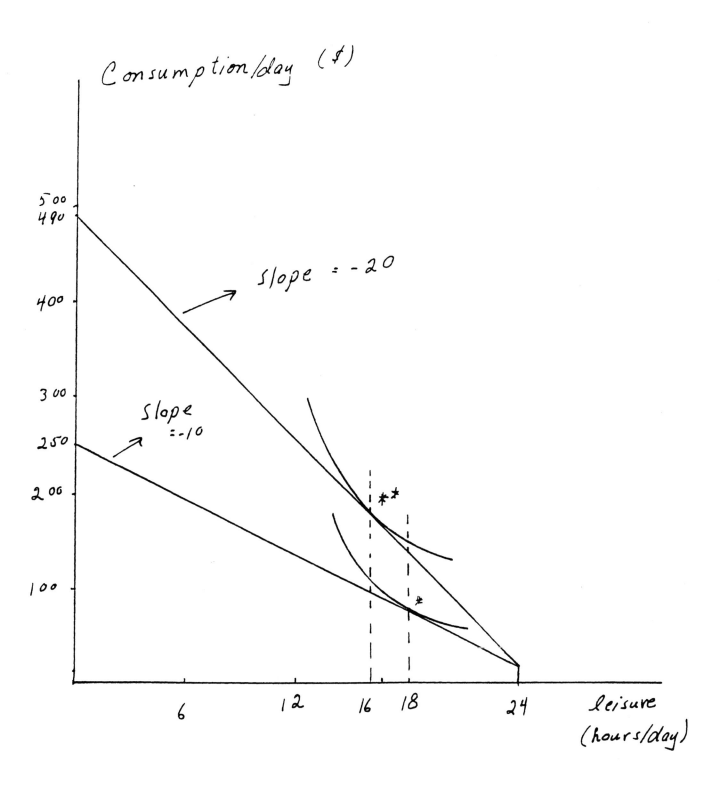

Consumption/day ($)

500
490

400

300
250

200

100

slope = -20

slope
= -10

6   12   16 18   24

leisure
(hours/day)

Figure 6.2

In Exercise 6.2 we began to explore how a consumer would respond to a change in either the wage rate or unearned income. We discovered the odd fact that a rise in the wage rate might actually induce a consumer to reduce his labor supply. The reason is that the wage increase makes him richer, and one of the goods he wants to buy with this new income is more leisure.

More important, we discovered that the consumer selects a point of tangency between the budget constraint and an indifference curve; that is, he goes to a point where the slope of the indifference curve is equal to the price ratio -w/p (which in our special case is just -w, see footnote 2).

The Demand for Labor

In Figure 6.2 and Exercise 6.2 we analyzed the forces which govern the amount of labor a consumer would **supply** to the market. The answer depends upon the consumer's preferences (indifference curves) and upon the budget constraint (unearned income and the wage rate). Next we need to explore the forces which govern the amount of labor that will be **demanded** by entrepreneurs. That is, for any given wage rate, how much labor will entrepreneurs want to hire?

From the perspective of an entrepreneur, what are the consequences of hiring more labor? Hiring more labor brings forth both good news and bad news. The good news is that, with a bigger labor force, the firm can produce and sell more output; the bad news is that the firm has to pay for the additional labor.

The firm's decision is really pretty straightforward: If the good news is bigger than the bad news, then hiring the additional labor increases profit. So let's look explicitly at the two components of news which result from hiring one more person-hour of labor:

The Bad News: This is as simple as it seems it should be: in order to get an extra person-hour of labor, the firm has to pay **w**, the hourly wage rate.

The Good News: Whe a firm hires a bit more labor, the **rate** at which output rises is

$$\frac{\Delta C}{\Delta L} \tag{1}$$

This is merely an algebraic way of writing the extra C that is produced per extra hour of labor; we refer to this ratio as the **Marginal Product** of labor. If the firm used to be at * in Figure 6.3, hiring one more person-hour is represented by a move to **; this moves the firm from Isoquant 8 (output is 8) to Isoquant 8.3 (output is 8.3). The marginal product of labor, in this example, is the extra output (.3) divided by the extra labor (1). So the marginal product is 0.3.

We now know that if the firm is at * it can get 0.3 of extra output by hiring 1 more unit of

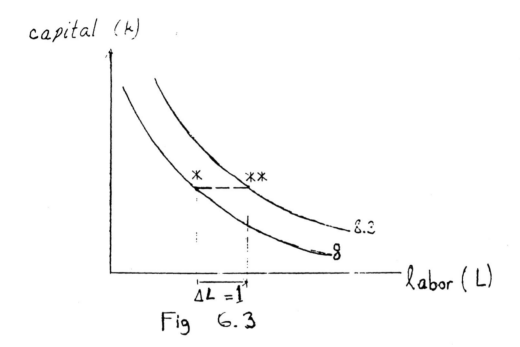

Fig 6.3

labor. But we don't know how good this is for the firm, because we know the price of C[4]. Producing 0.3 of extra C is better news for the firm if C sells for $10 each than if it sells for $.50 each. The firm's good news is the marginal product, multiplied by the unit price of output, or

$$\frac{\Delta C}{\Delta L} \cdot P_C = (VMP_L)$$ (2)

This expression is dollars of extra revenue which come from the hiring of one more person hour of labor. We refer to this as the Value of the Marginal Product of Labor (VMP$_L$); that is, what the marginal product is worth. When the firm hires a little more labor, profit rises by the good news less the bad news:

$$\Delta \Pi = VMP_L - w$$ (3)

The firm's profit-maximization rule is fairly simple: Hire more labor if $\Delta \Pi$ is positive, don't hire more labor if it is zero, and fire labor if it is negative. The firm is satisfied with the size of its labor force only when adding labor would neither raise nor lower profit. So the firm's rule for maximizing profit is, keep expanding the employment of labor up to the point where

$$VMP_L = w$$

- ☆Exercise 6.4: For reasons we will explore below, the marginal product of labor generally declines as the firm hires more labor (so long as it doesn't hire more capital at the same time). Table 6.1 below gives a firm's total output for various amounts of labor. As you can see, as the firm hires more labor it is able to produce more output. But also, as it hires more labor, the **increments** to output get smaller and smaller.

---

[4]Right now we're dealing with the special case in which $P_c = \$1$. But it's useful to know how to express the "good news" when we are not making this special assumption.

Table 5.1

labor	output
1	10
2	20
3	29
4	37.5
5	45.5
6	51.5
7	55
8	59
9	62

i.   Reproduce Table 5.1, with four blank columns. Label the columns: Marginal Product, Value of Marginal Product, Incremental Labor Cost, and Incremental Profit.
ii.   Calculate the marginal product, for each level of labor usage, and fill in the appropriate column of your table. (For labor = 1, the marginal product is the extra product from hiring the first worker; the marginal product is 10.)
iii. Assume the price of the good is $10; calculate and fill in the column labeled Value of Marginal Product.
iv.   Now assume the wage rate is $50. Fill the column labeled Incremental Labor Cost (there are no tricks here; this is as simple as it seems).
v.   Finally, for each increment of labor, calculate the incremental profit (the amount by which profit changes as labor is increased). Is it always profitable to employ more labor? Is it always profitable when $w < VMP_L$? Why?

In working Exercise 6.4, you should be able to see that increasing labor usage increases both revenue (by VMP_L) and cost (by w). By simply comparing the gain with the loss, one can see whether profit will be raised by hiring more labor. When $w = VMP_L$, the good news is just balanced by the bad news; this is the point at which it stops being profitable to hire more labor.

The Law of Diminishing Returns

Equation (6.3) tells us what happens to the firm's profit if it hires one additional unit (person-hour) of labor. We now need to ask whether we know what happens to VMP_L as more and more labor is employed. This question is answered by the Law of Diminishing Returns:

▶   The Law of Diminishing Returns: After some point, in the presence of a fixed input, subsequent equal increments of a variable input yield ever smaller increments of output.

Notice first that the Law of Diminishing Returns tells us how the marginal product of labor should behave; increments of output produced by increments of a variable input. Also, it refers to a fixed input.

The easiest way to see that the Law of Diminishing Returns makes sense is to imagine that the "fixed input" is an acre of land. The Law of Diminishing Returns asserts that, after some point, adding more farmers to this acre of land will yield ever smaller increments of output. Whereas the third farmer added to the land might have added 4 bushels to the land's yield (thus his marginal product is 4), the fourth farmer adds only 3 (more) bushels, the fifth farmer 2.5, and so on. Surely, by the time we have employed 100 farmers on a single acre of land, the 101st farmer will not be able to raise output very much.

There is no way to "prove" that the Law of Diminishing Returns is valid; in fact, in some highly unusual circumstances it probably is not valid. We assert it as a Law because it is intuitively plausible, and because it seems to agree with reality almost everywhere we look. We will make heavy use of the Law of Diminishing Returns a bit later in this chapter.

●   Exercise 6.5: Check to see whether the numbers in Table 6.1, as described in Exercise 6.4, display the Law of Diminishing Returns. Check all of the phrases in the Law:
i.   Is there a fixed input?
ii.   Is there a sequence of equal increments to a variable input?
iii.   After some point, do the increments of output get ever smaller?

The Leisure-Consumption Production Possibilities Curve

The economy is capable of "producing" two consumer goods; consumption and leisure.[5] If it is capable of producing these two goods, there must be a production possibilities curve with consumption and leisure on the axes. Let's see what it looks like:

●   Exercise 6.6: Suppose the economy has 1000 consumers; in addition, it possesses a fixed stock of land and capital.
i.   If the economy produces no consumer goods (that is, nobody goes to work) how much leisure can it "produce?" Draw a graph which consumption on the vertical axis and leisure on the horizontal, and plot the "nobody works" point.
ii.   Now let's suppose that everybody works for 1 hour per day, and as a result the economy

---

[5]We already know that "consumption" can be divided into Corn and Wheat, or for that matter into the thousands of distinct consumer goods which exist in the economy. But we can also aggregate all of these consumer goods into one "composite" commodity, consumption. This aggregation is useful when we are studying the tradeoff between consumption and leisure.

produces some consumer goods. Draw a point on your graph which depicts this change.

iii. Now set the work day at 2 hours; and then 3 hours, etc. When you connect these dots, you should get a production possibilities curve.

iv. Write an algebraic expression for the slope of the production possibilities curve (that is, write an expression for the rise over the run). Have you seen this expression earlier in this chapter (HINT: take a look at Equation 6.1).

In Exercise 6.6iv you should see that the slope of the production possibilities curve is minus the marginal product of labor ($-\Delta C/\Delta L$). You may have gotten $\Delta C/\Delta l$ (l is leisure, remember), but after all, $\Delta L = -\Delta l$, so the expression we suggest is right too.

In Exercise 6.6iii, you were asked to draw a production possibilities curve, but nothing in the Exercise itself required that it look "normal." You may have drawn a "normal" one because by now it feels right, but we need to check and see whether it really is right. We can check that it is right in two ways. First, we'll construct the production possibilities curve in Exercise 6.7, relying on numbers that you make up when you complete Table 6.2:

Table 6.2

Project	ΔC	ΔL	$\Delta C/\Delta L$
1	20	100	0.2

● ☆Exercise 6.7: Make a table like Table 6.2 above, with room for 10 "projects".

i. Design 10 "projects" numbered 1 through 10. Each "project" requires a specific amount of labor, ΔL, and yields an increment of the consumer good, ΔC. Project #1 needs 100 hours of labor and yields 20 units of consumption goods. Fill in whatever numbers you want for Projects 2-10, but make sure the total labor used on all 10 projects (the sum of the ΔL entries) just adds up to 24000 (the number of person-hours that exist in the economy).

ii. Now rank the projects from highest $\Delta C/\Delta L$ to lowest.

iii. Draw the resulting production possibilities curve (begin with all leisure and no consumption, and one-by-one adopt your projects, reducing leisure and increasing consumption by the amounts associated with the "current" project. Is this curve bowed out like a "normal" production possibilities curve? Would it be possible to change the numbers in your table in such a way as to make the curve bowed in?

In Exercise 6.7, you produced a production possibilities curve almost exactly the way we did back in Chapter 3, and it is bowed out for the same reason. No matter what the individual projects look like, once we rank (and adopt) them going from best to worst, we necessarily get a production possibilities curve that is bowed out.

● ☆Exercise 6.8: Make another graph; on the horizontal axis plot labor (it must run from 0 up to 2400. On the vertical axis plot $\Delta C/\Delta W$; the maximum value for this axis needs to be the highest value for $\Delta C/\Delta W$ that you got in your table from Exercise 6.7.

i. The horizontal coordinate of your first point should be ΔL from the most productive project on your list; the vertical coordinate should be ΔC/ΔW from that same project. This point gives the marginal product of labor if only the first project is carried out.

ii. The x coordinate for the second point should be ΔL from the first project **plus** ΔL from the second project; the vertical coordinate should be ΔC/ΔW from the second project only.

iii. Continue to add points to the graph in the same manner, until you have plotted a point for each project. Connecting the dots, you have a graph plotting the marginal product of labor (ΔC/ΔL for the last project adopted) against total use of labor. You should end up with a point at 2400 person-hours of labor (all the nation's labor is used) and the marginal product of the worst project.

In exercise 6.8, you should have gotten a downward sloping curve; this curve depicts the fact that the marginal product of labor declines as the amount of labor used in the economy increases. This happens because of the way you constructed the production possibilities curve. The first labor employed (your first project) was applied to the most productive project; less productive projects were adopted only after we had already devoted labor to the more productive ones.

- Exercise 6.9: Look at the marginal product of labor curve you drew in Exercise 6.8.

i. Just is you did in Exercise 6.5, check to see whether the marginal product curve you got is an example of the Law of Diminishing Returns.

ii. Try to make up numbers for your Table 6.2 which will cause the Law of Diminishing Returns to fail.

Moving along the production possibilities curve from the all-leisure-no-consumption pont to the all-consumption-no-leisure point, we are applying more and more increments of labor to the nation's fixed stock of land and capital. Notice that this is precisely the set of circumstances described by the Law of Diminishing Returns. And the production possibilities curve is bowed out because the Law of Diminishing Returns holds. The first increment of labor applied yields a big bang (depicted respectively in the steep slope of the production possibilities curve near the x axis) and the large value for ΔC/ΔL for your first project in Exercise 6.7. But subsequent increments of labor yield smaller increments of output; this is exactly what the flattening of the production possibilities curve depicts.

Efficient Allocation of Human Time

We have now studied all of the pieces required to address the question of efficient allocation of human time between work and leisure. We proceed in a very familiar manner; we look for possible transactions that help one consumer without harming another.

Figure 6.4a shows the nation's production possibilities curve between **C** (Consumption) and **l** (leisure), and Figure 6.4b shows an indifference curve between **C** and **l** for one consumer.

Figure 6.4

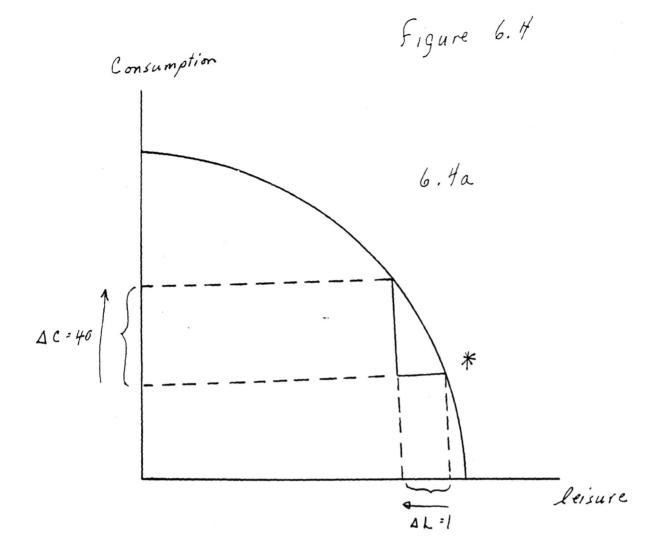

6.4a

Consumption

$\Delta C = 40$

leisure

$\Delta L = 1$

*

6.4b

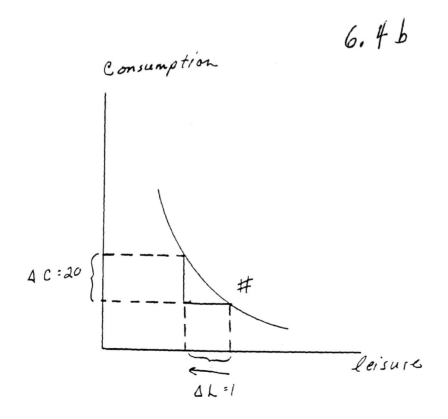

Consumption

$\Delta C = 20$

#

leisure

$\Delta L = 1$

Production is presently occurring at *, and the consumer is at #.

- Exercise 6.10: Copy or trace Figure 6.4 onto your own paper.
i. If this consumer were to work for one additional hour, how much extra output could the economy produce? (Depict it on the appropriate graph.)
ii. How much of the extra output you identified in Exercise 6.10i above **must** be given to this consumer, if he is to be happy with his decision to work an extra hour? Is there some **C** left over?
iii. Is the point (*,#) depicted in Figure 6.4 efficient or wasteful?

We have done exercises like 6.10 sufficiently often that it should be very straightforward by now; in fact you should probably be able to predict what is coming next.

- Exercise 6.11: Return to your work from Exercise 6.10. Under what circumstance would it be **impossible** to make this consumer better off (without making another worse off) by moving along the production possibilities curve?

At the starting point, *, of Figure 6.4a, it is possible to produce $40 of extra **C** with one extra hour of human labor, and our consumer is willing to provide an extra hour of labor in exchange for only $20 of extra **C**. Clearly the consumer should work the extra hour and take home somewhere between half and all of the extra output that results. Staying home would be wasteful.

Market Allocation and the Equilibrium Wage Rate

We already know a lot about how markets allocate human time:

Entrepreneurs continue to hire more labor up to the point where the **VMP of labor is equal to the wage rate.**

Consumers supply labor up to the point where **the wage rate equals the slope of the tanget indifference curve.**

Let's do what we did in Chapter 4; pick a wage rate and see how it works:

- Exercise 6.12: Figure 6.5 depicts an economy with only two consumers. Figure 6.5a shows the production possibilities curve, and 6.5b and 6.5c respectively show indifference curves for consumer 1 and 2. The budget constraints for the two consumers are drawn in; for each the slope is (as it should be) **-w**. Copy or trace these figures onto your own paper.
i. Deaw a line tangent to the production possibilities curve, whose slope is **-w** (the same as the slopes of the budget constraints).
ii. On Figure 6.5a, you should be able to identify the amount of labor that will be hired by

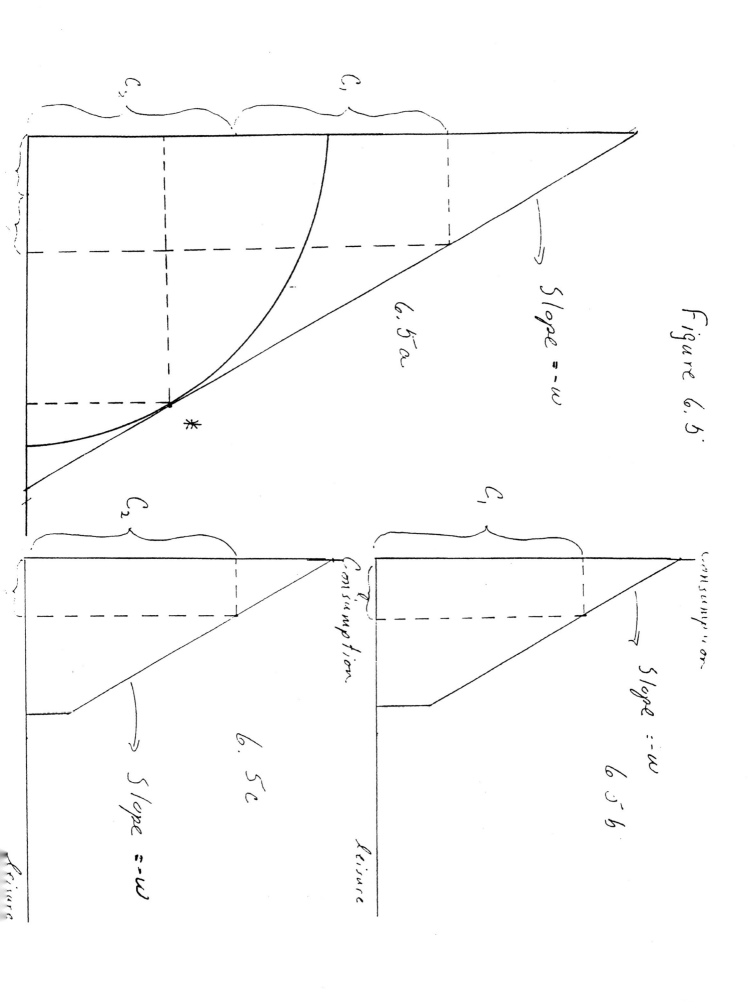

Figure 6.5.

profit-maximizing entrepreneurs [HINT: They hire up to the point where $VMP_L = w$; what is the slope of the production possibilities curve?]

iii. In Figure 6.5, is the amount of labor supplied by the two consumers greater or less than the amount of labor desired (demanded) by entrepreneurs?

iv. In a market economy, would you expect upward or downward pressure on the wage rate, beginning from the wage of Figure 6.5? Show the effect of this wage change on the amount of labor demanded by entrepreneurs.

The wage rate we picked in drawing Figure 6.5 is not an **equilibrium** wage rate; at that wage the amount of work offered by workers is greater than the amount of work entrepreneurs are willing to pay for. We would expect this to lead to downward pressure on the wage rate. After the wage rate falls, entrepreneurs will want to hire more labor, and consumers may want to supply less.[6] Eventually this wage pressure will eliminate the gap between labor supply and demand, and we will have an **equilibrium**, which looks like Figure 6.6.

In Figure 6.6, all three price lines have the same slope (namely **-w**) thus their tangencies describe respectively the optimal points for the entrepreneurs and the consumers (labor suppliers). Furthermore, it depicts an equilibrium wage, since the amount of labor demanded by entrepreneurs (L_d) equals the sum of the amounts supplied by the two consumers ($L_{s1} + L_{s2}$). From Figure 6.6, there is no pressure for the wage rate to either rise or fall.

Is the Market Allocation Efficient?

Once again we follow the method of Chapter 4 and (since it is repetitious) it is very easy to show that the market allocation of human time we have just described is economically efficient.

Look again at Figure 6.6; we know it is an equilibrium since
(i) everybody is responding optimally to the wage rate, and
(ii) the amount of labor supplied equals the amount demanded; there is no pressure for the wage rate to move.

Now imagine this same graph, with the actors still at *, $\#_1$, and $\#_2$ but without the price lines. Except for the fact that there is a second consumer in the picture this is identical to Figure 6.4; it depicts an economically efficient allocation of human time.

The labor market fosters economic efficiency because the wage rate contains two different pieces of information. It is

---

[6]As we have already seen (Exercise 6.2), workers might either increase or decrease their labor supply in response to the wage cut. Thus, without using some more advanced methods, we can't prove that the wage cut will reduce the gap between labor supply and demand. And with these more advanced techniques it is indeed possible to prove that the downward pressure on wages described above will eventually eliminate the gap between labor supply and demand.

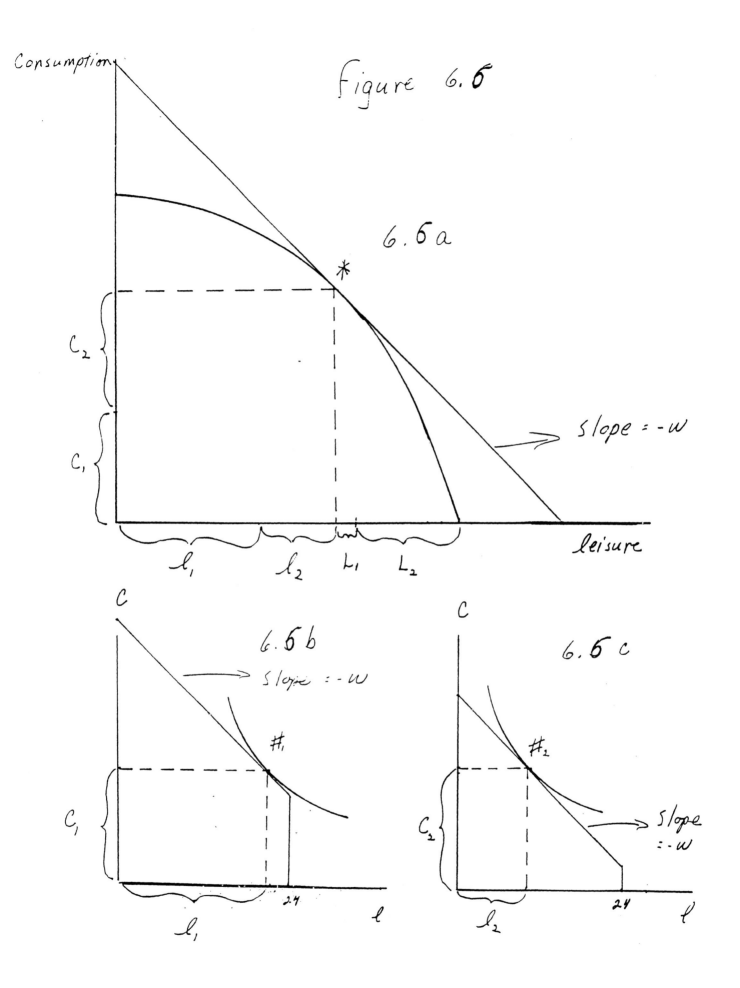

Consumption

figure 6.6

6.6a

*

C_2

C_1

slope = -w

leisure

ℓ_1 ℓ_2 L_1 L_2

c

6.6b

slope = -w

#₁

C_1

ℓ_1 24 ℓ

c

6.6c

#₂

C_2

slope = -w

ℓ_2 24 ℓ

(i) equal to the rate at which consumers are **willing** to sacrifice leisure in exchange for consumption (tangency with budget constraint), and
(ii) equal to the rate at which the economy is **able** to transform leisure into consumption goods.

Efficiency requires that these two rates be equal to one another, and the market, through the mediation of the wage rate, brings about this equality.

Conclusion

In many respects, this chapter repeats the path we covered in Chapter 4. Only the names of the main characters have changed; whereas Chapter 4 dealt with the production and distribution of Corn and Wheat, this capter deals with the production and distribution of Consumer goods and leisure. And in each chapter we have addressed two distinct questions:

(i) How does a smoothly functioning market system allocate human time between leisure and consumption, and
(ii) What is an efficient allocation of human time?

As in Chapter 4, we learned that the smoothly functioning market mimics the efficient allocation. Once again, though nobody tries to make it so, the allocation of resources generated by the un-coordinated selfish actions of entrepreneurs and consumers tends to allocate time in an economically efficient (waste-free) way.

Chapter 7
The Present vs the Future

The consumers of Chapters 2 through 6 never looked to the future; they spent their entire incomes on Corn and Wheat or Consumption and leisure; never did they borrow or save.

Similarly, entrepreneurs used the resources at hand to produce either Corn and Wheat or Consumption goods (leaving production of leisure to consumers themselves). Never did they engage in any capital investment which would have served to **augment** the stock of resources. In fact, we never said where the nation's stock of physical capital came from. But we all know the answer; physical capital has to be produced by some of our resources.

In this chapter, we will take consumers and entrepreneurs out of the timeless world of Chapters 2 - 6. We will see where capital comes from, and we will study the economic forces which determine the size of the nation's capital stock. And of course we will ask the other question which comes up repeatedly in this book: do economic forces tend to produce the efficient amount of physical capital?

Cosumers in a World with Time

The simplest way to think about time is to pretend that there are just 2 time periods; the present and the future, and that is what we will do in this chapter. And we will assume for simplicity that the future is one year away. This might not seem like much of an improvement over a model with only the present; after all, surely consumers think not only about this year and next year, but also about the year after that, and so on, on through the expected lifetimes of their children, grandchildren, and so on.

Whereas the relevant future certainly does contain more than just next year, there are two reasons for dealing only with this year and next year. First, we can continue to use geometry (the two dimensions of the graph will correspond to this year and next year), and second, everything we learn by considering only two periods carries over to a world with many future periods. So we lose little by sticking with the easier problem.

In this setting it is sensible to think of consumers as caring about two things: C_1 (Consumption in period 1; that is, today), and C_2 (Consumption in period 2; that is, next year). Now that we have collapsed everything consumers care about into two goods, we can draw indifference curves, as in Figure 7.1. And as is always the case, the consumer's objective is to get on the highest possible indifference curve.

We know the consumer wants to get to the highest indifference curve he can afford; the next question is: What can he afford?

Let's suppose that he earns income Y_1 in year 1 and Y_2 in year 2 (he presumably earns this

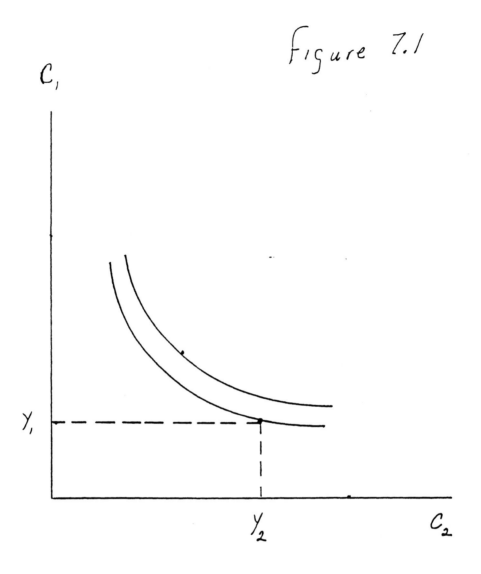

Figure 7.1

income by selling off some of his leisure, as in Chapter 6). We will stick with the simplification of Chapter 6, and set the price of Consumption equal to $1 in each period.[1] Straightaway, this tells us one point that the cosumer can afford; consume Y_1 this year and Y_2 next year; neither a borrower nor a lender be. This point is indicated as * in Figure 6.1. But (as in the case we have drawn), this might not be such a good idea. Since our consumer earns so much more income this year than next, he might find that the thrills of this year's consumption are no compensation for the penury of next year's. Better, perhaps, to save some of this year's income.

This leaves us in a familiar position: We must specify the **budget constraint** between C_1 and C_2.

- Exercise 7.1: Copy or trace Figure 7.1 onto your own paper. You know he can afford *, simply by spending this year's income this year and next year's next. Plot the combination he could afford if he simply kept $10 of his income in his wallet for a year, and spent it next year. Now plot out **all** of the combinations he could afford, by keeping various portions of his income in his wallet for a year.

In Exercise 7.1 you plotted one way (not the best way, generally) for a consumer to trade off this year's consumption for next year's. The consumer can afford any point on the "budget constraint" that you drew.

Note that the budget constraint you drew looks a bit strange. In particular, it stops in the middle of the quadrant; it never gets to the C_1 axis. In addition, it might occur to you that if you don't want to spend this year's income until next year, it's better to put it in the bank to earn interest than to keep it in your wallet. Let's deal with interest first.

- Exercise 7.2: Retrieve the graph you drew in Exercise 7.1
i. Assume that the consumer can put his money in the bank and earn 5% interest. Redraw the budget constraint you drew in Exercise 7.1. [If you need to, you can build it up as you did in Exercise 7.1; assume the consumer saves $10, then $20, and so on.]
ii. Now raise the interest rate to 15% and draw the budget constraint.
iii. Let's use the symbol **r** to stand for the interest rate. Write down an algebraic expression for the slope of the budget constraints you drew above [that is, write down an expression for the rise over the run].
iv. [More advanced and not necessary for the remainder of the chapter] Now suppose that

---

[1]As we have progressed through the book, we have tried to get out of the price-setting business and let market forces determine prices. So it may seem odd that we continue to set P_c ourselves. But in this particular instance it is harmless; we are simply defining the size of the Consumption "units" so that their price is $1.

the interest rate is 0 but the inflation rate is 5%.[2] Draw the budget constraint under this assumption. Now do the same assuming the interest rate and the inflation rate are both 5%.

v.   Write down a general expression for the slope of the budget constraint when there is both inflation and interest. (Economists generally use the symbol π to refer to inflation).

vi.   Economists generally refer to $(r-\pi)$ as the "real" interest rate. Can you see why this name makes sense?

In Exercise 7.2 we saw, not surprisingly, that the shape of a consumer's budget constraint, if he chooses to save part of this year's income, is determined by the interest rate. The slope of the budget constraint is $1/(1+r)^3$; thus the higher the interest rate the flatter the slope. But in Exercises 7.1 and 7.2 the consumer could only save; he couldn't borrow.

Suppose the budget constraint looks like Figure 7.2 (this is what you should have gotten in Exercise 7.2i). We have also drawn in the highest indifference curve the consumer can afford (so far). As you can see, he does not want to save at all; given the budget constraint as we have it so far, he just consumes Y_1 this year and Y_2 next year. But by looking at the graph, you might notice that the consumer would be better off if somehow the budget constraint were "extended" back to the C_1 axis. As we will see in Exercise 7.3, the consumer can do this, by borrowing.

●   Exercise 7.3: First, check your graph from Exercises 7.1 and 7.2 against the budget constraint in Figure 7.2; did you correctly draw the budget constraint for $(r = 5\%)$? Now make your own copy of Figure 7.2, including the indifference curve.

i.   Now assume the consumer can borrow at 5% as well as save at 5%. Draw in the "borrowing" part of the budget constraint. [If you need to, start at the Y_1, Y_2 point and have your consumer borrow $10. Plot the loss of C_2 and the gain in C_1.] What is the slope of this budget constraint? Is it the same as in the "saving" portion of the budget constraint that you drew in Exercise 7.2?

ii.   Does the option to borrow make the consumer better off?

iii.   Now draw a new budget constraint (on the same graph) under the following assumptions: Y_1 and Y_2 are the same as before, but now the interest rate is 15%. Check to see that your new budget constraint makes sense.

In Exercises 7.2 and 7.3 we determined the shape of a consumer's budget constraint. In Exercise 7.4 we will combine two questions: First, what does **efficient** allocation of C_1 and C_2 between two consumers look like? And second, do market forces tend to bring about this

---

[2] Inflation refers to an increase in the price level. Here you are asked to assume that, whereas $P_1 = \$1$, $P_2 = \$1.05$.

[3] For this expression to be right, you need to express the interest rate not as 5 (as in 5%) but rather as .05.

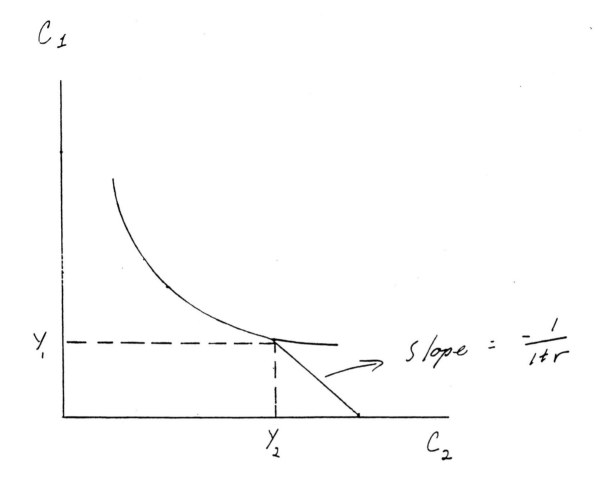

Figure 7.2

efficient allocation? This is almost identical to the questions we asked in Chapter 2, and we will use exactly the same method of analysis to answer the questions here. If you thoroughly understand Chapter 2, Exercise 7.4 should be very easy for you.

- Exercise 7.4: Draw two graphs, for consumers A and B; for each the vertical axis is C_1 and the horizontal C_2. Give each some Y_1 and some Y_2, as in Figure 7.1. For each consumer, draw an indifference curve through this endowment point (taking care to give the two consumers' indifference curves quite different slopes at their points of endowment).

i. Starting from the two points of actual endowment (the Y_1, Y_2 points for the two consumers), can you construct a possible deal between the two consumers which makes one better off without harming the other? [You should be able to find one.]

ii. Describe in detail the deal that these two consumers "should" be able to engage in (state specifically what each would agree to do).

iii. Continue to work with the consumers you invented at the beginning of this exercise. Leave them with the same initial incomes, but now give both of them the opportunity to borrow and lend at some interest rate **r**. Draw their budget constraints and sketch the points they will go to. Now is it possible to find a deal which makes one consumer better off without harming the other? Explain.

The option of borrowing and lending is the route through which consumers are able to "move" consumption from one time period to another, and the interest rate is the price at which these transactions are conducted. The higher the interest rate, the more costly it is to consume today rather than a year from now. (Look at the budget constraints you drew in Exercise 7.3, respectively for r = .05 and r = .15; you should see that the higher interest rate adds to the "reward" for postponing consumption until period 2 (or, what comes to the same thing, adds to the "punishment" for consuming in period 1).

So long as all consumers face the same prices (interest rates, in this instance), it is impossible for consumers to trade their consumption ("I'll give you some of my C_1 if you promise to give me some of your C_2) in a way that will make at least one consumer better off without making another worse off. In other words, the existence of a uniform interest rate ensures that any give national stock of this year's, and next year's consumer goods is allocated efficiently (without waste) among consumers.

Production of Consumer Goods Over Time

In the section we just finished, there was a **given** stock of consumer goods available in periods 1 and 2. The fact that all consumers face the same interest rate ensures that there are no trades left to be made among consumers that would make at least one better off without harming another. But by now we should be dissatisfied when either prices or quantities are "given." "Given," after all, is jsut a nice way of saying "made up by the textbook author." And in Chapter 4 we saw the kind of trouble this caused. So the next two questions to tie down are these:

(1) What determines the amounts of C_1 and C_2 that are actually produced in a market economy?

(2) What determines the interest rate?

When we answer these questions we can get out of the business of picking interest rates and production quotas ourselves. In answering these questions, we will be proceeding almost exactly like we did in Chapters 3 and 4, and again in Chapter 6.

If we want to know what combination of C_1 and C_2 will actually be produced in an economy, we must take the same steps we have taken before: First, figure out what combinations of C_1 and C_2 **can** be produced; and second, figure outwhich point among the possibilities **will** be produced by profit maximizers.

The Production Possibilities Curve

At any point in time, a society has a stock of resources. Among these resources is physical capital; plant and equipment, roads and vehicles, inventories of semi-finished and finished products, and so on. Another component of capital is not so tangible; the state of knowledge we have accumulated, and the level of training and expertise of our labor force.

All of these types of capital must be produced, and their production requires resources. If these resources were not devoted to making capital, they could be used to immediately produce consumer goods. The production of these capital goods is called **investment**.[4] Since investment diverts resources from the production of consumer goods, we know that an increase in investment does two things; it leads to an **increase** in our ability to produce consumer goods **next year**, but at the **cost** of **reducing** the production of consumer goods this year. And all of this, of course, can be depicted on a production possibilities curve, of the sort drawn in Figure 7.3.

By now it probably just "looks natural" for production possibilities curves to be bowed outward, as we have drawn it.[5] But once again it is important to understand **why** it is bowed out. In addition, it is important to know specifically what is measured by the slope of the production possibilities curve. We will explore these questions in Exercise 7.5:

● ☆Exercise 7.5: We'll begin by soliciting investment ideas from all of the nation's

---

[4]Notice that this definition of investment is different from another common definition of the word "investment." "Investment" in the stock market or the bond market, for example, is not an act which employs resources to produce plant and equipment or another resource which will assist in future production of goods and services. Therefore, putting your money in the stock market is not an act of investment, as we will use the term.

[5]In a moment we will discuss the flat component of the production possibilities curve near the C_1 axis.

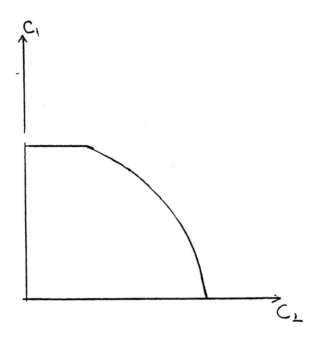

Fig. 7.3

entrepreneurs, and we'll record the pertinent facts concerning their ideas in a table or spreadsheet. We'll ask the entrepreneurs only two things about their investment projects:

1. How much will it cost? We'll measure this by asking, by how may dollars must C_1 fall if this investment is adopted?
2. How many dollars' worth of output (C_2) will the project yield next year? We'll label these as ΔC_1 and ΔC_2 respectively.[6]
i. Create a table with enough room for 15 projects, with a layout like that below. (We will tell you later what the "i" column represents). Make up any numbers you want for ΔC_1 and ΔC_2, with the following restrictions. (1) For most of the projects, make ΔC_2 bigger than ΔC_1, but make a few for which the reverse is true; (2) make one project for which $\Delta C_1 = \Delta C_2$, and (3) Make sure that the ΔC_1 entries add up to $2000. (4) In general, this exercise will go more smoothly if your ΔC_2's are not too different from your ΔC_1's (say between half as big and twice as big). But feel free to experiment.

Project	ΔC_1	ΔC_2	$\Delta C_1/\Delta C_2$	i
1	$20.00	$35.00	0.05	0.75

ii.   Rank the projects from lowest $\Delta C_1/\Delta C_2$ to highest and redo the table.
iii. If the economy adopts **none** of the proposed investment projects, assume that it has enough resources to produce $1500 of C_1. And even if it does none of the investment projects, it will be able to produce $1000 of C_2 next year. Plot this point on a new graph with C_1 on the vertical axis and C_2 on the horizontal. The highest value for C_1 you will need is $1500; the highest value for C_2 depends on the characteristics of your projects. (Add up the ΔC_2 entries for all of the projects in your table; you won't need a higher value than this.)
iv.   Now starting from the point you plotted in part (iii) we'll hypothetically adopt projects one by one. Move from the no-investment point you have already plotted by "adopting" the project with the lowest value of $\Delta C_1/\Delta C_2$; plot the resulting point on your graph. Keeping the first project in place, "adopt" the second one. Keeping the first two in place, adopt the third one, and so on.
v.   You should have run into trouble part way through step (iv) above; in particular, you should have discovered that your entrepreneurs dreamed up more investment projects than the economy can possibly afford. How is this revealed?
vi.   Now redraw the production possibilities curve (on the same graph) but don't adopt projects in the same order. Pick the projects at random. What does the new curve look like?

---

[6]These labels make sense: The cost of an investment project is the amount by which society's stock of C_1 must fall; of course it must fall by ΔC_1. And of course the investment makes it possible for us to produce ΔC_2 of additional C_2 next year.

like?

If you did part iv right, and if you smoothly connected the dots, you should have gotten a curve which looks something like Figure 7.4. The region below the horizontal axis is of course impossible; it corresponds to using more resources for investment than we actually have.

You should see that the curve is bowed out for the now-familiar reason: By the way you organized your table, you "adopted" the best investment projects first. So long as it is possible to rank the projects from best to worst, the production possibilities curve is bowed out. You should also see that the production possibilities curve is likely to have a flat portion like the one we have drawn; we will be able to produce some C_2 even if we do not invest anything at all this year. Some of our resources will still be here next year even if we don't invest at all this year.

The Rate of Return

The first project you adopted in Exercise 7.5 was the "best" available project, and you got a bowed-out production possibilities curve because you began by adopting the best, then the next-best and so on.

At this point it is useful to come up with a number which captures "how good" an investment is. In your table, you ranked projects from lowest $\Delta C_1/\Delta C_2$ to highest. The smaller is this ratio, the smaller is the **cost** of the project **per unit** of extra C_2 produced. Thus we could perfectly well use the ratio $\Delta C_1/\Delta C_2$ as our indicator of the quality of a project.

As it happens, both economists and the financial community have adopted a slightly different indicator number, which carries **exactly** the same information as $\Delta C_1/\Delta C_2$; it is referred to as the **rate of return** on a project.

Suppose we have a project which costs $100 (today) and produces $110 (a year hence). It is natural to think of the rate of return on this project as 10% (a year from now we get out 10% more than we put in). Without even thinking about it, in coming up with 10%, you did the following calculation:

$$ i \ = \ \frac{\Delta C_2 - (-\Delta C_1)}{(-\Delta C_1)} \tag{1} $$

where we use the symbol **i** for the rate of return (it's sometimes called the **internal** rate of return; that's where the i came from).[7] The numerator tells us how much more C_2 we get out than the C_1

---

[7]We need to keep putting minus signs in front of ΔC_1 because by itself ΔC_1 is a negative number (investing is an act of reducing C_1). So the negative signs convert what would otherwise be -$100 in the above example to $100.

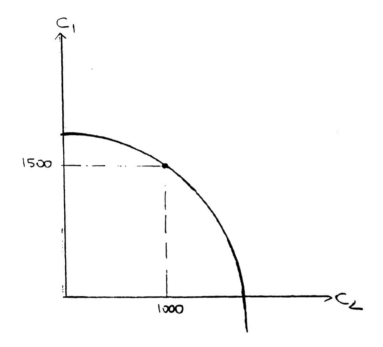

Fig 7.4

we had to put in (\$110 - \$100). And we divide by ΔC_1 so that we don't just say "\$10," but rather \$10 per \$100 of investment; 10%, or .10.

- ☆Exercise 7.6: Return to the table you made in Exercise 7.5 above; now we'll fill in the final column.
i. Calculate the rate of return on each of the projects. (You might first want to check to verify that we got the rate of return right on the project that appears in the problem itself.)
ii. Starting at the C_1 "end" of your production possibilities curve, check to see that in building up the production possibilities curve you "adopted" the investment projects with the highest rates of return first; only after these were in place did you adopt ones with lower rates of return.
iii. Look at the project for which $\Delta C_1 = \Delta C_2$; what is its rate of return? Does that make sense?
iv. Now look at the projects for which $\Delta C_2 < \Delta C_1$. If you applied the formula correctly, you should have gotten negative rates of return for these projects. Did you? Do you think a negative rate of return accurately describes such a project?

- Exercise 7.7: Make a new graph. On the x axis we will plot total investment; the maximum value you need here is \$2000. On the vertical axis we'll plot rates of return; the scale n this axis needs to run from the highest to the lowest rate of return on the investment projects in your table.
i. First, plot the most productive investment project (that is, its ΔC_1, against its rate of return).
ii. Next, plot the rate of return of the **second** project against the **sum** of the costs of the two projects (that is, the x value should be ΔC_1 for the most productive project **plus** ΔC_1 for the second project).
iii. Keep adding projects until you have added them all. You have just plotted the rate of return on the marginal investment project as a function of the total volume of investment which is carried out. We will use this below, when we discuss the entrepreneur's profit maximizing decision.

We now have thew following two pieces of information:

(1) The rate of return on an investment is equal to $(\Delta C_2 - \Delta C_1)/\Delta C_1$, and
(2) The slope of the production possibilities curve is $\Delta C_1/\Delta C_2$.

With a little bit of algebra, which you should be able to carry out, you can see that the slope of the production possibilities curve can be expressed, in terms of the rate of return on the marginal project, as

$$slope = -\frac{1}{1+i} \tag{2}$$

Exercise 7.8: (in case you have trouble seeing that expression (7.2) for the slope is right)

i.   On your own paper, wriite out the following expression

$$slope = -\cfrac{1}{1 + \cfrac{\Delta C_2 - (-\Delta C_1)}{(-\Delta C_1)}}$$

ii.   Notice that it is identical to equation 7.2, except that you have written out the alternative expression for **i** (from equation 7.1)).

iii. Now replace the "1" in the denominator of your equation with$(-\Delta C_1)/(-\Delta C_1)$.

iv.   Now simplify the expression:

$$slope = \cfrac{1}{\cfrac{-\Delta C_1 + \Delta C_2 - (-\Delta C_1)}{-\Delta C_1}}$$

$$= \cfrac{1}{\cfrac{\Delta C_2}{-\Delta C_1}}$$

$$= -\cfrac{\Delta C_1}{\Delta C_2}$$

From this exercise you can see that the two alternative expressions for the slope of the production possibilities curve are really synonyms for one another; they say the same thing and can be used interchangeably.

The Investor's Profit-Maximization Decision

We treated Exercise 7.5 as a compilation of all of the investment opportunities in the economy. But any individual entrepreneurs also has a mini-version of the table you created; a list of investment ideas which he could put into effect if it is profitable to do so. The problem is, the investor must pay (ΔC_1)[8] for the project now but he will only reap the proceeds (sale of ΔC_2) next year.

---

[8]So far we have only shown that the investment project's cost **to society** is ΔC_1; from the perspective of the entrepreneur, cost is the cost of the labor and other inputs required to build the project. We still haven't demonstrated that these two notions of cost are the same thing. Readers are asked to accept this on faith for one more chapter; we will turn to this question in Chapter 8.

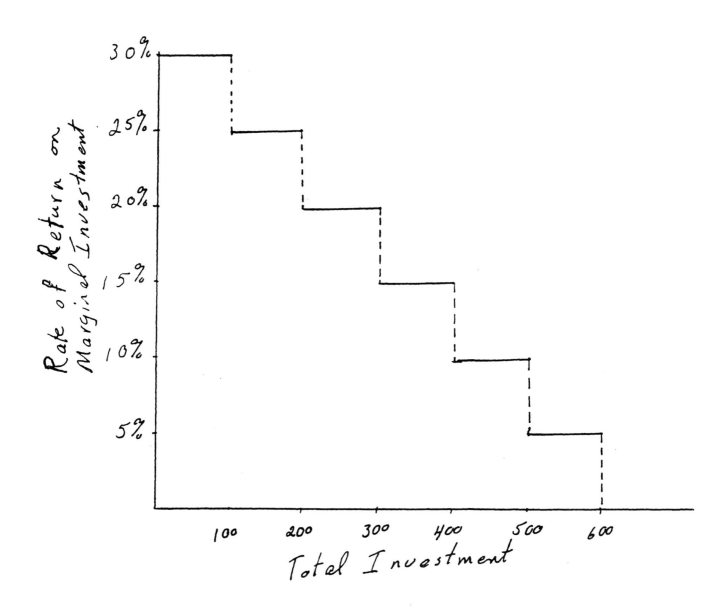

Figure 7.5

Given that he has to pay for the project before the proceeds flow in, we need to recogize that there are two possible ways of paying for it:

(1) He might be able to devote some of this year's profits to the purchase of the investment project, or

(2) He might borrow the funds from a lender.

First, we'll assume he borrows. Under this assumption let's see what his profit-maximization decision is.

● Exercise 7.9: The entrepreneur has already made a list of his feasible investment projects; has ranked them from highest to lowest rate of return, and has made a graph of total investment against the rate of return on the marginal investment (just like you did for the whole economy in Exercise 7.7). (as graphed in Figure 7.5.) As you can see, rates of return range from 30% down to 0 (he didn't bother to list any projects with rates of return less than 0). The entrepreneur chooses to borrow in order to pay for his investments; he will pay off the loans next year when the proceeds of the investments arrive. (You will notice that we have not smoothly connected dots, as we have usually done in this book. Rather, we are thinking of the investment projects as coming in discrete units of $100. We're doing this just to make the rest of this exercise a bit easier to interpret.)

i. Notice that the first investment project costs $100 (as do all the others) and that its rate of return is 30%. The interest rate is 10%. A year from now, after paying off both the principal and interest on his loan, what is the entrepreneur's profit from this investment?

ii. Now suppose the entrepreneur carries out the second project **as well as the first**. What will his total profit from both projects be after receiving his proceeds and paying off his loans?

iii. Make a graph with total investment on the horizontal axis and total profit on the vertical (you will need a horizontal scale of about $1000 and a vertical of about $300). Plot **total profit** against **total investment**, starting at no investment and going up to the last investment depicted on Figure 7.5. What is the profit maximizing level of investment?

iv. Make your own copy of Figure 7.5, and draw a horizontal line on it at 10%. This represents the interest rate; it is horizontal because that depicts the fact that the interest rate does not depend upon the amount of investment the entrepreneur carries out. At what level of investment does this line intersect the other one?

v. Now suppose the interest rate rises to 15%. On the same graph you used above, plot total profit under this assumption. What happened to the profit maximizing level of investment?

vi. On the graph you did in part (v) add another horizontal line for the new interest rate of 15%. At what level of investment does it intersect the rate-of-return line?

As we saw in Exercise 7.9, the higher the interest rate the fewer investment projects are profitable. In deciding which investment projects are profitable, entrepreneurs behave very much like when deciding how much labor to employ; they examine the good news and the bad news, and see which is greater:

7.11

The Good News: The good news from a project is the rate of return.
The Bad News: The bad news is the interest rate the entrepreneur must pay in order to fund the project.

The profit maximization rule is very straightforward: Carry out all investment projects up to the point where

$$\textit{Profit maximizer's stopping rule} \qquad i = r \qquad\qquad (5)$$

So long as the rate of return is greater than the interest rate, the project adds to profit; but any project for which i < r, if carried out, will reduce profit.

●   Exercise 7.10: Check that the stopping rule (equation 7.5) properly advises the entrepreneur in Exercise 7.9. (If the entrepreneur stops adopting more projects when r = i for the marginal project, does he maximize profit?

What if he doesn't have to borrow?

We have articulated the rule for maximizing profit assuming the entrepreneur has to borrow to finance the projects. But what if he doesn't need to borrow; for example if he has the money out of retained earnings? It turns out that the profit maximizing rule is just the same under these conditions, if we make one additional assumption: If the entrepreneur can borrow at interest rate r he can also lend at the same rate.[9] Under this assumption he can either invest his money in his own projects (earning i) or lend it out (earning r). Clearly, he should continue to invest in his own projects so long as i > r. But once all of those projects have been funded, he should stop investing in his projects, and earn r instead. So we see, the rule for maximizing profit is the same whether he borrows or uses his own funds to finance his investment projects.

The Total Level of Investment in a Market Economy

We already know what is possible -- everything on a production possibilities curve like that we show in Figure 7.3. We also know that every entrepreneur expands investment up to the point where the rate of return equals the rate of interest, because that is the behavior that maximizes profit. So in finding out how much investment will be carried out in the entire economy, all we need to do is find the place on the production possibilities curve where i = r.

For starters, we'll make up an interest rate; later in the chapter we will let economic forces determine the interest rate. We will proceed as we always have at this point; we'll draw a price line with the right slope, and slide it up or down until it is tangent to the production possibilities

_____

[9]Like all assumptions, this one might not be valid. And it is easy to think of reasons why it might not be. We will explore this possibility, and its implications, at the end of this chapter. But for now let's see what happens if it is true.

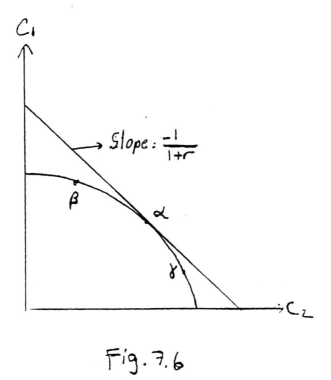

Fig. 7.6

curve.

Remember, we know that the slope of the production possibilities curve is $-1/(1+i)$, so all we need to do is draw a price line whose slope is $-1/(1+r)$, and slide it up or down until it is tangent to the production possibilities curve. We'll end up with a picture like Figure 7.6. At point α on Figure 7.6 the slope of the production possibilities curve is equal to the slope of the straight line, and we can express this as a simple equation:

$$\frac{1}{1 + i} = \frac{1}{1 + r} \qquad \textit{which is the same as}$$

$$1 + i = 1 + r \qquad \textit{which is the same as}$$

$$i = r$$

In other words, the very act of finding a tangency between the production possibilities curve and a line with slope $-1/(1+r)$ is equivalent to finding the point on the production possibilities curve where $i = r$. Profit maximizers obey the rule: Keep investing until $i = r$; then they stop. So the tangency point on the production possibilities curve, α, is the point which will actually emerge from the actions of profit maximizers.

- Exercise 7.10: Copy Figure 7.6 onto your own paper.
i.   If the economy is at β instead of α, show that there is (at least one) profitable investment opportunity which has not been exploited.
ii.   If the economy is at γ instead of α, show that somebody carried out at least one investment project which is not profitable.

The Aggregate Budget Constraint

As in Chapters 4 and 6, we began above by drawing a price line tangent to the production possibilities curve, picking the slope so that the tangency point would reveal the point of profit maximization. In Chapters 4 and 6, we then noticed two things about this price line:
(1) The slope of the price line is identical to that of a consumer's budget constraint, and
(2) The line itself is the aggregate of all of the consumers' budget constraints.

We can easily see that the first of these things continues to be true here; check back to Exercise 7.2, and see that the slope of a consumer's budget constraint is $-1/(1+r)$; just the slope we used in constructing the price line for the production possibilities curve.

Is it also true that, if we add up all of the budget constraints of the economy's consumers, we will recover the price line itself? It is indeed true, and for the same reason it was true in Chapter 4. The entrepreneurs of Figure 7.6 earn revenue by selling C_1 this year and C_2 next year. This revenue is all paid out in consumers' income (some to wages, some to interest, some to rent, and whatever is left to profit); furthermore, as we emphasized in Chapter 4, there is no other way for consumers to get income. Thus the sale of C_1 and C_2 represents all of the income earned by all of the consumers in the economy.

Equilibrium

Consumers think they can afford any point on the aggregate budget constraint, so when we add up all of the C_1 and C_2 they want to buy, we might get a point like **D** (for demand) in Figure 7.7 (many students will recognize this as just a repetition of material from Chapter 4; see especially Figure 4.4). And of course, the combination that consumers demand is not what is produced; in fact it would be impossible to produce that combination.

As in Chapter 4, this problem arises because the interest rate (the "price" in figure 7.7) is not right. Producers want to produce a lot of C_2 whereas consumers want to consume a lot of C_1.

If the interest rate were to rise, producers would want to shift from producing C_2 toward producing C_1, since some investments which are profitable at a low interest rate are unprofitable at a higher interest rate (we saw this in Exercise 7.9). And similarly, if the interest rate were to rise, consumers would tend to shift toward C_2 (borrowing has become more expensive and lending more attractive).

We know how to depict a rise in the interest rate in Figure 7.7; the price line (which is the aggregate budget constraint) becomes flatter. And we would expect upward pressure on the interest rate until a position like that of Figure 7.8 is achieved. At this interest rate, the amount of C_1 and C_2 that consumers demand is identical to that which entrepreneurs want to supply.

Saving and Investment

Suppose that consumers spent all of their year-one income on C_1 and saved nothing for year 2. If this were to happen, who would be available to lend money to entrepreneurs to finance their investment projects? You can't say that firms would do it; firms are owned by consumers and their profits are part of consumers' income. The firm has retained earnings to invest in new projects only if the consumer-owners of the firm decide to leave the profit in the firm (an act of saving) rather than distribute it to stockholders. The answer is that if consumers really decide to spend all of their income in year 1, **there will be nothing left for investment**. Investment is possible only when consumers do not spend all of their year-1 income on C_1.

Return to Figure 7.8. Notice that it would have been possible to produce C_1' in year 1, but in equilibrium only C_1'' is produced. The gap, labeled **I**, is the volume of C_1 which could have been produced but wasn't. The freed-up resources produce investment goods. Even if these investment goods had not been produced, the economy still would have been able to produce C_2' in period 2. But the investment goods make it possible to do better; to produce C_2''. The gap between C_2' and C_2'' is the return to the investment; it is labeled **R** in Figure 7.8.

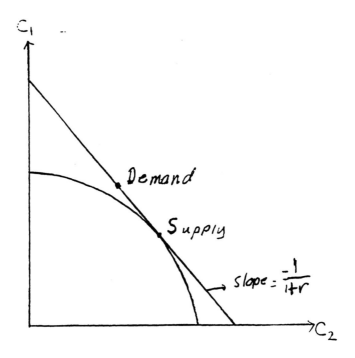

Fig. 7.7

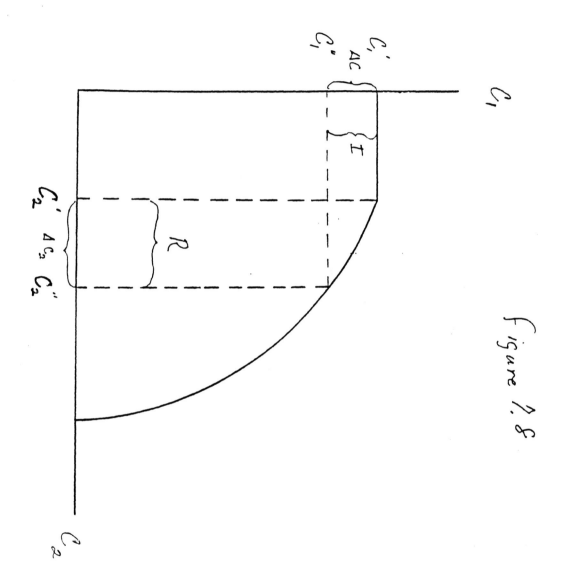

figure 7.8

We have used the label **I** (for investment) in Figure 7.8, but we just as well could have labeled it **S** (for saving), for it represents the amount of potential C_1 that consumers sacrifice (by saving) in order to increase their ability to purchase C_2. If consumers do not save, they spend all of their income on C_1, and all of the nation's resources must be devoted to producing C_1; no resources are available to produce any investment goods.

The graph you constructed in Exercise 7.9 can be thought of as a **Demand Curve for Investment** goods; for any given interest rate, it tells the amount of investment that entrepreneurs want to do. But the fact that entrepreneurs **want** to do the amount of investment depicted in the Exercise 7.9 graph does not mean they will be able to do so. It remains to be seen how much saving consumers wish to do, at various interest rates. In Exercise 7.11, you will build up a **Supply Curve of Savings** for an individual consumer.

- Exercise 7.11: Assume a consumer has Y_1 in year 1 and Y_2 in year 2; plot these points on a graph with C_1 on the vertical axis and C_2 on the horizontal, like you did in Exercise 7.1. Now, assuming the interest rate is 5%, draw the budget constraint.
  i. Draw in a consumer indifference curve tangent to the budget constraint, and indicate the amount of saving your consumer does.
  ii. Now raise the interest rate to 10%, and again indicate the amount of saving your consumer does.
  iii. Draw a new graph with r (the interest rate) on the vertical axis and S (saving) on the horizontal, and plot the point {S,r} from both part i and ii.

In Exercise 7.11 you plotted two points on a consumer's **supply curve of saving**. By experimentally changing the interest rate more, you could plot out the entire supply curve. Notice what the curve tells you; it gives the amount of saving the consumer will do for any given interest rate.

Imagine constructing such a supply curve for each consumer in the economy. Now for any given interest rate, we know the amount of saving that each consumer wants to engage in. Suppose that we have two such supply curves in Figures 7.9a and 7.9b. We can add them up, and get a curve like Figure 7.9c. And in a similar fashion we could add up all of the savings supplies of all the consumers in the economy.

Now we can combine the supply curve of savings with the demand curve for investment on one graph, as we do in Figure 7.10, below. This is another way of depicting the same information that appears in Figure 7.8, and in this graph it is perhaps easier to seethe forces at work when the interest rate is not an equilibrium. Suppose the interest rate is below equilibrium, as depicted by the line r_1. You see that the supply of savings from consumers is less than the demand for investment by entrepreneurs. (This depicts the same situation as does the price line ** in Figure 7.7 above.) Entrepreneurs, in their scramble for the limited (at interest rate r_1) supply of funds, will bid up the interest rate. This process will continue until there are enough funds to supply all investors' demands. And note that the rise in the interest rate does two things:

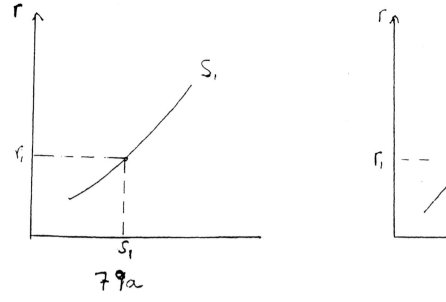

7.9a

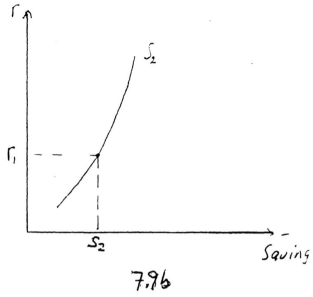

7.9b

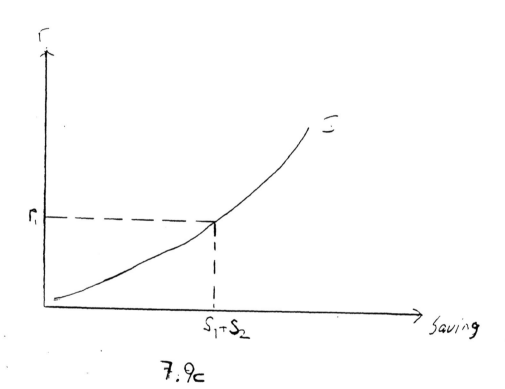

7.9c

Fig. 7.9

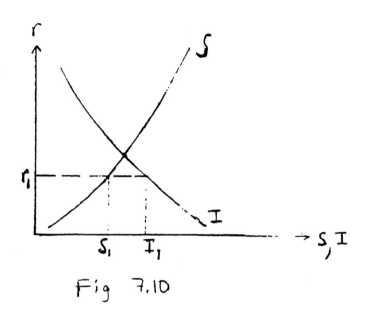

Fig 7.10

It tends to increase the stock of funds available and it dampens entrepreneurs' demand for funds.

Is the Equilibrium Efficient?

There are no surprises left in answering this question: Economic efficiency requires that the slope of the production possibilities curve (at the point of production) be identical to the slope of every consumer's indifference curve (at the point of consumption), as we have discussed above. Entrepreneurs, in their effort to maximize profit, go to a point on the production possibilities curve where its slope is equal to $-1/(1+r)$. Consumers, for their part, go to points on their indifference curves which are tangent to a budget constraint, whose slope is also $-1/(1+r)$. The market for loan funds (sometimes called the capital market) ensures that the economy makes an economically efficient "decision" regarding the allocation of resources between production of current consumption goods and capital goods which will enhance our ability to produce consumer goods in the future.

- Exercise 7.10: Figure 7.11 depicts an economy which has three consumers. Panel a is the production possibilities curve, along with a tangent price line whose slope is $-1/(1+r)$. Panels b, c, and d show the three consumers' budget constraints along with tangent indifference curves,

i.   Check that Figure 7.11 depicts an **equilibrium**. If it really is an equilibrium, the following must all be true:
    a.   Every consumer is on the highest indifference he/she can afford;
    b.   Entrepreneurs are maximizing profit;
    c.   Total supply of C_1 equals total demand for C_1;
    d.   Total supply of C_2 equals total demand for C_2;
    e.   S equals I.

ii.   Check that Figure 7.11 depicts an **efficient** allocation of resources. If it really is efficient, the following must all be true:
    a.   It is impossible for any two consumers to trade to their mutual benefit;
    b.   It is impossible to make any one consumer better off (except by harming another) by sliding along the production possibilities curve.

As in the case of two goods (Corn and Wheat) and as in the case of Leisure and Consumption, we have seen here that the forces of equilibrium between the present and the future tend to eliminate all economic waste.

But It Really Doesn't Work That Way

We have described a world which some would say bears only the faintest resemblance to reality. Most important, there is not only **one** interest rate. In reality, different people can borrow at different rates, and any one person faces a variety of interest rates. To take but one example,

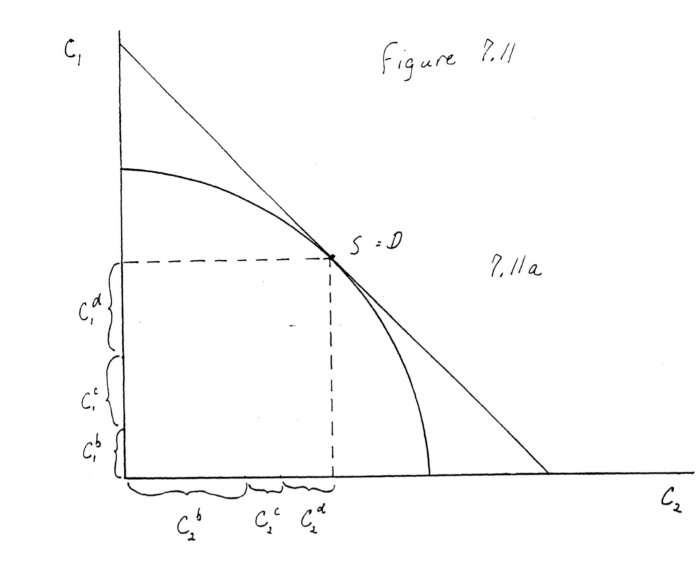

Figure 7.11

7.11a

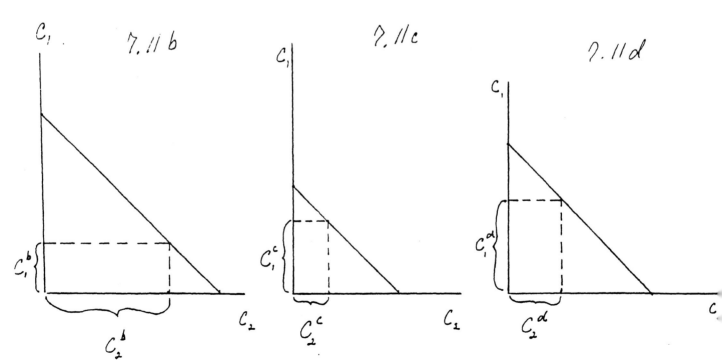

7.11b

7.11c

7.11d

mortgage rates are often less than half as high as credit-card interest.[10] And almost all of us face a higher interest rate when borrowing than saving (lending).

In Chapter 2, we discussed the economic force of arbitrage, and we argued that arbitrage tends to eliminate instances in which the same good sells for different prices. Thus if oranges sell for $1.00 in store A and $2 in store B, an arbitrageur is tempted to buy from store A and sell for $1.50 to customers entering store B. This force, then, **tends** to eliminate price spreads for a given good.

We pointed out in Chapter 2 that many instances of apparent price variability are in fact not two different prices for the same good, but rather two different goods. To take an extreme example, land in Manhattan commands a price hundreds of times higher than land in Montana.

Why has arbitrage not eliminated (or at least reduced) the spread between credit-card and mortgage debt? Is it another case of two different goods like land in Montana and New York, so we shouldn't expect price equality anyway, or is there something more going on?

In two important respects, the market for loans (as depicted in Figure 7.10) is fundamentally different from those we discussed above. In the market for debt, there are two important forces which are completely absent from markets for such goods as oranges.

The two forces are **risk** and **asymmetric information**. When an entrepreneur has an investment idea that costs C_1 and "promises" a return C_2, the lender is only sure of C_1 (the bad news). Even the entrepreneur can't know for sure that C_2 will really happen (and thus that he will be able to repay the loan). But beyond this "inherent" uncertainty, the lender is frequently faced with the task of deciding whether the entrepreneur is truthful in his claim for the profitability of the investment.[11]

The type of transaction envisioned in Chapter 7 is of much different character from that envisioned earlier in the book. In Chapter 7 we are dealing not in instantaneous exchanges (Wheat for dollars) but in promises (to repay the loan) which might not be kept. Lenders must devote a great deal of effort to determining the creditworthiness of their borrowers. And the

---

[10]The spread between mortgage and credit-card interest rates is greater than meets the eye, as you can see if you did the "real interest rate" segment of Exercise 7.x. Suppose inflation is 5%, the mortgage rate is 8%, and the credit card rate is 18%. The real interest rate on credit card debt is 5 times higher than that on the mortgage.

[11]Suppose the entrepreneur knows that there is only a 10% chance the investment will be successful; if it is not successful he will simply default on the loan. If the lender also knew of the 10% success probability, he would refuse to make the loan. The entrepreneur has an incentive to claim that the success prospect is not 10% but 90%, and frequently the lender has no way of knowing the truth.

creditworthiness of a borrower depends in part on why he is borrowing. Generally speaking, the greater the **collateral**, the smaller is the risk taken by the lender.[12] And not surprisingly, lenders are willing to offer lower-interest-rate loans for lower-risk investments. Unfortunately, not all entrepreneurs with good investment ideas have sufficient collateral, so frequently they have difficulty financing investment projects which in reality would be productive.

Whereas the economic forces discussed throughout this book work in the loan market to foster economic efficiency every bit as much as they do in the labor market or the orange market, we must recognize that there is also a special set of forces at work in the loan market which tend to prevent it from achieving the level of efficiency which might reasonably emerge in other markets.

---

[12]Collateral has a very long pedigree. Clay tablets found in the Hittite capital of Hattusas (approximately 14th century BCE) record loan agreements with detailed descriptions of the consequences of default. One tablet offers the merchant's wife as collateral.

Chapter 8
A Reconciliation, a Recapitulation, and a Preview

Reconciliation

Throughout this book we have defined "cost" to mean the value of alternative output foregone. The cost of wheat production is the forgone corn production; the cost of producing consumer goods is the forgone leisure; the cost of producing consumption goods for today is foregone future consumption.

Only in Chapter 3 did we look at cost from the perspective of a firm. In that chapter, we recognized that to a firm the cost of increasing the production of **x** is not the consequent national decline in the production of **y**. To a firm, the cost of producing a bit more **x** is what he has to pay for the extra labor, land and capital.

It is now time to ask whether these two notions of cost are the same thing (and we certainly hope to learn that they are). As in Chapter 2, we will assume that there are two goods, Corn and Wheat, and we will assume again that each is produced with just one input; for variety we'll call it labor.

We know that a Corn-producing firm which cannot influence price (a competitive firm) expands its output up to the point where

$$P_C = MC_C \tag{1}$$

P_c (price of corn) is the good news from expanding output, and MC_c (marginal cost of producing corn) is the bad news from the perspective of the firm. A corn grower thinks of MC as the cost of the extra labor required to grow the next bushel of corn:

$$MC_c = \omega \cdot \frac{\Delta L}{\Delta C} \tag{2}$$

(We're using ω to stand for the wage rate, to keep it straight from w, which stands for wheat.)

But we have found it useful to think of MC as what consumers **really lose** if corn production rises a little bit:

$$MC_c = P_w \cdot \frac{\Delta W}{\Delta C} \tag{3}$$

where the right hand side is the value of Wheat that can't be produced if we produce one additional bushel of Corn.

Now we need to think about what we know about the wage rate, ω. The wage rate is not just some number that we can pick; it is a specific number which is generated by the economic forces we described in Chapter 6. Suppose, for example, that the equilibrium wage rate is $10/hr. Labor sells for $10/hr for the following very simple reason: an hour of labor can produce $10 worth of wheat. Or to state it differently, the wage is equal to the value of labor's marginal product in Wheat production:

$$\omega = VMP_L$$
$$= P_w \cdot \frac{\Delta W}{\Delta L} \tag{4}$$

The wage rate, ω, **tells the corn producer how many dollars worth of wheat production will be lost** if he (the corn entrepreneur) hires one more hour of labor. And the corn farmer continues to hire labor only so long as the wage rate (the value of wheat foregone per hour of labor) is less than the value of the extra corn produced.

We can show this clearly with a little bit of algebra: Begin by replacing ω in Equation (8.2) with the bottom line in (8.4) (this, after all, is just a synonym for ω).

$$MC_c = \omega \cdot \frac{\Delta L}{\Delta C}$$
$$= P_w \cdot \frac{\Delta W}{\Delta L} \cdot \frac{\Delta L}{\Delta C} \tag{5}$$
$$= P_w \cdot \frac{\Delta W}{\Delta C}$$

In Equation (8.5) we began with marginal cost as the firm sees it, but with our own knowledge of the fact that the wage rate is equal to the value of the marginal product. Then, by the simple act of canceling the ΔL's, we ended up with marginal cost as we have been using it throughout this book.

Thus marginal cost as seen by an entrepreneur (the cost of the incremental inputs) is really marginal cost as we have used it (the value of the alternative output sacrificed). The corn farmer who stops expanding production when P = MC is doing just what he should do to promote economic efficiency; he expands corn production just up to that point on the production possibilities curve the last $1 worth of corn production requires a reduction of $1 in wheat production. Of course, the Corn farmer does not think about foregone Wheat production; he just thinks labor is expensive so he would be wise to use it sparingly.

Recapitulation

In the preceding chapters we have been addressing two quite different questions:

► Question 1: What does an economically efficient use of our resources look like?

► Question 2: What does the outcome of a market allocation of our resources look like?

There is no inherent reason why the answers to these two questions must be the same (and in the next few chapters of the book we will explore important instances in which they are not the same). And it is important to realize that the two questions are inherently different from one another. The first asks how an omnipotent benevolent[1] dictator would allocate resources; the second asks how resources will be allocated when nobody even tries to formulate an overall plan and every agent in the economy simply acts in his or her own selfish interest.

It is an amazing and remarkable fact that under a wide range of conditions, the selfish acts of individual consumers and entrepreneurs tend to bring about economic efficiency.

The price system, when it works, is a massive device which does two things:

► First, the price system disseminates information.

► Second, the price system greatly limits the amount of information that anybody needs to have.

Let's turn to the first point first. The ratio of prices (the slope of a consumer's budget constraint) tells each consumer the slopes of **all other** consumers' indifference curves, as well as the slope of the production possibilities curve.

The fact that a price ratio "conveys" so much information really means that nobody needs to know very much in order to play their role in the drama of efficient resource allocation. They need to know the prices of all of the goods that they might seriously contemplate buying or selling, and they need to know their own preferences.

Efficiency requires that each consumer consume at a point where the slope of his indifference curve is identical to that of every other consumer in the economy, and also equal to the slope of the production possibilities curve. But no consumer tries to do this; public spirited consumers do not interview their neighbors to find out the shapes of their indifference curves, nor do they interview the production possibilities curve to ascertain its shape. First of all, there is no

---

[1]Surely a benevolent dictator would want to allocate resources efficiently; it would be foolish to waste resources. But remember that there is a whole range of economically efficient allocations, since efficiency says nothing about who is relatively well off and who is not. So when discussing economic efficiency, we are leaving out an important component of the benevolent dictator's task.

reason to assume that consumers (and entrepreneurs, for that matter) are so public spirited. And even if they were so public spirited, they would surely be overwhelmed by the enormity of the task.

In fact, we don't need to hope that individual consumers and entrepreneurs care at all about economic efficiency. If all consumers face the same prices as one another, and so long as consumers and producers face the same prices, then selfish behavior, based on quite limited information, has a strong tendency to bring about economic efficiency. Whereas in principle I "should" care about the shapes of all consumers' indifference curves (either because I am public spirited or because I selfishly want to make a trade of the sort we saw in Chapter 2), all of that information is compacted into the ratio of prices.

The price system does all of this because prices convey and compress information. In general it is not necessary that the users of prices fully understand the information contained in the prices. You can see this clearly in the case we discussed above:

The wage rate "informs" the corn farmer that an extra hour of labor devoted to corn production will reduce the value of national wheat production by ω itself (since this is the value of the marginal product of wheat production). If the corn farmer were public spirited he would only hire additional labor up to the point where the value of the added corn production just offsets the value of the lost wheat production.

The price system saves us from two things: first, it is not necessary for the corn farmer to be public spirited; he will behave efficiently (expand output only up to the point where $P = MC$) because it is the profit-maximizing thing to do. Second, regardless of whether the corn farmer is public spirited, he does not need to be an expert in wheat farming (or in the production of all of the other consumer goods in the marketplace). The wage rate informs him of the productivity of labor in other industries, and therefore tells him the true cost of using it in his industry. Of course, the farmer has no reason to care that the wage rate contains all this information; all he cares about is that he has to pay it. If he is selfish, he will do exactly the same thing because it maximizes his profit.

Earlier in this book we argued that the price system might be the greatest labor saving device in the history of mankind. In Chapters 2 - 7, we have tried to give you the justification for that apparently ridiculous claim.

Preview

The economy of the first seven chapters works efficiently because prices convey all of the information that is necessary to induce selfish consumers and entrepreneurs to make efficient decisions. But in reality there are many times when this process does not work. Much of the study of advanced economics is the study of instances in which prices fail to do the job we analyzed in Chapters 2 - 7.

There are a large number of reasons why the price system might fail to deliver perfect efficiency. In the next few chapters we will discuss some of those reasons, and at the same time ask whether we can prescribe cures for these failures.

Perhaps the most straightforward class of breakdown occurs when prices **misinform** consumers or producers. Sometimes prices lie, for example when they fail to accurately depict marginal cost. This happens, for example, when monopolists set prices or when governments impose taxes.

Sometimes the very nature of the good makes it difficult to charge a price at all. It is difficult (though not impossible) to charge individual users for their receipt of broadcast radio and television signals.

We will explore these and other circumstances when prices do not deliver the right information in the final portion of the book.

Chapter 9
When Prices Lie: Monopoly

Introduction

The entrepreneurs of the first part of this book simply looked up the prevailing price in the newspaper and expanded output up to the point where $P = MC$. Even though we learned that output prices respond to forces of supply and demand, we assumed that each entrepreneur ignored this fact.

In many circumstances, it is appropriate for entrepreneurs to pretend that the price it can charge is just a number, beyond its control or power to explain. Many entrepreneurs lack any power to influence prices in any meaningful way. An individual wheat farmer is just given a quote for the price of wheat; it would be ridiculous for him to say, "I'll only sell to you if you raise the price by $.25/bushel." The buyer would respond that Kansas is a big state and that he really does not care whether this particular farmer sells or not.

The individual farmer is prevented from influencing the price by his very insignificance, and in much the same way it makes sense to think of individual consumers as having no power over the prices they pay.

So long as farmers believe that they have no control over the price itself, they will expand output to the point where $P = MC$. But what if the farmers all banded together? Then they could influence the price; in particular, they could agree to restrict output and therefore drive up the price.

In this chapter we will explore two questions:

(1) How does market equilibrium (like we discussed in Chapter 4) change when one industry is monopolistic; and

(2) What happens to economic efficiency when one industry is monopolistic?

The Monopolist's Profit Maximizing Decision

A monopolist is the only firm in the economy which sells a particular good -- the only firm in the industry.[1] Let's say that the monopolist produces good M (for Monopoly).[2] But of

---

[1]An **industry** is all the firms in the economy who produce one particular good; thus for example the Corn industry is all of the Corn farmers in the economy.

[2]Later we will briefly discuss **why** he is the only entrepreneur in the industry (that is, why other firms don't enter the industry and undercut his price. But for now we will just assume that

course, even a monopolist can't charge whatever price it wants to; if it sets the price too high nobody will buy his goods. He is restricted, in other words, by what consumers are willing to pay.

- ☆Exercise 9.1: Suppose the market demand curve[3] is made up as follows: At P = 10, quantity demanded is 1000; every time the price falls by $1, quantity demanded increases by 1000. (Thus, if P = 0, quantity demanded is 11,000).
i. Plot the demand curve, leaving room for another graph directly below the demand curve. The graph just below should have a horizontal axis identical to that for your demand curve (that is, quantity, going from 0 to 11,000). The vertical axis, labeled in dollars, needs to range from about -$15,000 to +$35,000.
ii. On the new graph, plot the **total revenue** that the monopolist could earn as a function of quantity (that is, the amount of revenue he could earn at output of 1000, 2000, 3000, etc). Bear in mind that he can only charge a given price if consumers are willing to pay that price.
iii. On the same graph we are now going to plot **marginal revenue** for the monopolist. Marginal revenue (MR) is the change in total revenue (the good news) that the monopolist receives if he expands output by one.
- For Q = 1000, plot the **increase** in the monopolist's revenue, which results from expanding output from 1000 to 1001.
- At Q = 2000, plot the amount by which the monopolist's revenue increases as he expands output from 2000 to 2001.
- Continue plotting these points, for Q = 3000, 4000,5000, etc. all the way up to Q = 11,000.[4]
iv. Take a look at your total revenue curve (drawn in part ii above). At what level[5] of output is total revenue maximized? At this level of output, what is marginal revenue equal to? Does this make sense?

---

he **is** a monopolist, and that he has no reason to fear competition from other firms.

[3]By "market demand curve" we mean the total amount that all consumers in the economy will buy, at various prices.

[4]We could have also asked you to calculate MR for 1001, 1002, etc. But it gets pretty boring, and besides, all such points lie on the line you just drew. (If you are comfortable with algebra, it should be very easy for you to show that this is true; if you are not, you can try a few points and see that we are right.

[5]We just asked you to plot revenue for 0, 1000, 2000, etc. As a result, you might not be able to tell **exactly** where total revenue is maximized. But you should be able to see that, the finer the steps you take in plotting total revenue, the more accurately you can answer this question. If you were to plot the points close enough together in Exercise 9.2ii (or use calculus if you know how), you would find that revenue is maximized at Q = 5500.

When analyzing the competitive firm's profit maximization decision, we compared the good news from expanding output (price) with the bad news (marginal cost). For a monopolist. the good news from expanding output is not just price, but marginal revenue. Let's explore this a little further.

Look at Figure 9.1a and b; this is the set of graphs you should have gotten in Exercise 9.1 above. First, check to see that you got it right. Second, let's see why marginal revenue looks the way it does.

Suppose output is now 2999; the monopolist considers expanding it to 3000. What will be the consequences? The first consequence is that he sells the 3000th unit of output; he can get $7 for it. But he has a problem; he has to charge the same price to all customers. So by expanding output to 3000, he has to cut the price on the "first" 2999 units from $7.001 to $7. Thus the good news is not $7, but $7 - $2.999 (2,999 units times $.001), or almost exactly $4. (Check to see that you got $4 for marginal revenue at quantity = 4 in exercise 9.1 above).

- Exercise 9.2: Return to your graphs from Exercise 9.1. You already observed that revenue is maximized at a quantity between 5000 and 6000, and if you had plotted the points between (or used calculus) you would have learned that revenue is actually maximized where Q = 5500.

i.   Look at the marginal revenue curve you drew in Exercise 9.1; what is the value of MR at Q = 5000? (If your graph is not accurate enough to give a definite answer to this question, calculate MR at Q = 5000 by hand.)
ii. Suppose now that the monopolist's production cost is zero. In that case he pretty obviously maximizes profit by setting output at 5500. See if you can formulate a "rule" that the profit maximizing monopolsit should obey, using the notion of marginal revenue.
iii. Now suppose unit cost of production is $3; that is, total cost is $3 times output. (Notice that **marginal** cost is $3). On the same graph you used in Exercise 9.1, draw a graph of the monopolist's total profit as a function of output. What is the profit maximizing level of output? What is profit at that level of output?
iv. In the last part of Exercise 9.1, you were asked to formulate a "rule" that the monopolist should obey if he is to maximize profit, incorporating the notion of marginal revenue (MR). But that was under the special assumption that the monopolist could produce the good at no cost. In Exercise 9.1iii above, you should see that the level of output declines as marginal cost rises. See if you can formulate the profit maximizing monopolists rule to live by under this more general assumption that marginal cost is not zero. [HINT: Just like a competitive firm, a monopolist expands output so long as the good news from doing so is grerater than the bad news; he stops expanding when they are equal.]

When you calculated marginal revenue in Exercise 9.1, you could have saved some time (and maybe you did) by applying the following formula:

Figure
9.1a

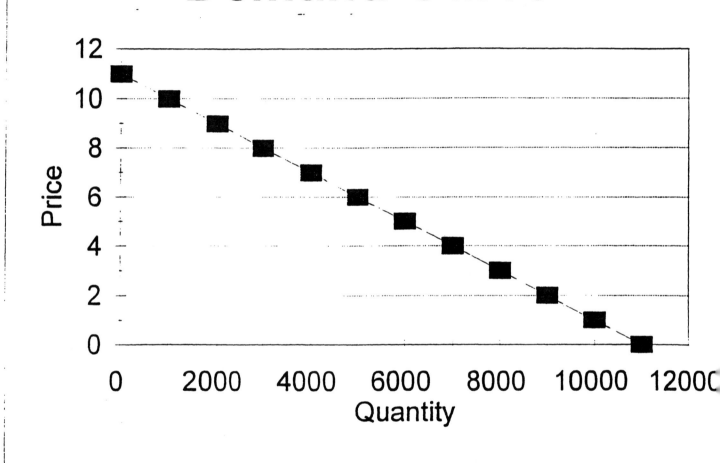

Demand Curve

Figure 9.1 b

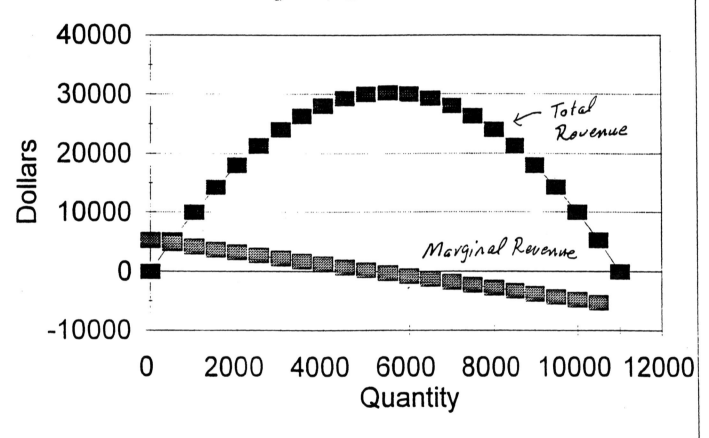

Total and Marginal Revenue

Total Revenue

Marginal Revenue

$$MR(i) = P(i) - [P(i-1) - P(i)] \cdot Q(i-1)$$

or in plain English, Marginal Revenue measured at output level (i) equals the price if he sells (i) units of output minus the price cut needed to expand sales from (i-1) to (i) multiplied by Q(i-1). The good news, P(i), is offset by the price cut required to sell more output, and the size of the offset is determined by the amount of output, Q(i-1) that would have been sold at the higher price, but for the expansion of output. Frequently we write this same expression as

$$MR(i) = P(i) + \frac{\Delta P}{\Delta Q} \cdot Q(i) \qquad (2)$$

where $\Delta P / \Delta Q$ is the amount by which the price has to decline per unit expansion in output.[6]

The Profit Maximizer's Rule

In exercise 9.2 you were asked to devise the profit maximizing monopolist's rule to live by. In our hint we suggested you compare the good news and the bad news from expanding output. The bad news of course is marginal cost, and you should see that the good news is marginal revenue. The profit maximizing monopolist continues to expand output so long as marginal revenue is greater than marginal cost, and therefore stops expanding output when

$$MC = MR \qquad \textit{which is the same as}$$

$$MC = P + \left(\frac{\Delta P}{\Delta Q} \cdot Q \right) \qquad (3)$$

The material inside the parentheses is negative, since the only way for the monopolist to expand output (positive ΔQ) is to cut the price (negative ΔP). So we know that the monopolist maximizes profit where

$$P > MC \qquad (4)$$

and because of this fact, we will see that the economic efficiency which emerged from the first part of the book fails to occur.

Throughout the first part of the book, prices truthfully revealed information to consumers regarding the shape of the production possibilities curve. In Chapter 4, the price line is tangent to the production possibilities curve because every producer expands output until P = MC. Now we

---

[6]Notice that $\Delta P / \Delta Q$ is itself a negative number (P must fall if Q is to rise), so the whole term enters the MR expression with a (+) sign.

must ask what the world looks like when the (only) producer in one industry fails to obey the P = MC rule.

The monopolist has an "accurate" picture of what marginal cost is. He thinks of marginal cost as the cost (to him) of the labor required to produce one more unit of output. Suppose for example that his MC is $10. In other words, the extra labor required to produce one more unit of output has a market cost of $10. The firm just thinks of this as $10 worth of labor, but since we have read Chapter 6 we know why the labor costs $10; The labor is worth $10 on the market because it is able to produce $10 worth of output in the competitive industry.[7] This means that

$$MC_M = -P_C \cdot \frac{\Delta C}{\Delta M} \tag{5}$$

In other words, the marginal cost faced by the monopolist is really the falue of the other output foregone when the monopolist expands output.

But remember, the monopolist charges a price greater than MC, so when it comes to pricing we have the following:

$$P_M > -P_C \cdot \frac{\Delta C}{\Delta M} \quad \text{which is the same as}$$

$$\frac{P_M}{P_C} > -\frac{\Delta C}{\Delta M} \tag{6}$$

P_M/P_c is the price ratio that consumers face in the marketplace. It is (negative) the slope of each consumer's budget constraint. Economic efficiency requires that this slope be equal to the slope of the production possibilities curve; this is what we saw in chapter 4.

Unfortunately, equation (9.6) tells us that the slope of the price line (the slope that consumers see in deciding which goods to buy) is not the same as the slope of the production possibilities curve. Equilibrium looks like Figure 9.2, below. The left hand panel, 9.2a, shows the production possibilities curve, with C (the good produced in a competitive sector, for which P = MC) on the vertical axis and M, the monopolized good, on the horizontal. The equilibrium price line cuts the production possibilities curve, reflecting the inequality shown in Equation 9.6 above. The combination supplied occurs at this intersection. And since we are discussing

---

[7]If you need to review this, re-read the first section of Chapter 8 (Reconciliation).

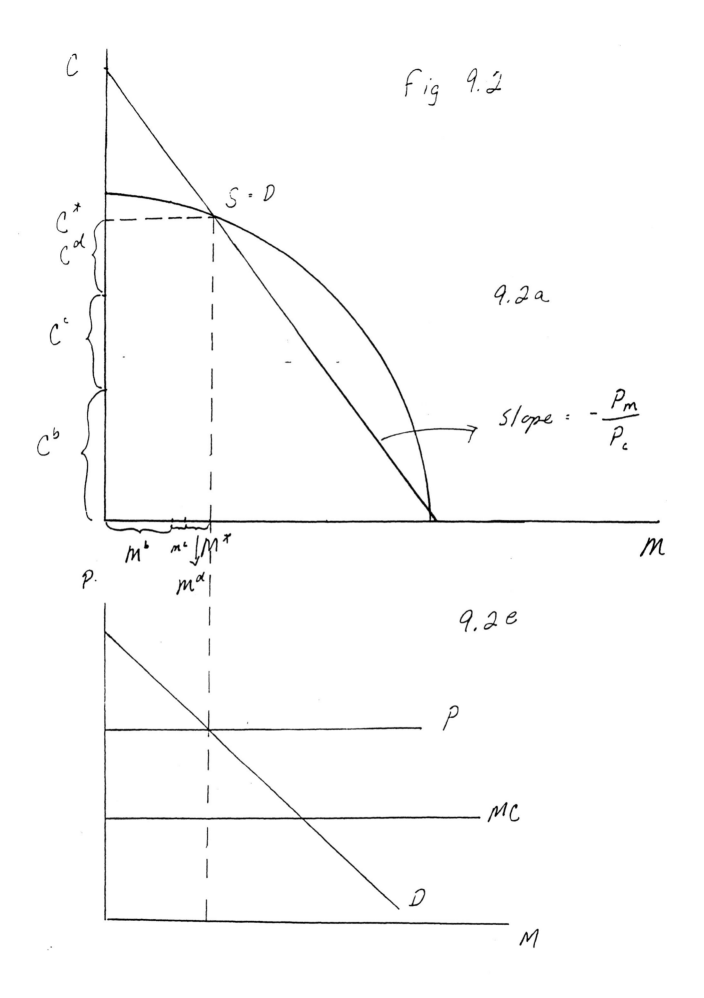

Fig 9.2

C

C^*
C^α

C^c

C^b

$S = D$

9.2a

$slope = -\dfrac{P_m}{P_c}$

m^b m^c $\downarrow M^*$

m^α

M

$P.$

9.2e

P

MC

D

M

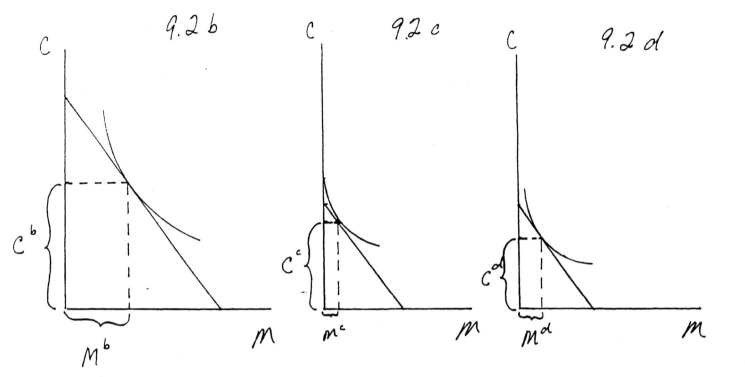

9.6

equilibrium prices[8] the quantity supplied equals the quantity demanded. There are three consumers in this economy[9]; in panels b, c, and d, we depict the consumers in this equilibrium. We know that their budget constraints must add up to the price line (they do) and that in equilibrium their demands for M and C must add up to the quantities supplied (again, you can check th see that they do).

Look carefully and verify that this picture is an equilibrium:

- For the monopolist, P > MC, as required by his profit maximization condition;
- For the competitive industry, P = MC, as required by their profit maximization conditions;
- Therefore, the price ratio is steeper than the production possibilities curve;
- The combination produced is on the production possibilities curve;
- Consumers' budget constraints add up to the price line;
- And (in equilibrium) supply equals demand.

Despite the fact that the equilibriuum looks different from the other ones we have seen, nobody in the system has an incentive to change behavior, and therefore it is an equilibrium.

Is it Efficient?

By this stage in the book you should be able to tell at a glance that the equilibrium of Figure 9.2 is economically wasteful; there exists a change from that equilibrium which, if only there were a way to induce people to do it, could make one consumer better off without harming any other consumer. And we know exactly what that change is: Any one of the consumers reduces his consumption of C by a small amount. This releases resources from the C industry, which are then instructed to produce a bit more M. Given the slopes of the indifference curves and the production possibilities curve, the consumer who took the initiative is made better off, and no other consumers are made worse off.

So Why Doesn't it Happen?

Now look at Figure 9.2e, directly below 9.2a. This is the demand curve for M, drawn so that the M scale on the demand curve lines up with the M scale on the production possibilities curve. The horizontal line labelled P_M represents the monopolist's profit maximizing price (the

---

[8]Recall the process of price adjustment, from Chapter 4, which ensures that supply equals demand. The same process occurs when one of the products is produced by a monopolist. Since we have already discussed the process of price adjustment, we will not repeat the discussion here. Instead, we just depict a situation in which the price adjustment has already occurred; that is, an equilibrium.

[9]There is no need to just draw three consumers; but on the other hand we don't learn anything by drawing more, so we will stick with three.

9.7

numerator in the ratio P_M/P_C depicted in Figure 9.2a, directly above). We've also drawn the monopolist's marginal cost curve.

Looking at Figure 9.2e, we can spot the same mutually beneficial transaction that we discussed in the last paragraph, and we can see why it won't happen.

- Exercise 9.x: Trace or draw the demand and marginal cost curves of Figure 9.2e onto your own paper. Starting at the equilibrium quantity, consider the possibility of expanding output of the monopolized good, M, by 1.
i. Measured in dollars, how much must output of C fall in order to make it possible to increase M by 1?
ii. How many dollars' worth of C would a consumer be **willing** to give up if he could get one more unit of M in the deal?

The key to Exercise 9.3 is the realization that the **height of a demand curve** measures the willingness of a consumer to pay for one more unit of the good; at the equilibrium above, the consumer (all consumers, actually) is willing to pay P_M to get one more unit of M.[10] But the very act of paying P_M is equivalent to the act of giving up P_M worth of the other good. That's why the height of the demand curve depicts the number of dollars worth of the other good that the consumer is willing to pay to get one more unit of the good.

So long as price is greater than marginal cost, consumers (who see the price but not the marginal cost) would be willing to give up more than marginal cost in order to acquire a bit more of the monopolized good, M. Thus the answer to Exercise 9.3i is, "Output of C **must** fall by MC_M in order to produce one more unit of M." The answer to Exercise 9.3ii is, "A consumer would be willing to give up $\$P_M$ worth of C in order to consume one more unit of M."

In effect, the consumer would like to strike the following deal with the monopolist: The monopolist produces one more unit of M, at cost MC. The consumer pays something between P_M and MC for the good. The consumer is better off than before; he got the unit for less than the maximum he was willing to pay for it, and no other consumer is worse off. And the owner of the monopoly (also a consumer) is better off.

The very telling of this story both shows the specifics of the "deal" waiting to be struck and reveals why the deal doesn't actually come off. The monopolist (in most circumstances) cannot cut a special deal for one consumer; if he offers a reduced price to this consumer, he will have to do so for everybody. So the monopolist will never agree to the "deal" that our consumer proposed, despite the fact that the **direct** effects of the deal are all beneficial. Unfortunately for the monopolist, and therefore for our negotiating consumer, the side effect more than offsets the direct benefits.

---

[10]This is not quite right; each consumer was willing to pay P_M for the last unit of M; they would be willing to pay a bit less than P_M for the next unit.

Now look back at equation 9.2, which describes the monopolist's marginal revenue. The final term in this equation, $Q \cdot \Delta P / \Delta Q$, is the "side effect" that we referred to in the last paragraph. This term tells us how much the monopolist loses because, as a consequence of expanding output, he needs to reduce the price to all of his customers.

You can also see the "direct effect" and the "side effect" of expanding by using a demand curve; turn to exercise 9.4.

- Exercise 9.4: Make a new copy of the demand curve you drew in Exercise 9.1, but now re-label the x axis as follows: Where the first graph says 1000, just say 1; replace 2000 with 2, etc.
i. Assume $Q = 3$; draw a vertical line through the demand curve to reflect this, and a horizontal line representing the price if $Q = 3$. The area of the rectangle you have drawn is the firm's total revenue.
ii. Now think about expanding output to 4, and draw the lines which will enable you to define the box of total revenue at $Q = 4$.
iii. Notice that you have made two thin rectangles; a vertical one between $Q = 3$ and $Q = 4$, and a horizontal one between $P = 8$ and $P = 7$.
iv. Write an algebraic expression for the area of the vertical box, and then do the same for the horizontal box. Can you relate these expressions to the two components of marginal revenue, from Equation 9.2?

Your vertical box above should have area $(4-3) \cdot P_4 = P_4$. Your horizontal box should be the side effect: $3 \cdot (P_4 - P_3)$. The horizontal box is the side effect that tends to deter the monopolist from expanding output even when there is a mutually advantageous deal to be struck.

Of course, output price falls by just as much if a comeptitive firm cuts output as if a monopolistic firm cuts output; what becomes of the "side effect" if a competitive firm cuts output?

- Exercise 9.5: Return to your worksheets in Exercise 9.1. When MC = 3, we saw that the profit maximizing level of output is 4000, where MC = MR. Now suppose that the industry is not monopolistic; rather it is competitive, and each firm is very small. For concreteness we will assume that there are 1000 firms, of equal size. If they are (together) producing the monopoly price/quantity combination, each firm is producing 4 units of output[11] and selling at $P = 7$.
i. Calculate the marginal revenue of a competitive firm, bearing in mind that if he expands output by 1, the price will have to fall. Specifically, suppose one firm raises its output from 4 to 5. What are the direct and side effects of this action.
ii. When this one firm raises output from 4 to 5, what happens to the revenue of a typical

---

[11]A "unit" might be a ton or 100 tons, so don't worry about the small number of "units" that the competitive firms are producing.

other firm in the industry?

iii.   What happens to the sum of the revenues earned by all of the firms in the industry?

In Exercise 9.5i, you should have found the following: When a competitive firm expands output by 1, the price has to fall from $7 to $6.999 (the only way to expand output is to cut the price so additional consumers will buy). So the competitive firm gets $6.999 on the additional output, but loses $.001 on each of the 4 units that it was already selling. Its marginal revenue is $6.995.
The typical other firm in the industry sees the price fall by $.001, and thus loses $.004.
The losses suffered by all of the 1000 firms in the industry add up to $4.

In this exercise, we can see that the "side effect" still happens when a competitive firm expands output. However, virtually all of the side effect falls on other firms, the competitors of the one firm that raised output. That is why a competitive firm ignores the side effect (it's not his side) and the monopoly does not ignore the side effect.

Discriminating Monopoly

The monopolist fails to expand output as much as he "should" because of the side-effect term in marginal revenue; if he cuts the price for one consumer he must cut it for all. Why do we assume this? The firm is after all a monopolist and therefore consumers can't get the good from anybody wlse.

In most settings we assume that a monopolist is forced to charge the same price to everybody because of the presence of **arbitrage**, which we first introduced in Chapter 2. Arbitrage, remember, is the profitable art of buying low and selling high. If a monopolist sells part of his wares at a discount to one consumer, there is frequently nothing to prevent that customer from reselling it to somebody who otherwise would have paid full price. Pretty soon the monopolist notices that his discount customer is the only person buying his goods.

In addition to arbitrage, the monopolist trying to sell at two different prices faces another problem: When the customer says, "I am not willing to buy any more of your goods at your regular price, but if you give me a discount I'll buy some," how does the monopolist know that the consumer is telling the truth? If he can't tell whether the customer is telling the truth or not, he will not offer special discounts of the type we described above; all of his customers will claim that they are unwilling to pay the posted price.

But there are some circumstances in which the monopolist at least partially escapes both the arbitrage and the truth-telling problem. He can escape the arbitrage problem whenever it is physically impossible to resell the good (surgery and college education come readily to mind).

In addition, there are times when a monopolist has at least some ability to distinguish between customers who are willing to pay high prices and those who are only willing to pay low prices. An obvious example is airlines, who give discounts for consumers who stay over a Saturday night. These are typically family travellers who are willing to pay less than business travellers; business travellers, on the other hand, are generally unwilling to stay over Saturday night.

Let's suppose the extreme case of **perfect price discrimination**, a monopolist who knows his customers so well that he is able to sell every single item for the maximum price that the consumer is willing to pay. Under this extreme assumption, what is the monopolist's marginal revenue? You should be able to see that under perfect price discrimination, the second term in Equation 9.2 (the side-effect term) disappears. The only thing that happens when a monopolist sells an additional unit is that he receives **P**; he does not need to cut the price on the other units he sells, and so there is no mitigation to the good news he gets by selling one more unit.

And you can see very directly that under this assumption, **all possible mutually beneficial transactions occur**. Every time a consumer is willing to pay more than the marginal cost of the good, the deal goes through. Strange as it seems, an economy with a perfectly discriminating monopolist is perfectly efficient. (Notice; if airlines were forced to charge the same price for all fliers, many weekend family fliers might be priced out of their trips.)

Are Two Monopolies Better than One?

Return to Figure 9.2, the production-possibilities-curve depiction of equilibrium in the presence of a monopoly. Look at Panels **a** and **b** and pretend that the price lines are not there (all you see is the production possibilities curve with the point of production and one consumer's indifference curve with the point of consumption). From this picture you know that to restore efficiency, we need to produce more of **M, and therefore less of C** (there's no other way to produce more M). In other words, in terms of efficiency, the problem of monopoly can be described as either the production of too little M or too much C.

This suggests that there might be two alternative ways to cure the problem: either break up the M industry and make it competitive or allow the C industry to collude and form a monopoly.

It is indeed **possible** that two monopolies are more efficient than one; the distortion wrought by one monopoly might be partially undone by the formation of a second. Of course, it would be better still if there were no monopoly at all. And even if one monopoly is inevitable, it is very difficult to determine the precise conditions under which efficiency is enhanced by allowing another to exist. Almost all economists agree that society is **very** likely better off with fewer rather than more monopolies.

Conclusion

In this chapter, for the first time, we have observed an economic equilibrium which is economically wasteful. With monopoly, consumers are misled regarding the shape of the production possibilities curve; they are led to mistake "expensive" for "costly." By "expensive" we mean how much the consumer must pay for the good; by "costly" we mean how much society must sacrifice in order to produce the good.

We know that consumers don't really make mistakes at all when facing monopolists; consumers care only whether a good is expensive, not whether it is costly. Only when prices accurately reflect costs do consumers act as if they cared about cost. The (efficiency) problem with monopoly is that prices do not reflect costs, and therefore consumers do not line up the slopes of their indifference curves with the slope of the production possibilities curve.

Chapter 10
When Prices Lie: Taxes

Introduction

So far, government has played essentially no role in our economy; there have been neither taxes nor government expenditures. We have pretended that all of a nation's production possibilities are devoted to producing goods and services which will be purchased by consumers.

In reality, there are many types of goods for which private markets either work poorly or not at all. One obvious example is national defense. Though this is a product which requires some of our resources to produce, and which makes us better off as consumers, it is clearly not the kind of good that individual consumers can buy in stores.

To the degree that our national defense protects us from foreign invaders, we all receive the same level of protection. It is physically impossible for one consumer, individually, to take less national security and more apples. Unlike corn or wheat or leisure, or any of the other goods we could have used as examples in the first part of the book, national defense has the peculiar property that when I enjoy its benefits, I in no way diminish your enjoyment of its benefits (the same statement cannot be made for apples, for example). Such a good is called **nonrival**.

In addition to being nonrival, national defense is **nonexcludable**; it is physically difficult to prevent a consumer from enjoying its benefits. I receive the benefits merely by living within the borders of my country, and there is no effective way to deliver national defense to some citizens but not others.

Goods which are both nonrival and nonexcludable are referred to as **public goods.** Most public goods are provided by governments, since there is no effective way for entrepreneurs to provide such goods profitably.

In addition to public goods, the government provides another important service that the market economy is incapable of providing: **income redistribution**. We have emphasized that the market economy creates a powerful set of forces which tend to bring about economic efficiency. But we have also said that economic efficiency is only one objective that we might assign to an economy. Most of us also care about the distribution of income; who is rich and who is poor, and the relative incomes of the rich and the poor. Of course we do not all agree on acceptable levels of income inequality, but in most societies a majority of the population seems to agree that there is a public obligation to redistribute income from the rich to the poor.

In this chapter we will just assume that there are tasks which must be left to the government, and that these tasks require resources. We will not discuss the amount of resources which the government should require for these tasks; that is a question for a course in public finance. We will assume that the government requires some specific level of resources to carry out the functions which have been assigned to it by the voters. Our task is to ask how the government acquires resources, and to look at the consequences.

Government Requires Some Resources

Let's suppose that the government uses a certain portion of our resources, leaving the private economy with the rest. We can easily represent this as in Figure 10.1. The outer production possibilities curve represents the combination of corn and wheat (the goods produced in the market economy) that could be produced if all of the nation's resources were left in the hands of private citizens.

But in fact the government will use some of the resources, leaving only the inner production possibilities available for Corn and Wheat.

And with this inner production possibilities curve, we can ask the same question we asked in Chapters 2 - 8: does the market mechanism allocate the resources efficiently?

The answer to this question depends crucially on **how** the government gets access to the resources it needs. In this chapter we'll consider the most frequently used method of getting resources into the hands of the government: taxation.

Taxation and Prices

To be concrete, let's suppose that the government charges a tax of t% on every bushel of Wheat sold. Thus entrepreneurs actually receive some price P_w^e for their Wheat[1], but consumers pay $P_w^e(1+t) = P_w$. What does equilibrium look like? Let's start building it up.

First, the price line, as seen by entrepreneurs, is tangent to the (inner) production possibilities curve at the point of production. Its slope is the ratio of prices actually received by producers, $-P_w^e/P_c$.

Second, the slope of each consumer's budget constraint is given by the prices that the consumers actually see, namely P_c and P_w (where, because of the tax, P_w is equal to $P_w^e(1+t)$).

Third, prices must adjust until total supply equals total demand.

Such an equilibrium is depicted in Figure 10.2, where 10.2a shows the production possibilities curve with the price line as seen by producers, and 10.2b, c, and d show the

---

[1]The superscript e stands for entrepreneur; P_w^e thus refers to the price of wheat received by the entrepreneur. P_w without a superscript refers to the price that the consumer actually has to pay.

economy's three consumers' budget constraints (steeper than the price line tangent to the production possibilities curve; the price of Wheat is higher in the eyes of consumers than producers). The three consumers go to points of tangency and, since the prices are equilibrium prices, total demands of consumers add up to total production. This is a true equilibrium; supply equals demand, and neither entrepreneurs nor consumers have any desire to change their behavior.

The Inefficiency of Taxes

It should be clear that Figure 10.2 depicts an inefficient allocation of **the resources that are left to the private sector**. The problem is not that the government took some resources; we recognize that if the government is to perform services for us it needs resources. The problem is that **in the act of taking resources the government has damaged the ability of the price system to efficiently allocate the resources** which are still available to the private sector of the economy.

In many respects the analysis of taxation is similar to that of monopoly (compare Figures 10.2 and 9.2). In each instance something causes consumers to see price lines which are not tangent to the production possibilities curve. And we can continue to explore the similarity with monopoly by asking the next two questions that arose in Chapter 9.

What Prevents the Mutually Beneficial Transaction from Occurring?

In Chapter 9, we noted that a monopolist would like to go ahead and strike all of the possible mutually beneficial transactions. But he is frequently deterred from doing so by the prospect of a side effect; he cannot cut the price for one consumer without cutting the price for all.

●   Exercise 10.1: Relying on Figure 10.2, draw a transaction that helps one consumer and makes nobody else worse off. Describe the type of negotiation that the consumer would engage in when trying to work out such a deal. Such a transaction has a well-known name; see if you can figure out what it is.

The name you should have come up with in Exercise 10.1 is **tax evasion**, and we know why it (generally) does not occur. But notice that under a certain set of (admittedly very farfetched) conditions, nobody (not even the government) loses as a result of tax evasion.

Suppose the equilibrium of Figure 10.2 has occurred. One consumer writes to his Congressman, stating the following:

Dear Congressman from a Wheat Producing State:

"I have already purchased all of the Wheat I am willing to buy at P_w (which, as you know, includes a tax of t% per bushel). However, I would be prepared to buy an additional 10 bushels

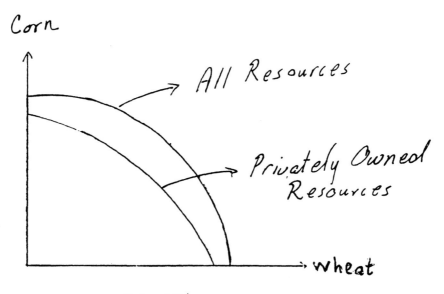

Fig 10.1

at the lower price P_w^c. I know any one of the farmers in your district would be happy to sell to me at this price; after all, that's the price they get now. So the farmer gains, I gain, and the government doesn't lose, since I am already paying all of the taxes I am willing to pay. Please introduce a special bill authorizing me to buy 10 bushels of wheat, at whatever price I can negotiate with one of the farmers in your district, without paying taxes on it."

Sincerely,
Honest Constituent

The problem is pretty obvious: There is not the slightest reason to assume that the constituent is honest. Nevertheless, it is worth noting that the tax evasion proposed by our constituent, if he really is telling the truth, tends to undo the efficiency damage inflicted by taxes.

Are Two Taxes Better than One?

We can describe the inefficiency revealed in Figure 10.2 in one of two ways: too little Wheat production or too much corn production. And this is very similar to what we said about monopoly: too little M or too much C; they are two ways of describing the same problem.

You may have already spotted a straightforward way to fix the inefficiency introduced by the wheat tax: tax Corn at the same rate[2]. Just as we saw that it might help to "fight" one monopoly with another, so we might balance the distortionary effect of one tax with another tax.

Let's suppose that the government levies a t% tax on both goods (or more generally, on all goods). Now the prices, as seen by entrepreneurs and consumers, bear the following relationship:

$$P_w^e \cdot (1+t) = P_w \quad and$$

$$P_c^e \cdot (1+t) = P_c;$$

therefore

$$\frac{P_w^e}{P_c^e} = \frac{P_w}{P_c}$$

If the tax **rate** is the same on both goods, then the **price ratio** between Wheat and Corn is the same for both producers and consumers. This of course means that the slope of the equal-revenue line which motivates producers is the same as the slope of every consumer's budget constraint. Figure 10.2 becomes Figure 10.3, which looks like our familiar everything-is-efficient picture.

---

[2]Presumably, now that both corn and wheat are being taxed, the tax **rate** can be lowered.

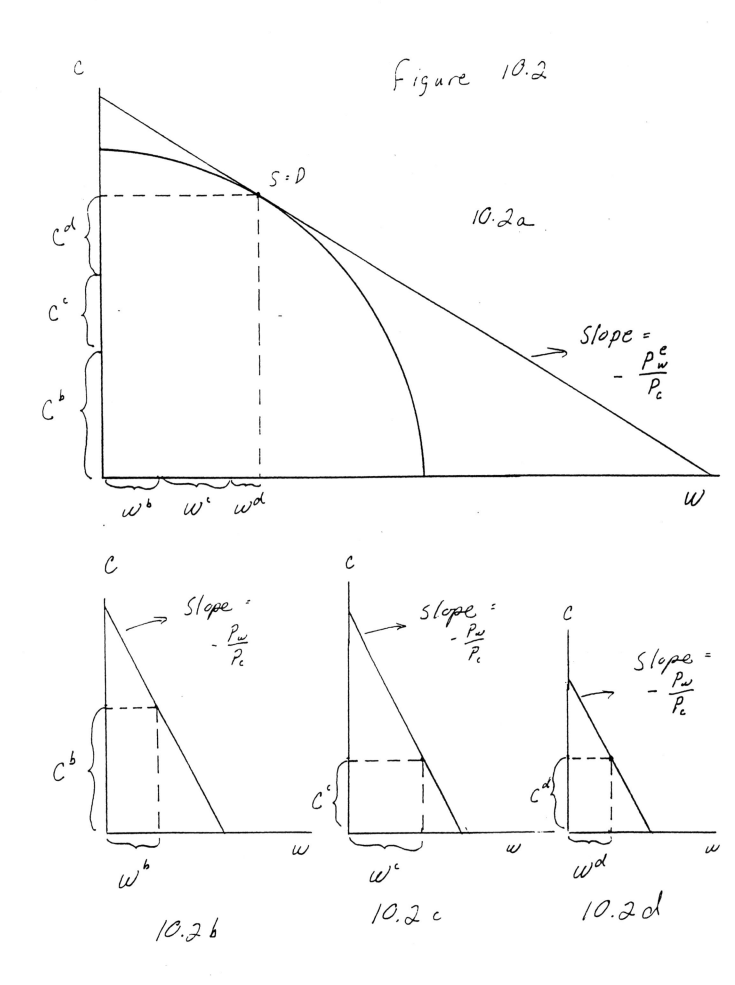

Figure 10.2

10.2a

Slope = $-\dfrac{P_w^e}{P_c}$

10.2b

Slope = $-\dfrac{P_w}{P_c}$

10.2c

Slope = $-\dfrac{P_w}{P_c}$

10.2d

Slope = $-\dfrac{P_w}{P_c}$

Figure 10.3 makes it appear that a government can tax its citizens without damaging the integrity of the price system.

Unfortunately, when we look more deeply, it turns out that governments in general **cannot** tax citizens without damaging the price system. To see this, let's take another look at the tax system described in Figure 10.3. Corn and Wheat, collectively, are "consumption," and we need to study the effect of taxation on the amount of consumption produced. For simplicity, we'll assume that corn and wheat are produced with just labor, and as we did in Chapter x, we will draw a production possibilities curve between consumption and leisure; it is depicted in Figure 10.4a. Our task now is to draw the relevant price lines and analyze the equilibrium combination of consumption and leisure.

- Exercise 10.2: As in Chapter 6, we will assume that $P_c^e = \$1$; that is, the price of consumption **that the entrepreneur receives** is $1. Draw two pairs of axes, each with consumption on the vertical and leisure on the horizontal axis. On the first, draw a production possibilities curve; leave the second one blank for now.

i. Pick a wage rate and the profit maximizing combination of consumption and leisure. In doing this, write down the expression for the slope of the production possibilities curve and the rule that a profit-maximizing entrepreneur would obey in deciding how much labor to employ. (This is simply a review of Chapter 6; look in particular at Exercise 6.4). Show the profit-maximizing point on your production possibilities curve.

ii. Now draw a representative consumer's budget constraint on the second graph. Remember, the consumer must not only pay P_c^e (=$1) for his consumption, but also must pat the tax. Thus he faces a price of $(1+t)$. Now draw in a tangent indifference curve.

iii. Let's suppose that the wage rate you selected in parts i and ii happens to be an equilibrium. (In other words, if you were to draw graphs like your indifference-curve/budget-constraint graph above for all other consumers, the aggregate of leisure and consumption demands would add up to the profit maximizing point on the production psosibilities curve). Is the equilibrium economically efficient? If possible, describe a specific trade which would serve to improve efficiency.

As you saw in Exercise 10.2, a tax on all consumption goods creates **inefficiency in the allocation of time** between production and leisure. Consumers have to give up a lot of leisure (enough to produce the good **and** pay the tax) in order to acquire consumer goods. The tax on consumer goods makes leisure more attractive than it would be if there were no tax. In fact, as we'll see in Exercise 10.3, a proportional tax on consumption is very much like a proportional tax on labor income.

- Exercise 10.3: Start just as you started Exercise 10.2; with a production possibilities curve between consumption and leisure in panel **a** and a blank graph in panel **b**. But now we will suppose that there is no tax on consumption goods, but rather a tax on labor income (an income tax).

i. Firms have to pay a wage rate **w** (and sell consumption at price $1). Draw the price line

Figure 10.3

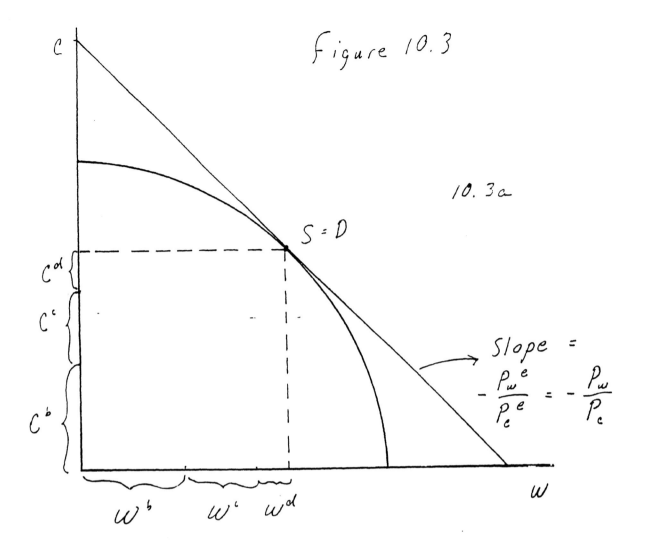

10.3a

$S = D$

Slope =
$-\dfrac{P_w{}^e}{P_c{}^e} = -\dfrac{P_w}{P_c}$

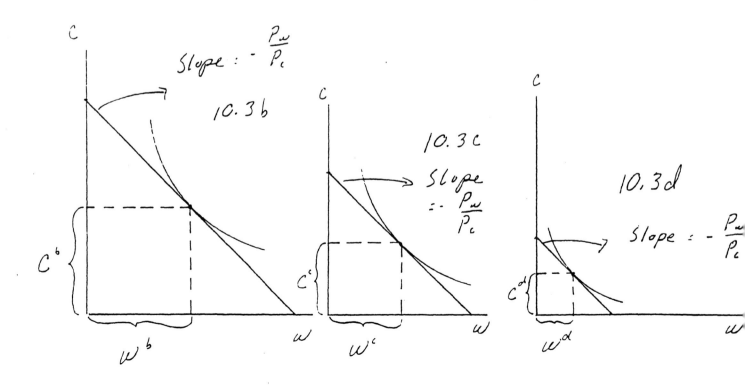

Slope $= -\dfrac{P_w}{P_c}$

10.3b

10.3c

Slope
$= -\dfrac{P_w}{P_c}$

10.3d

Slope $= -\dfrac{P_w}{P_c}$

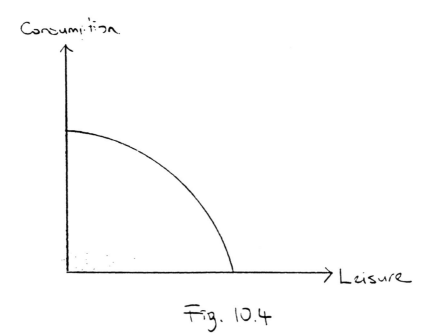

Fig. 10.4

which enables you to see what combination of leisure and consumption will be produced, and specify its slope.

ii.   On panel **b**, draw the budget constraint of a representative consumer, bearing in mind that the consumer has to pay an income tax at the rate **t**. Thus the consumer's "take-home" wage is **w(1-t)**. Draw an indifference curve tangent to this budget constraint and indicate the combination of leisure and consumption that the consumer will demand.

iii.   Assume that the wage rate you picked was an equilibrium (check Exercise 10.2iii, if you need to, to see what this means). Is the equilibrium economically efficient?

iv.   Does your answer to Exercise 10.3 look a lot like your answer to Exercise 10.2? (It should.) Why are Exercise 10.2 and 10.3 in effect the same exercise?

An income tax and a tax on consumption goods both do the same thing: they cause consumers to "believe" that transforming leisure into consumption is more costly than it really is. If the (pre-tax) wage rate is $10/hour, this tells us that it is **possible** to produce $10 worth of consumption with an extra hour of labor.[3] If the consumer would prefer $10 of extra consumption to the extra hour of leisure, then efficiency dictates that he go to work and receive the $10. But if the income tax rate is 20%, he doesn't get $10 worth of consumption for giving up an hour of leisure; he only gets $8. Thus he is less inclined to go to work than he should be. An income tax tends to discourage work effort.

A tax on consumption does precisely the same thing. Instead of getting $10 of consumption from an extra our of work, the consumer only gets $8, because of the $10 he pays for consumption goods, $2 goes to taxes.

Are Three Taxes Better than Two?

We began this chapter with a tax just on Wheat. We then saw that by extending the tax to Corn as well, we eliminated the inefficiency as between Corn and Wheat. But looking more deeply, we saw that there was still an inefficiency between consumption and leisure. Can we use the same trick again -- extend the tax even more broadly and eliminate the inefficiency between consumption and leisure as well?

In Figure 10.5, [Savas: this should be 10.5a (a ppc between consumption and leisure, and 10.5b,c, and d (consumers' indifference curves and price lines including the tax). Be sure total consumption for the 3 consumers, of both C and leisure, adds up to the corresponding amounts on the ppc.] we reproduce the equilibrium you should have gotten in both Exercises 10.2 and 10.3 (check to see that you got them right). We can describe the "problem" in one of two equivalent ways: there is too much leisure in equilibrium, or there is too little consumption. We

---

[3]If you can't quite remember why this is right, remember that the profit maximizer's rule is to continue to hire labor until w = VMP, where VMP is the value of the extra output that can be produced with an extra hour of labor. And as far as the firm is concerned the wage rate is the pre-tax wage; that's what he has to pay.

can't fight this problem by removing the consumption distortion, except by abolishing the tax. Since we assume the government needs the resources, that option is not acceptable.

Let's describe the problem as "too much leisure." Then, in principle, the government has two possible ways of undoing the damage it caused by levying the consumption (or equivalently the income) tax. It could subsidize labor or tax leisure. Either would encourage people to take less leisure.

It's pretty clear that subsidizing labor isn't the answer; under this program the government would simply return to workers the very money it collected in consumption (or income) taxes; it would leave the government with no money.

And it is hard to imagine that taxing leisure is a practical idea. The very statement of the "proposal" sounds silly. Suppose that the consumption tax is 20%. In order to get the slopes of all of the price lines equal again, we should impose a leisure tax equal to 20% of the wage rate. That is, if your wage rate is $10/hour, you must pay the government $2 for every hour you stay home. If your wage rate is $20/hour, you must pay $4 per hour of leisure. Without pursuing this foolishness any farther, let's just accept the fact that there are some goods which simply cannot be taxed, and that among the most important of non-taxable goods is leisure.

Once we accept the non-taxability of leisure, there is no escape from the inefficiency of Figure 10.5. Every system of taxes that a government might impose does two things:
(i) It takes resources from the private sector for use by the public sector (this is the intended purpose of the tax); and
(ii) It leaves the private sector with a damaged price system. The very existence of taxes compromises the ability of the price system to convey information; inevitably, in a world with taxes, prices are unable to tell the whole truth to consumers and entrepreneurs.

Confiscation

There is one way that governments might get resources from the private economy without compromising the price system: it could simply confiscate property at random from the public.

Suppose that the government raised its revenue by sending out IRS agents in the middle of the night to randomly steal property from consumers. They might take cars, houses, groceries, or bank deposits, and they might take from the rich or the poor. When consumers wake up in the morning they discover that they are poorer than they thought they were. But since no taxes are levied **on transactions** in this scheme, such IRS depradations do no damage to the information-dissemination ability of prices. An extra hour of labor enables a consumer to buy an extra $10 of consumption goods, and the same hour of labor can be converted into $10 of consumption goods by entrepreneurs.

As this section should make clear, taxes lead to inefficiency not because they take

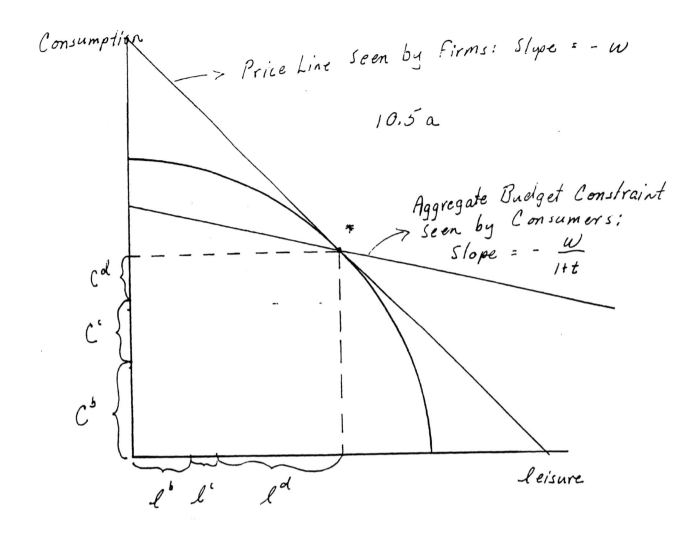

Consumption

Price Line seen by Firms: Slope = -w

10.5 a

Aggregate Budget Constraint seen by Consumers; Slope = -$\frac{w}{1+t}$

C^d

C^c

C^b

ℓ^b ℓ^c ℓ^d

leisure

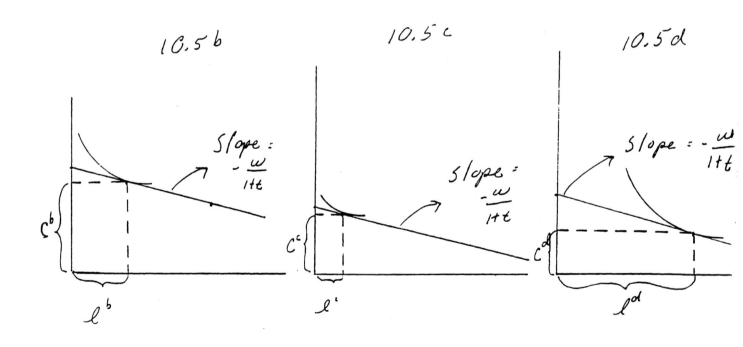

10.5 b

Slope = -$\frac{w}{1+t}$

C^b

ℓ^b

10.5 c

Slope = -$\frac{w}{1+t}$

C^c

ℓ^c

10.5 d

Slope = -$\frac{w}{1+t}$

C^d

ℓ^d

Figure 10.5

resources from us, but because they cause consumers and producers to see different prices.

Taxing Land: Confiscation that Looks like a Tax

- Exercise 10.4: Copy all four panels of Figure 10.5 onto your own paper, but **do not draw in the indifference curves**.
- v. Give the consumer a set of L-shaped indifference curves, and draw one of these "curves" just touching the budget constraint at the same point where the smooth indifference curve touched the budget constraint in Figure 10.5. (this obviously is the highest indifference curve that the consumer can afford). Notice that these indifference curves do not (quite) violate the basic rules: they don't cross, they are the most extreme possible form of being bowed in toward the origin, and they do not slope upward.
- vi. Can you think of a pair of goods for which L-shaped indifference curves actually make sense? Explain.
- vii. Is your modified Figure 10.5 a depiction of an equilibrium? [HINT: to be an equilibrium, total supply must be equal to total demand, and neither the producer nor any of the consumers can have any incentive to change their behavior.]
- viii. Can you spot a trade that would make this consumer better off without harming another? [First, try reducing his leisure and giving him the extra consumption that can be produced; then give him more leisure and insist that he give up the consumption that can no longer be produced.]

In Exercise 10.4 it is impossible to make one consumer better off without harming another **even though the price ratio fracing the consumer is different from the price ratio facing the entrepreneurs.**   The reason is that the consumer (the provider of labor) behaves exactly the same **regardless of the price ratio**; therefore, it doesn't matter that he faces a "wrong" price ratio. In general, prices are important because they influence people's behavior. But when people are so rigid that their behavior is not influenced by price ratios. then it does not matter what the price ratio is.

With this in mind, suppose that the government levies a tax on land, say $10 per acre per year. Will this tax have any effect on economic behavior? Let's think of the possibilities:
(1) The tax won't affect the total stock of land; the physical size of the nation is not responsive to the tax rate.
(2) The tax won't affect the manner in which land is used. If a parcel of land earns $20 more in wheat production than in corn production (say $100 in wheat and $80 in corn) it still earns $20 more after paying the tax ($90 vs $70).

Taxing land does not create inefficiency because neither the stock of land nor the use of land is sensitive to the tax rate. In those rare instances where economic behavior does not respond to prices anyway, the government can levy a tax without creating economic inefficiency. Unfortunately, there are very few such goods, and therefore governments are forced to rely upon taxes which do distort the price system and therefore do generate economic inefficiency.

If you study public finance you will discover the topic of **optimal taxation**; this is a set of guidelines that economists have developed which help government officials design tax systems which minimize (but can't eliminate) the damage to the price system.

Income Redistribution and Economic Efficiency

One of the most durable topics of political rhetoric is welfare reform; politicians of all persuasions argue that the current welfare system is harmful and destructive, and that it must be changed so as to help people get off welfare. If all politicians agree on this, why is the system so persistent? The answer to that question goes far beyond the scope of this book; nevertheless, the insights we have gotten so far enable us to achieve some significant insights into the problem.

- Exercise 10.5: Suppose you believe that every family needs at least $5000 per year of income, to meet basic needs, and that if they are unable to provide this for themselves the government has a responsibility to help them. Suppose you also believe that if a family earns as much as $10,000 the government is not under any moral obligation to give them income assistance.

i. Envision a welfare system that gives every penniless family $5000 per year. As income rises, the government cuts the welfare payment just sufficiently so that the family receives no welfare payments when its income reaches $10,000. Under such a system, calculate the amount by which the family's take-home income (wages plus welfare) rises for each dollar of extra earned income.

ii. Let's assume that the welfare recipient has a wage rate of $5/hour (thus, by working 50 weeks per year at 40 hours per week he can earn $10,000). Other than welfare, he has no source of "unearned income." Draw his budget constraint both before and after the existence of the welfare program described in part i.

iii. In part (i) you should have found that the consumer takes home only $0.50 for every dollar of earned income; thus in part (ii) you should have seen that the welfare program flattens the budget constraint by 50%. You can think of the $.50 that the welfare recipient loses on each dollar of earnings as a tax, and in fact you can see that it has the same effect on the budget constraint as the income tax we analyzed above.

iv. Suppose you believe that a 50% tax[4] on the incomes of welfare recipients is bad policy; it is economically inefficient and it tends to discourage work.[5] You have decided that the tax rate should be no higher than 20%. Calculate the earned-income level at which the consumer no longer receives any welfare if you cut welfare payments by only $.20 for

---

[4]In fact, the welfare system in the United States generates tax rates much higher than 50% for many welfare families; indeed, some families stand to lose more than $1 for every $1 they earn; a tax rate of over 100%.

[5]You should know that these are two ways of saying the same thing; the 50% "tax" discourages work which, on efficiency criteria, should occur.

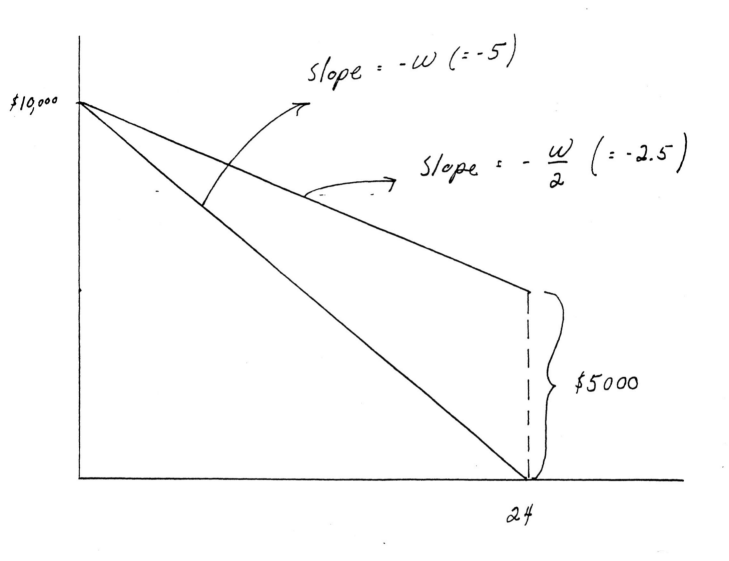

Figure 10.6

each dollar of earned income.[6] Look up median after-tax family income in the United States (you can find it in the Statistical Abstract of the United States or in any good Almanac) and compare it with the "break-even" income you just calculated.

Under the welfare program you analyzed in Exercise 10.5iv above, every family whose income is less than $25,000 per year receives some financial support from the government; all government programs, including welfare, are paid for by families whose incomes are above $25,000.

Many people feel that there is no need for the government to support families whose incomes are as high as $25,000. But as you should see from Exercise 10.5, there are only two ways to avoid paying welfare to people in this income range:
(i) reduce the basic payment to people with no income, or
(ii) increase the "tax rate" faced by welfare payments.

It is mathematically impossible to design a welfare program which does all of the following:
(i)   provides a decent income for society's poorest citizens;
(ii) imposes only a moderate tax rate on welfare families; and
(iii) phases out welfare by the time families are reasonably well off.

Perhaps the above is a bit too stark; after all "mathematically impossible" and "reasonably well off" don't usually belong in the same sentence.   But if you follow the basic format of Exercise 10.5, adjusting the numbers in any way you want, you will see that there is a very important sense in which the statement is right.   This is a big part of the reason that the problem is more difficult than the politicians would have us believe.

Conclusion

Governments must collect taxes in order to carry out functions which the private economy cannot perform. And most citizens also believe that we, acting through our government, have a moral obligation to provide assistance to the poorest members of our society.

In this chapter we have seen the unfortunate fact that governments **cannot** levy taxes, or help the poor, without distorting incentives and damaging economic efficiency. The very act of collecting taxes causes prices to misrepresent the relative scarcity of various goods. And in much the same way, the very act of providing welfare which declines as the recipient gets richer reduces the welfare recipient's incentive to get richer.

---

[6]We refer to this level of income as the "break-even" income; people poorer than this receive payments from the government; people richer than this pay the taxes to support both the welfare program and all other government activities.

This particular lesson from economics is rather negative; the more positive lesson, which you can study in courses like public finance, is that the study of economics **can** help policy makers design tax and welfare systems which minimize the damage to the price system, and therefore to incentives.

Chapter 11
When Scarce Resources Have no Owners: Externalities

Introduction

Economizing is the act of deciding how to use **scarce** resources. Some resources, even extremely valuable resources, are not scarce. Therefore we do not need to economize on their use. Air in central Montana is not scarce; despite its crucial importance to Montanans, it is so plentiful that we do not need an economy to allocate it among competing users.

You can test for the scarcity of a resource by asking if we would be better off with a bit more of it. And it is the scarce resources which must be allocated with care.

In the price mechanism we analyzed in Chapters 2 through 9, scarce resources are allocated to their most productive activities because the **owner** of each resource sells it to that entrepreneur who offers the highest price.

There is a hidden assumption in that analysis: **Every scarce resource has an owner**, who has the power to sell the resource or withhold it from the market and use it himself. This assumption looks pretty harmless and usually it is. But there are important instances in which scarce resources are not actually owned by anybody; therefore they cannot be sold and have no prices associated with their use.

Frequently when nobody in particular owns a resource, entrepreneurs and consumers use the resource without paying anybody for its use (there is no owner to demand payment). And since they do not pay for the use of the resource, they make no effort to use it economically. It is the prospect of paying for a resource that gets the attention of a consumer or an entrepreneur, or to state it differently, it is the prospect of paying that forces the economic agent to consider the consequences of using a resource.

The use of a scarce resource without paying for its use is one important example of an **externality**. The term is meant to suggest that the taking of the resource is external to, or outside, the system of prices. More precisely

- An **externality** is any action taken by one economic agent (a consumer or a producer) which harms or helps another, but for which no payment is rendered. Notice how an externality is different from a normal economic transaction. In any transaction, one agent takes something from another, but this taking is compensated by a payment, usually rendered in money. These types of transaction are **voluntary**, in that both parties agree to the terms. But as we will see, there is a class of actions where one agent is able to simply take a scarce resource without paying the victims of the taking, and without their consent.

Some Non-Owned Resources

We mentioned above that air in Montana is not a scarce resource; Montanans can use it pretty much as they wish without diminishing its usefulness to others. But the same is definitely not true of air in Los Angeles. Human activity makes the air in Los Angeles dirty, and the residents suffer as a result. The carrying capacity of the air over Los Angeles is scarce, in exactly the same way that tomatoes are scarce in Los Angeles. The use of Los Angeles air is not efficient because the people who stand to lose if the air is dirty have no ready way to sell or withhold the right to dump pollution into the air.

Now think about a trip on a Los Angeles freeway; the freeway is congested so the trip takes a lot of time. Each commuter wishes that the freeway were less congested -- that there were more road space per car. But you can't buy road space per car in Los Angeles; nobody owns the road space, and therefore nobody can sell it to you. (Legally, of course, the State owns the freeways. But there is no mechanism whereby the State could rent a moving slice of the freeway to you exclusively, to ensure that you get to work quickly.)

In the case of air pollution, the lack of ownership (and therefore the possibility of a price-based allocation system) results from the fact that the air moves around in ways that any potential owner could not control. As a practical matter, it is very difficult to imagine a mareket for air.[1]

In the case of freeway congestion, on the other hand, in some cases it is possible to charge prices for the use of the road and to limit access. And of course sometimes this is done.

In this chapeter we will explore the economics of the allocation of resources which cannot easily be owned or bought and sold.

Resource Allocation when a Scarce Resource is "Free"

We'll consider the production of a specific good, Electricity (called E below); the production of E requires the use of purchased inputs (I), such as coal and labor, as well as the discharge of smoke (S) into the environment. Any combination of I and S shown on the isoquant in Figure 11.1 can produce one unit of E. We'll collapse I into an aggregate of all purchased inputs, and measure it as dollars worth of I.

- Exercise 11.1: Copy or trace Figure 11.1 onto your own paper. Now draw a firm's equal-cost line for the E-generating firm tangent to this isoquant. [If you need to, refer to Exercise 5.2, when we first used equal-cost lines.] What is the slope of your equal-cost line, and why?

---

[1]By contrast, individual citizens do have the power to prevent others from dumping solid waste on their property. Neither solid waste nor land move around; it is easy for somebody to "own" land. Notice that a crucial aspect of ownership is the power to determine how the property is used, and to demand payment from those who use it.

11.3

In Exercise 11.1 you should have drawn a horizontal equal-cost line, reflecting the fact that the E-generating firm pays nothing to dump smoke into the air (nobody owns the air, and therefore nobody can sell or withhold the right to dump smoke into it). Along this horizontal equal-cost line the **firm's** cost does not change. Notice that the slope is what it "should be," namely the negative of the price ratio between I and I ($P_I = \$1$ and $P_S = 0$, so $-P_I/P_S = 0$). When the polluter does not have to pay for dumping smoke, he will continue to dump smoke right up to the point where the marginal product of dumping smoke is zero. The reason is that the alternative is to use more I, and he has to pay for I.

How do consumers feel about this? The air they breathe is dirty, which they don't like. On the other hand their E is cheap. Would they be willing to pay more for E in exchange for cleaner air? This is of course an economic efficiency question, and we can address it using the same techniques we have used throughout this book. That is, we can characterize the equilibrium, and ask whether it would be possible to move from that equilibrium in such a way as to make one consumer better off without harming another.

Consumers care about two things in the current context; C (Consumer goods) and Clean Air (A). Figure 11.2 depicts one indifference curve for one consumer. At present the consumer has the combination marked *. He buys C*, but does not buy A*; this is just the quality of air that exists after the E-generating firm decides how much to pollute it.

Before going on we need to tidy up one detail about units: We're measuring Air Quality and Smoke in the same units; A goes up by 1 every time S goes down by 1. Thus the emission of one unit of S by the factory reduces A by one unit; a movement to the right in Figure 11.1 translates dierctly into an equal movement to the left in igure 11.2.

Point * in Figure 11.1 and * in 11.2 represents an equilibrium. The consumer spends his entire income on C (the only product available for sale in the marketplace), and the E-generating firm produces E in his least-cost way.[2] Notice that the consumer never **decided** how much A to "buy;" the amount of A he has is simply the byproduct of a firm's decision, and nowhere in this decision-making process did the firm ask, "How badly would the consumer like to have cleaner air?" By contrast, the E-generating firm did (in effect) ask, "What would the consumer rather have, more consumption or more leisure?" He posed this question by offering a wage rate equal to the value of the marginal product of labor.

From the equilibrium of Figures 11.1 and 11.2, let's see if we can find a move that makes our consumer better off without harming any other consumer.

---

[2]As you know, there are many components of equilibrium which we have not bothered to draw. We have not drawn in the other consumers, the trade-off between leisure and consumption, or the trade-off among the various components of consumption. All we have drawn is the components of equilibrium that we want to study in the current setting.

Figure 11.1

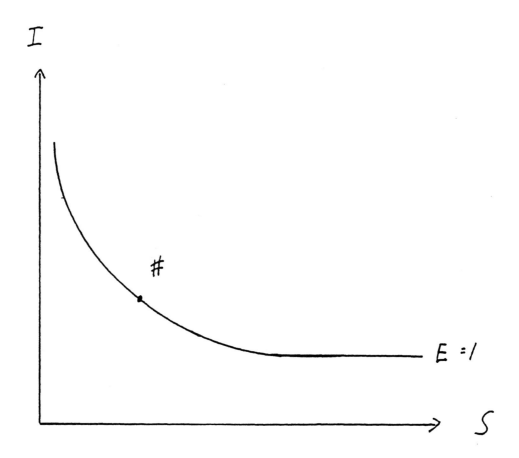

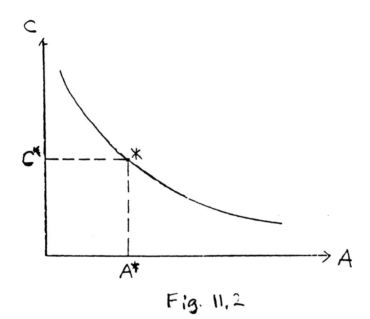

Fig. 11.2

- Exercise 11.2: Redraw Figures 11.1 and 11.2 onto your own paper.
i. In Figure 11.1, contemplate a reduction in S from * to # (and therefore an increase in A for our consumer of the same amount; we'll get to that later). Show the extra amount of I that will be required to keep output of E constant. Call this amount ΔI (remember, it is measured as dollars worth of purchased inputs). What happens to cost of production as seen by the firm?
ii. How many dollars' worth of C must some consumer give up if the move from * is actually to be carried out? [Hint: Go back to Chapter 8, if you need to, and ask why the extra I has a market value of ΔI.]
iii. Now let's suppose that the consumer depicted in Figure 11.2 (labeled Consumer 1) reduces his own consumption by the amount you determined in 11.2ii just above. Is he better off than before? Is anybody else worse off?
iv. Now let's imagine a whole series of S-reducing steps along the isoquant of Figure 11.1, with the consumer of 11.2 always volunteering to absorb the requried reduction in consumption. Try to depict the appearance of the two graphs when the last trade which actually helps our consumer has been carried out. At that set of points, what are the slopes of the isoquant and indifference curve? Why?
v. For the S-reducing steps you carried out in 11.2iv above, our depicted consumer kept getting better off and no other consumer became worse off; no other consumer lost either A or C. Was any other consumer made better off?

The equilibrium of Figures 11.1 and 11.2 is economically wasteful, and in Exercise 11.2 we explored **one** of the reasons for this. Our consumer would like the E-generating plant to use less smoke and more I (thus reducing the production of consumer goods but cleaning up the air). But the firm has no incentive to do so, **because he doesn't have to pay for the use of the air.** Since he doesn't have to pay for the air, he has no incentive to do the economizing that the consumer would like.

Figure 11.3a and b show the answer to Exercise 11.2iv; our consumer continues to sacrifice C in exchange for A, as dictated by the firm's isoquant, until the slopes of the indifference curve and isoquant are identical. You can see in Figure 11.2b that the consumer became better off in the process.

Many Consumers and Many Polluters

Looking at Exercise 11.2, it appears that the inefficiency can easily be remedied. It can't be that hard, after all, for the consumer to go to the firm and offer to pay him to reduce pollution. And if in fact there were only one consumer, and only one polluter, this would be right. But that is not generally the situation.

Look again at your answer to Exercise 11.2v. Always before in this book, we have been able to discuss deals that affected the two deal-makers, but which had no effect on anybody else. In the case of something like smoke, it no longer works this way. When our factory cleaned up his E-generating process in response to Consumer 1's proposed deals, he cleaned up the air not only for Consumer 1 but also for all of that consumer's neighbors. They all breathe and look through the same air. Thus the consumer of Figure 11.3b is doing his neighbors a favor by negotiating a reduction in pollution.

Now we must ask, if all of the neighbors somehow banded together, would they want a different level of air pollution from the one negotiated by just one consumer in Exercise 11.2iv?

- Exercise 11.3: The economy of Figures 11.1 and 11.2 consists not of just one consumer but three (we could draw more but would just get clutter without learning anything more). The other two consumers' indifference maps are drawn in Figure 11.3c and 11.3d. Copy them onto yoru own paper. Before any of the "trades" carried out in Exercise 11.2, consumers 2 and 3 are at the points labeled * in their indifference maps.

i. Look again at part iii of Exercise 11.2; Consumer 1 gives up some C in exchange for cleaner air. As a result of Consumer 1's action, show what happens to Consumers 2 and 3.

ii. Now let's suppose that all of the mutually beneficial transactions between the firm and Consumer 1 have been carried out (we moved from * to # in both Figure 11.3a and 11.3b). This moves Consumers 2 and 3 from points * to # in Figure 11.3c and 11.3d (they both get free A as a result of the deals between Consumer 1 and the firm). Also, we will suppose that (by chance!) the slopes of all three consumers' indifference curves at # are identical.[3] And to keep things simple below we will tell you that this slope, which is the same for everybody, is -1. (This is the situation depicted in Figure 11.3a-d, at the points labelled #.) Does any one consumer have an incentive to make any more deals with the E-generator? Explain.

iii. Now suppose that the three consumers act as a group. They agree that each will reduce his C by an equal amount. What is the **total** amount of C that the three consumers are willing to give up in order to reduce S by 1? Is it possible for the coalition of consumers to strike a deal with the E-generator which will make them all better off and not hurt anybody else?

iv. See if you can state the condition under which it is no longer possible for this coalition of three consumers to make a deal that makes them all better off without harming anybody else. In other words, see whether you can come up with a general characterization of economic efficiency when there is an externality. [A NOTE OF ENCOURAGEMENT: In 19__, Paul Samuelson received the Nobel Prize in economics. He made many important discoveries in economics; one of them was the answer to Exercise 11.3iv.]

---

[3]Consumer 1 was the only one who took any action; he kept trading with the E-generator until the slope of his indifference curve was identical to that of the isoquant. Then, because there were no more gains for him, he stopped dealing. There is no reason at all why this process should lead to a point where **all** consumers' indifference curves' slopes are identical to that of the production possibilities curve. In this exercise, we just pick such an outcome for convenience.

When our Consumer 1 of Exercises 11.2 and 11.3 made his deals with the E-generating plant, he was (unintentionally) doing a favor for his neighbors. As long as he continued to do this on his own, his neighbors were undoubtedly happy to sit back and enjoy the fruits of his deals. But if pressed, they would have been willing to pay him to continue to make deals beyond his own selfish stopping point. When the economy is at the # points of Figure 113.a-d, each consumer would be willing to give up $1 of consumption per unit of Smoke removal. But **collectively**, the three consumers would be willing to give up $3 of C ($1 each). Since the actual cost of reducing S by 1 is only $1, there is a possible deal which makes all three consumers better off; they each give up $.33 of consumption to bring about cleaner air, and keep the other $.67 they would have been willing to give up if pressed.

The total willingness to pay for each unit of smoke removal is found by **adding the ΔC's from the indifference curves of all consumers.** Hence the economically efficient level of smoke removal occurs where the marginal cost of smoke removal (ΔC/ΔS on the E-generator's isoquant) is equal to the **sum** of the marginal willingness to pay (ΔC/ΔS on the consumer's indifference curve) for all consumers. Such an outcome is depicted in Figure 11.4a (the firm's isoquant) and 11.4b-d (the three consumers' indifference curves).

Study Figure 11.4 carefully. In the "last step" which got the economy to the points labeled ☺ on each of the panels, the E-generator reduced the total C available to the economy by ΔC, which we have labeled as ΔI (=-ΔC) in Figure 11.4a. He did this by using ΔI worth of other inputs in producing E, and we know that these ΔI worth of inputs could have produced ΔI worth of extra C had they not been diverted to the production of E. Thus the rise in I for the Electricity producer is just equal to the fall in consumption produced by the other firms in the economy. That's why we can label it as ΔI(=-ΔC).

By using the ΔI in producing its electricity (E), the firm is able to cut back on Smoke by the amount ΔS(=-ΔA). And since S **fell** by the amount ΔS, **every** consumer's air quality **rose** by the same amount. So on each consumer's indifference map we draw a ΔA equal to (but in the opposite direction) the ΔS from Panel A.

Now some combination of the three consumers must give up the ΔC that was sacrificed to clean up the air. And we can see that the "final step" was just barely a good idea. The three consumers, together, are not willing to give up enough C to pay for any more removal of air pollution. The point represented by the ☺'s in Figure 11.4 is economically efficient.

Markets With Non-owned Resources

In the case of an allocation problem like air quality, we now know what the economically efficient outcome looks like. Now we must ask whether markets will spontaneously lead us to a point like ☺ in Figure 11.4.

Always before in this book, we have assumed that individual consumers and entrepreneurs

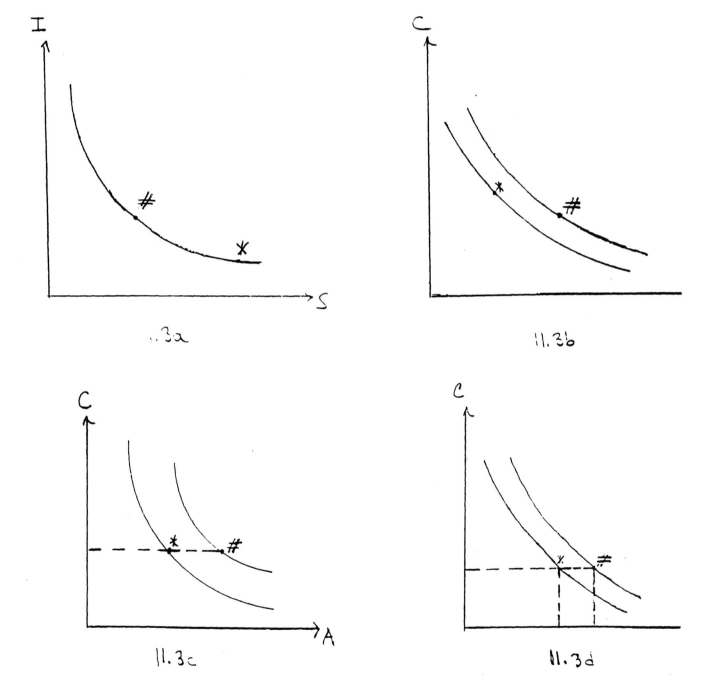

Fig. 11.3

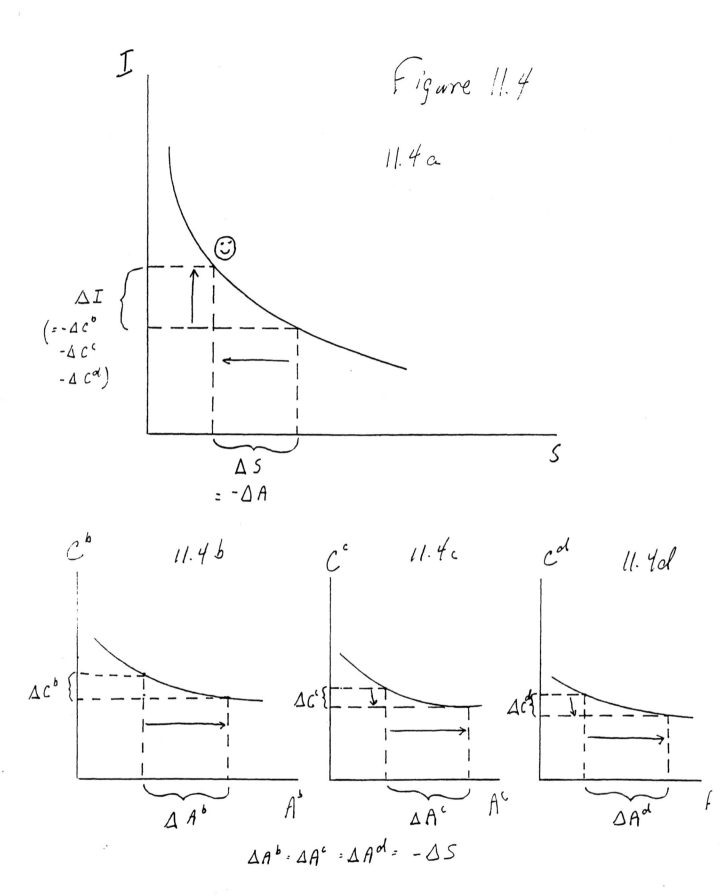

Figure 11.4

11.4 a

ΔI

$(= -\Delta c^b$
$\quad -\Delta c^c$
$\quad -\Delta c^d)$

ΔS
$= -\Delta A$

11.4 b

Δc^b

ΔA^b

11.4 c

Δc^c

ΔA^c

11.4 d

Δc^d

ΔA^d

$\Delta A^b = \Delta A^c = \Delta A^d = -\Delta S$

acted in their own selfish best interest. And in the model of Chapters 2 -8, this selfish behavior led to economic efficiency because the only people affected by any one transaction were the very people who (voluntarily) carried out the transaction.

If a consumer and a grocer can agree on a sale of tomatoes, we can assume that both the consumer and the grocer gain from the transaction, and nobody else is affected one way or the other. And if a worker accepts a job offer at wage w, we know, merely from the fact that the job offer was accepted, that efficiency is enhanced when the worker goes to work.

The problem with externalities is that the consequences of actions extend to people other than those who agree to the actions. This means that we can no longer count on private uncoordinated action to lead toward economic efficiency. In exercise 11.3ii, we saw that the level of air pollution resulting from uncoordinated action is higher than it "should" be.[4] Only by coordinated action will we achieve an economically efficient outcome.

The problem with coordinated action is that the coordination itself is difficult. First of all, somebody has to bring the consumers together to actually form a coalition. When there are only three consumers affected by a factory's pollution, it is certainly plausible to imagine that they will take the trouble to get together and decide how much to offer the polluter for each unit reduction in pollution. But suppose, as is frequently the case, that there are thousands or millions of consumers affected by the level of pollution. Then, there really doesn't seem a practical way for them to get together, report on the slopes of their indifference curves, and strike a deal with the firm.

Two important things change when we go from the realm of ordinary goods like corn and leisure to goods like smoke and traffic congestion. First, in the case of externalities, efficiency requires that somebody gather a great deal of information, which is likely to be difficult. Second, in the world of externalities, we need to worry about whether consumers or producers will be honest in revealing the relevant information.

Information

We found an efficient outcome in Figure 11.4 by finding a point where the slope of the isoquant is equal to the **sum** of the slopes of the consumers' indifference curves. One can imagine a group of three consumers negotiating with a polluter and finding a point such as ☺ in Figure 11.4. But it is not a very straightforward exercise, and it would require patience on the part of all of the participants. But the problem becomes a practical impossibility if there are hundreds, thousands, or millions of consumers. All would have to report on the slopes of their indifference curves, not just at the current points of consumption but over all of the possible outcomes which might be considered. Then somebody would have to load this information into a computer, to

---

[4] By 'higher than it "should" be, we mean 'higher than it would be at an economically efficient outcome.'

figure out how much the group of consumers is willing to pay for each of an array of pollution reductions. Finally the negotiator would have to take this information to the polluter and try to strike a deal.

Compare this with the information coordination needed to run the price system when none of the goods is afflicted with externalities. Consumers do not need to report the shapes of their indifference curves to anybody. Each consumer needs to know his or her own preferences, and the prices of the goods. The coordination that was required in Figure 11.4 is simply not necessary if there are no externalities.

Honesty

When the goods being exchanged are apples, grapes, and human time, consumers have no incentive to lie about their preferences. If the price of grapes is $1/lb, and if a pound of grapes is worth more than $1 to me, I would be foolish to lie to the grocer and say that they are only worth $0.80. If I am dishonest about my preferences, I harm myself and help nobody else.

Unfortunately, this self-enforcing honesty is not a feature of the world of externalities. Now everybody has an incentive to lie. To see this, think about Consumer 3 in Figure 11.4. His neighbors tell him that they are thinking of collectively asking the E-generating company to cut pollution. It might be in his interest to deny that he likes clean air, hoping that the other two consumers will go ahead without him and pay the firm to cut smoke emissions. He gets cleaner air without paying at all. Of course, the air is not as clean as it would have been had he joined the group; with all three consumers helping they would have bought more smoke removal. But on the other hand he didn't pay anything for the pollution removal that he did get.

The incentive to lie about one's desire for clean air is known as the **free rider** problem; each consumer knows that his neighbors want clean air, and each consumer hopes his neighbors will pay for it and he'll get it for free.

We can see pretty clearly that the free rider problem more severe in bigger groups. In our three-consumer example, if any one consumer refuses to join the group he gets air cleanliness for free, but he substantially reduces the pool of money available to pay for smoke reduction. So he gets significantly less clean air than if he joined the group. But if there are a million people in the community, any one consumer loses essentially nothing from refusing to participate.

The problem, of course, is that **every** consumer wants his neighbors to pay the entire bill, and as a result nobody has an incentive to tell the truth about his or her desire for clean air.

Summary of the Problem

Externalities are allocation problems which require collective action. It is physically impossible to clean up Los Angeles air for one consumer without cleaning it up for all, just as it is impossible to make a freeway less congested for one commuter without making it less congested for all. The fact that the action must be collective means that we cannot count on individual optimization behavior to bring about efficient resource use. The purpose of the preceding parts of this chapter is to demonstrate that the market forces which work so elegantly in other settings are unable to efficiently determine levels of such activities as air pollution and the use of congested roads.

Solutions to the Problem

The problem of externalities appears to cry out for government intervention. One action (a level of pollution for all consumers to live with) needs to be taken on behalf of everybody, and government is the only institution which can effectively play this role. But saying that government must deal with the problem is only a first step. Now we have to ask specifically how government might go about this.

Historically, governments have approached the problem of externalities in a variety of ways; probably the most frequent method has been direct regulation. The appropriate government agency makes some determination about the acceptable level of pollution, and orders polluters to take some specific action to reduce pollution. Of course, the regulator's problem is to decide how much pollution reduction he should insist on.

Economists generally recommend a different approach to externalities; one which is based on prices. We have seen in Chapters 2 - 8 that in the right conditions prices can do a wonderful job of allocating resources. So it is not surprising that economists would try to bring the power of the price system to bear on one other resource-allocation problem.

Let's return to the example of the electric generating firm above. The heart of the economist's solution to this problem is this: Charge the polluter a price, or pollution fee, for each unit of pollution that it emits into the air. Later we'll turn to the hard part: getting the price "right." For now notice that this is just backwards from the way we approached the problem in Exercise 11.3. In that exercise, consumers paid the firm **not** to pollute; now we are proposing that the firm pay the government (on behalf of consumers) for the right to pollute. Either approach induces the firm to reduce its emissions of pollution, and in terms of efficiency it does not matter which approach is used.

You can think of the world of Exercise 11.3 as follows: The firm owns the right to use the air as a smoke-disposing ground; it can either dump smoke or sell its right to consumers (and thus refrain from dumping smoke). In the paragraph just above, in effect we turned that around: Consumers own the right to clean air; they can either insist that it stay completely clean or sell off part of their rights to firms, who would like to use the air as a place to put their smoke. For the price mechanism to work efficiently, it is crucial that **somebody** own the rights to the air, but it

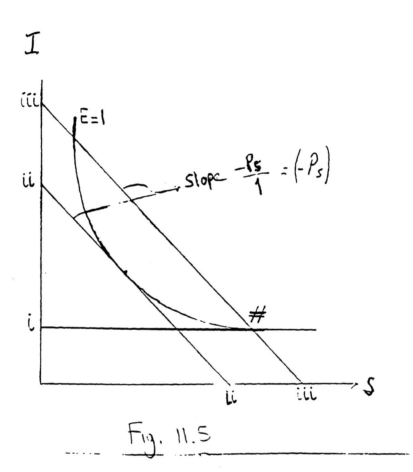

Fig. 11.5

doesn't much matter who.[5]

- Exercise 11.4: Return to Figure 11.4, which depicts an efficient mix of pollution and other inputs in the generation of electricity. Suppose the government recognizes that no coalition of consumers can really stick together to make the deal that brings about point ☺; the problems of coordination, information, and free riding are too great. The government therefore decides to charge the firm a pollution fee.

i. Plot the equal-cost line representing the fee that the government "should" charge.
ii. Remember that the I axis is denominated in dollars (worth of I). On this axis you should be able to read off the per-unit cost of generating electricity, as seen by the firm, before the pollution fee was instituted. See if you can find it.
iii. On the same axis, try to find the point representing the cost faced by the firm after the imposition of the pollution fee.
iv. Finally, on the same axis, try to find the point corresponding to the **true** cost of producing a unit of electricity before the imposition of the pollution fee. (by "true cost" we mean the cost of the purchased inputs plus the damage done to consumers by the pollution. In other words, we mean the value of other goods (consumption plus air cleanliness) that consumers forsake to get one more unit of electricity.

By now you likely know the pattern we follow in this book: in the next paragraph we will give the answer to Exercise 11.4, and then we will discuss it. But despite the easy access to the answer, you will learn the material much more thoroughly if you try to do it yourself before reading on.

Figure 11.5 reproduces Figure 11.4, including the firm's tangent equal-cost line when it can dump smoke into the air without paying. The I intercept of that (horizontal) equal cost line is the amount of I the firm must purchase to produce one unit of E, if it makes no effort to cut down on S (smoke). So this intercept, labeled *i*, is the firm's unit cost of producing E if there is no pollution fee (the answer to 11.4ii above). If the firm is competitive, *i* also represents the price it would charge for a unit of electricity.[6]

The equal-cost line tangent to the isoquant, labeled *ii* at both ends, is the line the polluter would face if he had to pay the efficient pollution fee. The slope of this line is $(-P_s/1)$ where P_s is the price the government charges for the right to pollute (s stands for smoke) and 1 is the price of I (since we are measuring I in dollars worth of other inputs). Every point on this line costs the

---

[5]Of course, if consumers own air rights and can sell them to the firm, they are richer than if the firm owns the rights and consumers have to buy their air cleanliness. So when we say it doesn't matter, we are only talking about efficiency. Once again, you can see that economic efficiency is blind to the important question of who is rich and who is poor.

[6]Remember, competitive firms set price equal to marginal cost; they pass all of their own costs on to consumers, but no more.

firm the same amount, and the point of tangency represents the most electricity that can be produced for this amount.

Now notice that the I-axis intercept of the *ii-ii* line costs the firm the same amount as any other point on the line. So the point *ii* on the I-axis directly tells us the cost the firm must incur in producing electricity if it has to pay the pollution fee. In other words, the cost to the firm rises from *i* to *ii* when it has to pay the fee. And of course it will pass this cost increase on to consumers. (This gives the answer to Exercise 11.4iii.)

In exchange for the price increase from *i* to *ii*, consumers get cleaner air. Is the cleaner air worth the extra cost of electricity? One way to answer this question is to ask, "what was the cost that consumers truly incurred in exchange for electricity before the imposition of the pollution fee?" The firm was using the mix of I and S designated by # in Figure 11.5; the cost of I (passed on to consumers through the output price) is *i*. But in addition, every unit of electricity makes the air dirtier, and consumers suffer as a result of this pollution. If the pollution fee of Exercise 11.4i is "right" in the sense that it truly reflects the harm suffered by consumers per unit of pollution, then the equal-cost line labeled *iii-iii* plots all of the combinations of I and S which cost the same as point #. That is, all points on the *iii-iii* line impose the same number of dollars' worth of harm on consumers.[7] In particular, we now know that the point *iii* on the I-axis represents the same true cost as does the point #. The I-axis is a handy place to read the cost, because it is already in dollars. So the point *iii* tells us the true cost of producing a unit of electricity using the input combination #.

● Exercise 11.5: Draw a graph with I (for purchased inputs) on the vertical axis and S (for smoke) on the horizontal. Plot the point # from Figure 11.5 (you don't need to be precise). We know that the firm has to pay $1 for each unit of I. Now let's suppose that it also has to pay P_s for each unit of smoke.

i. Draw in all of the points that cost the firm the same amount as point #. What is the slope of the line you drew?

ii. Study the vertical (I-axis) intercept of this line. This point costs the same amount as # (right?). At this point, how much S is the firm discharging? How much does this combination of I and S cost the firm?

iii. Since we are measuring I in dollars worth of I, do you see why the vertical intercept of this equal-cost line directly tells you the dollar cost of any input mix on the line? In particular, assure yourself that the cost of the I-intercept and # are the same. Also, verify that the cost of the I-intercept is the intercept itself. [If you are not sure that this is right, work through the following numbers: At #, S = 500 and I = 100; P_I = $1 (as it has been all along), and P_s = $2. With this information you can calculate directly the cost of #.]

Now let's try to pull all of this together. If it doesn't have to pay a pollution fee, the firm

---

[7] We will show this in detail in Exercise 11.5, in case you have trouble visualizing it now.

produces a unit of electricity using the I, S combination represented by #. In doing so, the firm itself faces a cost of i in doing this (since it just pays for the I, not the S). This cost is passed on to consumers, so the price of electricity is i.

When the firm has to pay not only for I but also S, two things happen. First, **its** cost inevitably goes up, and second, it economizes on S.

Getting the Pollution Fee "Right"

In most of this book, we have been able to count on economic forces to determine prices. The prices which emerge from the selfish behavior of consumers and entrepreneurs tend to be precisely those prices which induce consumers and consumers and entrepreneurs to behave efficiently, and no government agency needs to help guide prices to their efficient levels. The elegance of the price system lies in the fact that each consumer, and each entrepreneur, by his or her own selfish action, does a little bit to make the price system behave efficiently.

When there are externalities -- scarce resources which nobody owns -- this system fails to deliver economic efficiency. Citizens need to rely upon somebody else to do the work which the price system cannot do. But it is not an easy task.

In Figure 11.5 above, we showed the consequences of the imposition of a pollution fee. Because of the pollution fee, the polluter now treats air quality as a scarce resource, and economizes on its use. But the outcome of imposing this fee is efficient **only** if the fee is right.

In principle, we "know" what the fee should be; it shoud be just high enough to drive the polluter to point ☺ on Figure 11.4i. But that doesn't help much; in order to know where point ☺ is, we have to know the shapes of all consumers' indifference curves.

The higher the price the more assiduously the firm will try to cut down on pollution. But the harder he tries, the more cost he imposes on consumers in the form of foregone consumption. We cannot know how much the firm should try to reduce pollution until we know how badly consumers would like to have cleaner air. Only when we know the **value** of clean air, from the perspective of consumers, can we know the right pollution fee to charge firms.

Economists have devised many techniques which are designed to **estimate** the value that consumers place on clean air, and **to the extent that these estimates are reliable**, this gives us some ability to advise the government as to what represents an economically efficient pollution fee. Textbooks in environmental economics[8] give detailed discussions of these estimation methods; here we sketch out one of the methods that is employed, just to give a feel for the way the issue can be approached.

---

[8]See for example, Baumol, W., and Wallace Oates, Environmental Economics.

Due to wind patterns, topography, and so on, most cities have areas which are generally more polluted, and other areas which are generally less polluted. Suppose we were able to find an apartment in the more polluted section of the city and an **otherwise identical** apartment in the less polluted section. So long as we can be sure that they are truly otherwise identical, the only difference between these two hypothetical apartments is the level of pollution. If the one in the polluted section of the city rents for $400 per month and the other for $450, we can conclude that cleaner air is worth $50/month per household. Now suppose that there are 1000 apartments in the polluted neighborhood. The total damage to consumers, brought about by the extra pollution in the dirty neighborhood, is (estimated to be) $50,000 per month. This tells us how much we should charge a firm for adding enough pollution to a neighborhood to transform it from our "less polluted" to our "more polluted" neighborhood.

You can undoubtedly think of many things that are potentially wrong with the approach we described above. And in this context, it is important to make two points: First, the estimation methods which economists actually use are much more sophisticated than that sketched out here (though many of them do operate on the basic principle described in the preceding paragraph). But second, regardless of the sophistication of economists' methods of estimating the value that consumers place on clean air, there is of necessity a great deal of uncertainty as to the "right" value for pollution fee. Almost certainly, a carefully estimated pollution fee leads to a more efficient outcome than no action at all. But no economist believes that it is really possible to implement a set of pollution fees which allocate air and water quality truly efficiently.

Are Fees Better than Regulation

Why do economists generally recommend the use of pollution fees rather than direct regulation of polluters? The answer is that getting direct regulation "right" is even harder than getting the pollution fee "right."

Look again at Figure 11.4; the efficient point, ☺, occurs where the slope of the polluter's isoquant is equal to the **sum** of the slopes of the consumers' indifference curves. In order to get the pollution fee "right" the regulator needs to know the sum of the slopes of consumers' indifference curves.[9] Once the regulator knows how much consumers care about clean air (as revealed by the slopes of their indifference curves) he passes this information on to the polluter in the form of a pollution fee. At this point the polluter must decide whether it is more profitable to reduce pollution and avoid the fee or continue to pollute and pay the fee.

Now, by contrast, suppose the regulator sought to **tell** the polluter how much to cut back on pollution. In order to get it right, the regulator would need to know the slopes of all consuers' indifference curves (as in the case of pollution fees) and in addition he would have to know the slope of the firm's isoquant. That is, if the regulator knows that a certain reduction of pollution is worth $50,000 to consumers (determined by studying apartment rents and the like), he doesn't

---

[9]This is what we attempt to learn by looking at apartment rents, for example.

know whether to order the firm to reduce pollution until he knows whether it would cost more or less than $50,000. In addition to the difficult task of learning how badly consumers want cleaner air, the regulator now has to know how difficult it would be for the firm to reduce air pollution.

The fee-setting regulator avoids this last piece of information gathering: He simply says to the firm, "If you put that last unit of pollution into the air, the government will charge you a fee of $50,000; if you don't, we won't." The firm will pollute if the cost of avoiding pollution is greater than $50,000, and will refrain from polluting if the cost is less.

In other words, by relying on the pollution fee, the regulator saves himself the considerable trouble of learning how electricity is generated. And beyond this, there are two other benefits as well.

Honesty

Suppose the regulator simply orders the firm to cut back on pollution by a specific amount. The easiest thing for the firm to do would be to announce either that the pollution cutback is an engineering impossibility or at least that it would be prohibitively expensive. Almost invariably, the polluting firm knows more than the regulator about the possibilities for reducing pollution, and frequently the regulator will have little choice but to take the firm's word for it.[10]

If instead the regulator imposes a pollution fee, he is free to admit that he doesn't know how expensive it would be to cut pollution. The firm is free to decide for itself, as part of its profit maximizing strategy, whether to pay the fee or cut pollution.

Incentives for Innovation

If firms are ordered to cut pollution by a given amount, and if they are unable to talk their way out of the regulation, they will presumably find the cheapest possible way to cut pollution and then do it. Having satisfied the government's rules, the firm will devote no more effort to reducing pollution. (By contrast, firms are always on the lookout for ways to cut labor and capital costs, for the simple reason that labor and capital are expensive.) By contrast, the presence of a pollution fee serves as a constant prod to look for cleaner ways to manufacture.

Conslusion

Externalities arise when scarce resources are not owned by anybody. Since they are not owned they are not sold. And since they are not sold economic agents use them without regard

---

[10]This is almost exactly what happened when the government first proposed automobile emissions standards in the 1960s. Members of Congress were put in the impossible position of trying to determine how much it would cost to produce cleaner cars. The only people who truly knew (executives of automobile manufacturing companies) were not very helpful.

to their scarcity.

This chapter's first task was to demonstrate that in the presence of externalities the price system fails to allocate resources efficiently.

The second task of the chapter was to introduce the notion of pollution fees, a potentially fruitful way to harness the power of the price system to assist with the allocation of these non-owned resources.

To many students such a system of pollution fees probably looks quite cumbersome. And indeed it is cumbersome. A carefully designed system of pollution fees can surely be of great assistance in allocating certain resources. But even at its best, such a system surely cannot match the efficiency of the regular price system. The allocation difficulties caused by externalities should serve to heighten our appreciation of the power of the price system to allocate most of society's resources.

Chapter 12
When a Price Has Too Many Tasks: Insurance

Introduction

In this chapter we will discuss one more instance in which prices are unable to perform their optimizing as smoothly as in Chapters 2 - 8. We will deal with the issue of insurance, and to keep it specific we will discuss health insurance.

In many ways health-care expenditure is like any other kind of expenditure. Just as purchases of food tend to keep us from being hungry, purchases of medical care tend to keep us from being (or continuing to be) sick. Economic efficiency dictates that we purchase medical care up to the point where we would prefer that the next dollar be devoted to other kinds of consumption. The price of health care keeps us from using doctors to treat minor ailments that will mend themselves, such as headaches, hangnails, and the like. The price, in other words, induces us to **economize** on medical care.

But unlike our demand for food, our desire for medical care is often unpredictable; at any one time we don't know either when we are going to get sick or how sick we are going to become. Furthermore, many types of medical care are extremely costly. Because of the cost and unpredictability of medical care, most of us find it desirable to purchase medical insurance. In this chapter we will explore the benefits of medical insurance. But at the same time we will see that medical insurance, like many medical procedures, has undesirable side effects.

The Demand for Medical Care

So far in this book we have had little cause to use the concept of a **demand curve**; nevertheless it is a very useful tool for economists, and it will prove useful in analyzing health care.[1]

Figure 12.1 shows a market demand curve for medical care.[2] It is important to understand that this is a **market** demand curve; for each price on the vertical axis, the curve tells us how many units of medical care are purchased (demanded) by all of the consumers in the economy. The curve slopes downward, revealing that as the price of health care falls, consumers will purchase more of the good.

---

[1]Demand curves can be derived from a consumer's indifference curves, along with various hypothetical budget constraints. We show how to do this in the Appendix.

[2]Of course, with a complicated product like medical care, it is not very clear what we are measuring on the horizontal axis. Medical care does not come in well-defined units like bushels. We must think of a "unit" of medical care as a useful abstraction; in this chapter you can think of it as something like one hour of physician time.

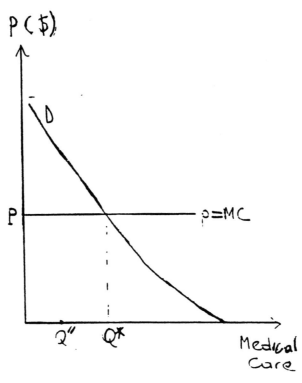

Fig 12.1

Now let's suppose that the price of medical care is **p**, shown by the horizontal line in Figure 12.1, and let's further assume that

$$P \quad = \quad MC$$

so that there is nothing like monopoly, taxes or externalities to cause price to deviate from cost. In this case, the price is a truthful signal of the cost of medical care, where we remember from previous chapters that cost means the value of other goods forgone.

For the moment we will pretend that medical care is like any other good, and for one last time review the sense in which markets help bring about economic efficiency.

- Exercise 12.1: Copy Figure 12.1 onto your own paper. Assume that the amrket is in equilibrium, so p = p* and Q = Q*.
- i. If medical care rises by one unit, by how much (how many dollars worth) must consumption of other goods fall?
- ii. How many dollars worth of consumption are consumers willing to sacrifice in order to acquire one more unit of medical care?
- iii. Is the equilibrium Q* economically efficient?
- iv. Now suppose that the actual level of medical care used by consumers is at Q" in Figure 12.1. What is the maximum amount a consumer would be willing to pay for one more unit of medical care? Is this the same as the number of dollars worth of the other consumer good that some consumer would be willing to give up?
- v. If medical-care output is Q", is it possible to make one consumer better off and no other consumer worse off by expanding output a little bit?

As we have seen before, we see that the intersection of the demand curve and the marginal cost curve (in this case just the horizontal line **p**) yields the economically efficient level of consumption. The reason is that the height of the demand curve measures the value of other goods that consumers are willing to give up for one more unit of (in this case) medical care, and the height of the marginal cost curve measures the amount of the other good which must be sacrificed in production.

The Complication of Unequal Needs and Uncertainty

On average, Americans spend about 15% of their income on health care[3]. However, expenditure on medical care is distributed very unequally across the population; most people spend virtually none of their income on health care, and a few spend a great deal. Some consumers (with the help of insurance) spend considerably more than their incomes.

---

[3]This 15% figure includes not only direct out-of-pocket expenditure but also medical bills which are paid by insurance companies.

Of course, the mere fact that some consumers spend a lot and some a little is no problem by itself; the same is true of many goods. One of the virtues of the price system is that it easily accommodates consumers with very different tastes. We don't think it strange, or a cause for concern, that some of us spend a great deal on baseball tickets and others spend nothing.

But medical care is different from baseball tickets for the following important reason: frequently we do not know in advance how much medical care we will want to purchase. An individual's demand for health care can increase by a factor of several hundred as a result of a single accident or illness.

Most of us find it prudent to **insure** against the possibility of an expensive accident or illness. We would prefer to pay a relatively small amount **regardless** of illness rather than none when we are healthy and a lot when we are ill. By purchasing insurance when I am healthy (and thereby reducing my consumption when healthy) I can reduce the possibility of financial ruin if I get sick. Even if I know that the average consumer pays more in premiums than the cost of the health care, the peace of mind is worth the price. Let's look at how a simplified version of health insurance would work.

A Simple Model of Insurance

Look again at Figure 11.1. If consumers buy Q* of medical care, at price **p**, total expenditure on medical care is **Q*·p**; it is geometrically represented by the area of the box with Q* and p at opposite corners. We already know that a large fraction of this expenditure is devoted to a small fraction of the population, and that many consumers spend little or nothing.

Now let's suppose that an insurance company offers consumers the following package. Every consumer pays a premium, which we will call π, and in exchange the insurance company agrees to pay all consumers' medical bills.

To keep things simple, let's say that the insurance company is not trying to make a profit (or alternatively, due to competition from other insurance companies is not able to make a profit). So all it has to do is to calculate the premium it must charge in order to break even. This break-even premium is

$$\pi* = \frac{Q*·p}{n} \tag{2}$$

where **n** is the population. The right-hand side of this equation is simply per-capita medical-care expenditure (total medical expenditure divided by the population). If the insurance company charges a premium equal to per-capita expenditure, it brings in (just) enough money to pay all the medical bills.

With this insurance, some consumers pay more in premiums than they would have paid in medical expenses, and some pay less. But it could well be that **all** consumers regard the insurance as a good deal, when they buy the insurance itself. All consumers buy the peace of mind that comes from knowing that their medical bills will be paid for if they get sick.[4] Consumers are likely to prefer the sure thing represented by the insurance premium to the gamble represented by the high probability of low medical expenditure and a low probability of catastrophic expenditure.

The Side Effect

- Exercise 12.2: Return to your copy of Figure 12.1, from Exercise 12.1.
i. After the introduction of insurance, how much must any consumer pay for one more visit to a physician? What is the price of a visit?
ii. How much medical care will consumers wish to consume, at this new price?
iii. Now suppose that the health-care industry adjusts the supply to accommodate any change in demand brought about by the introduction in insurance. Show the total amount of health care that will be provided.
iv. As a result of the changes you analyzed in parts i, ii, and iii, what has happened to total health-care costs in the nation?
v. Look at the (break-even) insurance premium that was calculated in equation 12.2. Will the insurance company still be able to break even if it charges this premium?

The problem you analyzed in Exercise 12.2 is known as **moral hazard**; the problem of moral hazard can be stated as follows: The introduction of insurance does more than pool the financial risks associated with illness; it also changes the price[5] of medical care and therefore changes consumers' behavior. Moral hazard is an unwanted side effect of insurance.

In Exercise 12.2i, you should see that for a consumer who has the type of health insurance we are discussing here, the **price** of medical care is zero. Since the insurance company agrees to pay all medical bills, the consumer pays nothing for an extra trip to the doctor. Consumers will continue to go to doctors right up to the point where the last trip is worthless to them.[6]

So long as somebody pays the bills, let's assume that the health care industry simply expands to accommodate the new demand brought about by moral hazard. This is depicted in

---

[4]Unfortunately, to actually **show** that insurance makes consumers better off in this kind of a setting is fairly complicated, and we will not be able to do it in this book

[5]The price of medical care is the out-of-pocket expense that the consumer must incur if he makes a doctor's visit.

[6]Of course, real insurance policies are more sophisticated than the one we laid out above, and there are many checks against the kind of behavior that is described here. But the extreme version of insurance is useful to highlight the problem of moral hazard. And as we will see below, it is impossible to design an insurance policy with no unwanted side effects.

Figure 12.2, which is what you should have gotten after parts i and ii of Exercise 12.2. The box whose opposite corners are p and Q** now represents the nation's total health care bills (the answer to part iii).

The insurance company has agreed to pay all medical bills, in return for the premium. But when we calculated the premium in Equation 12.2, we (mistakenly) assumed that the introduction of insurance would not increase the demand for medical care, so we only calculated a premium big enough to cover Q*·p. But now we know that total expenditure will be Q**·p, so the insurance premium has to rise to cover the side effect:

$$\pi^{**} = \frac{Q^{**} \cdot p}{n}$$

The insurance policy we have analyzed not only insures but it also cuts the price as seen by consumers (in this case to zero) which causes consumers to ignore the true scarcity (cost) of the resources which are needed to produce medical care. Consumers buy medical care which has very little value to them when, if faced with the right options (that is, the right prices) they would prefer less medical care and more of other types of consumption.

In this simple model, consumers do of course pay for all of the medical care they consume; total insurance premiums equal total medical bills. But each consumer's insurance premium depends not on his own use of medical care, but on **average** use of medical care. His own extra trip to the doctor has almost no effect on the average medical bill, so it has no effect on his premium. So from the consumer's perspective, each trip to the doctor's office is free.

Minimizing the Side Effects

Let's suppose that some insurance company figures out a way to eliminate the moral hazard problem. It could offer insurance at a premium π^* instead of π^{**}; consumers would prefer its product (though they get only Q*' instead of Q**, they pay π^* instead of π^{**}) and he would drive the other insurance companies out of business. So we know that insurance companies have an incentive to look for ways to eliminate the problem of moral hazard. How do they do it?

Coinsurance

In the example above, the problem of moral hazard arose because, after insurance, consumers faced a zero price of medical care. In fact, health insurance policies generally only pay a fraction of medical bills. The remainder must be paid by the consumer and is referred to as coinsurance. In effect, the idea is to force the consumer to pay a price for each doctor visit so as to discourage frivolous visits. Let's see how it works.

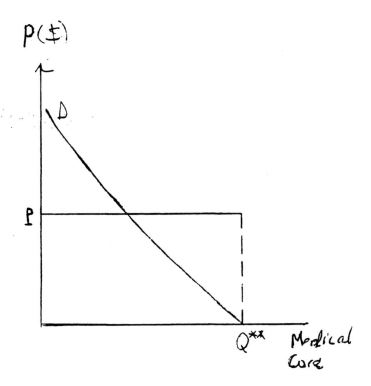

Fig. 12.2

- Exercise 12.3: Redraw the graph from Exercise 12.2 (in case you have lost it, we have drawn this graph as Figure 12.2). Now we will assume that the insurance company charges a premium, and agrees to pay 80% of the medical bills. If there is no medical insurance at all, check from Exercise 12.2 to remind yourself that total health care expenditure is the box whose corners are p and Q*.

i. Assuming that the quantity of medical care remains unchanged after insurance is introduced, show the effect of an insurance policy in which there is a premium π^*, and the insurance company agrees to pay 80% of health care bills. (You should get a graph like Figure 12.3; the box of medical-care cost is divided into 20% at the bottom, paid by consumers in the form of bills to the doctor (coinsurance) and 80% at the top, paid by consumers to the insurance company in premiums and then to the medical industry by the insurance company.)

ii. So far we are assuming that consumers do not change the quantity of medical care they purchase in response to the insurance. Given this assumption, does insurance change the total amount that consumers pay for medical care?

iii. As seen by consumers, what is the price of medical care in the presence of the insurance? Do they have an incentive to consume medical care which is not worth the (true) cost?

iv. Given what you saw in part iii, what do you think happens to the equilibrium quantity of medical care after the insurance is offered?

v. Has coinsurance eliminated the moral hazard problem? Has coinsurance made the moral hazard problem less severe than it was under the insurance sheme you analyzed in Exercise 12.2?

As you saw in Exercise 12.3, health insurance which pays 80% of medical bills (and leaves the patient to pay the other 20%) serves to cut the price by 80% (better than the 100% in Exercises 12.2, but still quite a bit). In deciding how much health care to buy, consumers act like it is very cheap, and they buy more than if they faced a price which was truthful about the cost.

In exercise 12.3, you should have gotten a graph like Figure 12.3. Marginal cost is equal to p*; physicians will charge this amount per visit regardless of insurance. Insurance pays 80% of the cost of each visit, so consumers face a price of $0.2 \cdot p^*$. Now, if consumers face a price of $0.2 \cdot p^*$ they will purchase Q' of medical care.

In both Exercises 12.2 and 12.3, the moral-hazard side effect of health insurance revealed itself through excessive consumption of medical care. But the side effect might show up in quite a different way, and it is useful to explore this possibility.

- Exercise 12.4: In Exercises 12.2 and 12.3 we assumed that, when insurance increases the demand for medical care, the health care industry will simply expand enough to satisfy the new demand. For example, in Exercise 12.2, we assumed that with no insurance the price of medical care is p and quantity demanded is Q*; with health insurance the quantity produced and consumed rises to Q** and the price remains at p. In this Exercise, we are going to assume that it is **impossible** to expand the supply of medical care at all; even if

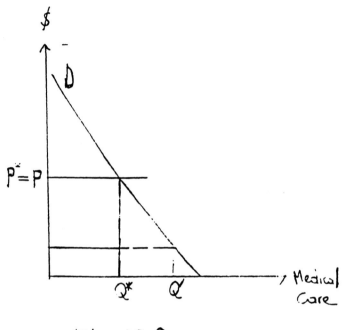

Fig. 12.3

consumers want more health care it is simply not available. Begin by redrawing the demand curve for medical care that you used in Exercises 12.2 and 12.3. Indicate the level of output Q* on the horizontal axis, and draw a vertical line from that point. You can think of this vertical line as the **supply** curve of health care. It depicts oru special situation, whereby no matter how high the price of medical care goes, the supply is always Q*.

i. First, notice the following: even with your vertical supply curve, without insurance the equilibrium occurs at p,Q*, so without insurance total expenditure on health care is just what it was in Exercises 12.2 and 12.3.

ii. Now let's consider the insurance scheme of Exercise 12.3; the insurance company charges a premium and agrees to pay 80% of medical bills. See if you can figure out how to depict the equilibrium. [HINT: Remember; in equilibrium, the price actually faced by consumers must be just that level which will cause them to demand the amount which is supplied.]

iii. What happens to total medical payments (insurance premiums plus direct payments to physicians) when the insurance scheme is offered?

iv. What happens to consumers' direct payments to physicians as a result of the introduction of insurance?

v. To what degree does this insurance protect consumers against the possibility of large medical bills?

Your graph should have looked like Figure 12.4. The vertical line labeled S is the supply curve under the assumption that supply is equal to Q* regardless of price. Given the demand curve, the equilibrium price with no insurance is p*, and total expenditure is Q*·p*. This is where we started the chapter; the problem is that Q*·p* is made up of huge medical bills for some consumers and very small ones for others, and consumers would like to insure against the risk of huge bills. To deal with this risk, we introduce insurance. But to deal with the problem of moral hazard, we analyze an insurance policy with 20% co-payments (or coinsurance) by consumers.

As a first step, the expenditure box Q*·p* is divided 80-20 betewen direct payments and payments through the insurance company (labeled coinsurance and insurance, respectively, in the expenditure box). But now comes the side effect.

With this insurance program, each consumer sees the price of medical care not as p but rather as 0.2p (that's all they pay when they go to the doctor). If the price is only 0.2p, consumers want to purchase Q** of health care. But Q** isn't available at price 0.2p, nor for that matter at any other price. Before any further adjustment, demand for health care exceeds supply. And since demand exceeds supply, we would expect the price to rise until demand is equal to supply.

How far must the price rise in order to eliminate the gap between supply and demand? It must rise all the way to its original level, p*! Only when the price that consumers face for each visit to the physician is equal to its original level p will consumers no longer demand more medical care than is available.

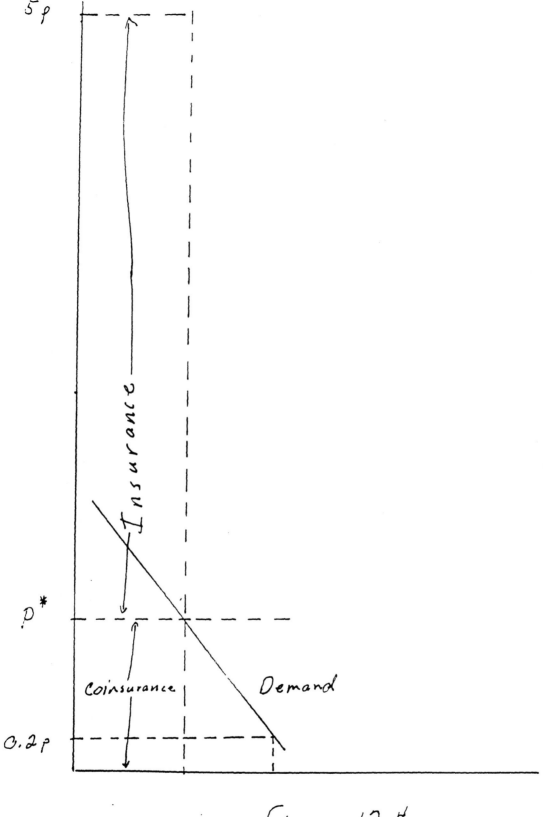

Figure 12.4

In equilibrium, the total cost of medical care in this extreme model has risen by a factor of 5, as depicted in Figure 12.4. Insurance pays 80% of the bills and consumers pay the other 20% directly. Though they only pay 20% of the total cost directly as bills (they pay the rest as premiums) the cost of health care has risen so much that they face exactly the same risk as they did before insurance was introduced. There is no benefit to insurance whatsoever; everything has disappeared into side effect. The only effect of health insurance, under this extreme assumption, is that the cost of health care has risen by a factor of 5.

Of course, it is not realistic to assume that the supply of medical care is absolutely fixed; the truth lies somewhere between the extremes of Exercise 12.3 and 12.4. Health insurance surely does mitigate the risk we introduced at the beginning of the chapter, but it also generates some side effects, which show up as some combination of a rise in the price of medical care and an excessive level of consumption of medical care.

Limitation of benefits

The problem of moral hazard arises because insurance reduces the price of medical care, and as a result consumers wish to buy more medical care. We noticed above that coinsurance -- forcing consumers to pay part of medical bills directly -- might diminish the problem, but will not eliminate it.

Insurance companies often address the moral hazard problem in a different way as well: they impose limits on payments. Frequently health insurance policies pay a specific dollar amount for a given diagnosis. Whereas this surely does diminish the demand for frivolous medical care, it is a very cumbersome system, in which physicians frequently must in effect get permission of insurance carriers before carrying out medical procedures. This too is one of the inevitable side effects of insurance.

Other Insurance

To be specific, we have concentrated on health insurance in the discussion above. But readers shold be aware that the problem of moral hazard plagues almost all types of insurance. The severity of moral hazard varies from one type of insurance to another. For example, it is not much of an issue with life insurance.

To take a case at the other extreme, consider unemployment insurance. We would like to buy insurance against the risk of losing our jobs. But the private-sector insurance industry never offers unemployment insurance.[7] The reason is very simple: If we were fully insured against the

---

[7]Of course, in the United States and many other countries, the government gives payments to laid-off workers. But unlike the private sector, the government has the power to tax workers and firms to pay for the benefits. In other words, the government does not have to pay benefits out of voluntarily-paid premiums.

12.9

risk of being laid off, we would be as well off without a job as with a job. Since it takes no real effort to get fired from a job, most of us would arrange to get fired and then collect our unemployment insurance.

Life and Death

Medical care does more than treat minor illnesses; frequently medical care keeps us alive. And many people feel that it makes no sense to talk about prices and costs and trade-offs when our very lives are at stake. Surely the importance and sanctity of life itself raises it above the banality of economics and economizing.

Unfortunately, wishing that human life were beyond the pale of economizing does not make it so. Whenever resources are scarce we must make difficult choices. We will conclude the book by sketching out the role that the principles of economic efficiency can play in helping us make the most difficult decisions of all.

Figure 12.5 is a production possibilities curve; its general shape by onw should be very familiar. On the vertical axis we plot consumption per year of live; on the horizontal we plot (average) length of life itself.[8] Let's explore some of the properties of this curve.

First, notice that consumption does not begin at zero but rather at some level which we designated C*. This is the minimum amount of consumption required to stay alive and healthy. Once we have allocated enough resources to produce C*, there is a pool of resources left over; these can be devoted either to more C or to activities which lengthen our lives. Some life-lengthening activities are extremely productive (yield a lot of life-lengthening for not much of a C sacrifice), and some are less productive. Just as we did in defining the production possibilities curve between consumption and leisure (Exercise 6.6) or between current and future consumption (Exercise 7.5) we can rank life-lengthening activities from most productive to least productive. Now, beginning at point * on the production possibilities curve (Figure 12.5), we can hypothetically carry out the possible life-lengthening activities, beginning with the most productive and ending with the least productive. This exercise, just as it has in previous chapters, gives us a bowed-out production possibilities curve.

It is an inescapable fact of life (and death) that we must choose a point on or inside the production possibilities curve. There is no escaping scarcity.

It is probably most useful to think of Figure 12.5 as representing a production possibilities curve for a given individual. And individual consumers, we must choose our favorite point along our own personal production possibilities curves. We choose whether to smoke, whether to wear

---

[8]Notice that the horizontal axis is **average** or expected length of life. We generally do not know when we are going to die. But we all know of actions we can take which improve our prospects for a long life.

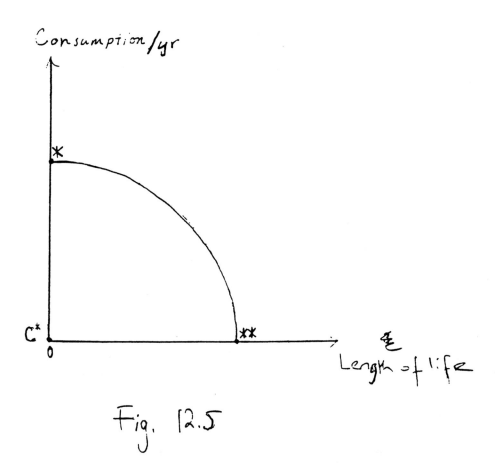

Fig. 12.5

seat belts, whether to eat foods that taste good or are good for us, and how often to get a physical exam. All of these choices represent trade-offs between the quality of life and the expected length of life. Virtually none of us choose the point represented by ** in Figure 12.5; most of us are willing to accept some shortening in our (expected) life spans in exchange for more fun while we are here.

It makes sense to think of individuals as facing production possibilities curves like Figure 12.5. We can spend our income (and our time) on either consumption or life-lengthening activities. We can buy safer cars, smoke alarms, and health foods. We can drive slowly, or even walk to work. We can choose jobs with good safety conditions (other things being equal, safe jobs generally pay less than risky jobs; employers have to pay workers not only to do the job but also to endure the risk of injury or death). Of course, the height of an individual's production possibilities curve depends upon a number of things, including his income. Rich people can afford to buy more consumption and more (expected) length of life.

All we need to do now to depict the consumer's decision is to draw indifference cuves. Let's suppose that a consumer chooses a point like **d** (for demand) in Figure 12.6. The fact that point **d** was chosen indicates that the consumer must have an indifference curve tangent to the production possibilities curve at point **d**; and we have drawn in such a curve.

The slope of the indifference curve is the rate at which the consumer is willing to trade off an additional year of (expected) life for extra consumption per year.

Application to policy

Economics does not tell us the point that any consumer "should" choose on his or her production possibilities curve; that depends upon the shape of the production possibilities curve itself and the preferences of the consumer. But economics does help us to see that the trade-off between length and quality of life is made in the context of the same scarcity of resources as any other trade-off. And as we will see, the notion of economic efficiency enables us to address the question of economic waste, even when the commodity at stake is saving lives. We will see this in Exercise 12.5.

- Exercise 12.5: In Figure 12.5a and b, below, we have drawn two consumers' production possibilities curves, and tangent indifference curves, between length and quality of life. Copy these onto your own paper.

i. We have drawn the two graphs so that at **a**'s tangency the slope is -1/1000, meaning that the consumer would be willing to sacrifice 1 year of expected lifetime in exchange for an extra $1000 of annual consumption. For consumer **b**, the slope is -1/1500. Can you think of a trade that consumers **a** and **b** could make that would make one better of without harming the other?

ii. For this part, ignore any trade you may have been able to devise for part i; return the consumers to the tangency points for the original figure. The government, acting on

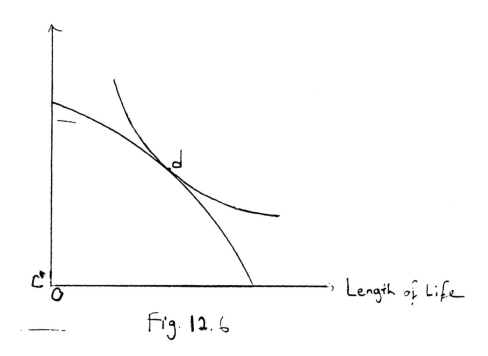

Fig. 12.6

behalf of the consumers, is thinking of spending tax money to increase highway safety. At an annual cost of $1000 per person, highway safety can be increased enough to save 100 lives per year; this in turn increases life expectancy by 0.1 years. Starting from the tangency points in the graph above, trace in the effect of this program for the two consumers. Are they made better off or worse off by the government's action?

iii. Can you devise a rule that the government should obey in deciding whether to undertake actions which increase life expectancy?

In Exercise 12.5i you were confronted with two consumers who had indifference curves of different slopes, at their points of consumption, and you were asked to try to devise a trade between the two that would make them both better off. You know that if the goods were apples and oranges this would be easy (see Exercise 2.2 -2.4). Furthermore, you know that in a market economy such a different-slopes outcome should not happen. Since all consumers face identical price ratios, they will all be driven to points of equal slope on their indifference curves (see Fact 2.2).

But such trades are more difficult to pull off when one of the goods is life expectancy. Suppose I am consumer **a** above, willing to pay $1000 per year for an extra year of life expectancy, and you are **b**, willing to pay $1500. In order to make a deal we must find a way for me to give you part of my life expectancy and you to give me part of your consumption. Frequently, there is simply no practical way to carry out such trades, and we end up in a world in which different people place different values on extending their lives.

But now turn to part ii of the above problem. No consumer is willing to sacrifice more than $1500 in order to secure an additional year of life expectancy; yet the proposed highway-safety program costs $1000 per person in exchange for only a 0.1-year increase in life expectancy. For both of our consumers, this is a bad deal.

There are two ways to see that the highway safety program is a bad deal. The first is what you already noticed in Exercise 12.5ii; neither consumer is willing to pay for it. We can express the same fact in the following way: if either consumer wanted to acquire an extra 0.1 year of life expectancy, he could do so much more cheaply than the $1000 cost of the safety program, simply by sliding along his own production possibilities curve until life expectancy rises by 0.1 years.

If the government decides that increasing life expectancy is a worthwhile public policy, Figure 12.8 tells us that the highway safety program is a bad way to do it; not only does it move consumers to lower indifference curves; it also moves each consumer inside his production possibilities curve.

Finally, it is difficult to find a sound answer to part iii of the Exercise. Different consumers value increasing life expectancy differently, as we saw in part i. Thus different consumers would advise the government differently as to how much public money should be devoted to life-saving. But the principles of economic efficiency do give us considerable guidance; it is economically wasteful for the government to pursue life-saving activity when the cost is higher than any consumer would be willing to pay for an increase in his own life expectancy, and it is wasteful to pursue expensive ways to save lives when there are cheaper ways that have not yet been pursued.

We can see one intriguing application of this principle in the national speed limit. In the aftermath of the 1973 energy crisis, the Federal government imposed a national 55-mile-per-hour speed limit. After the limit was imposed, many people noted that highway deaths declined, and they argued that the reduction in deaths was an additional benefit of the 55-mph speed limit.[9] This argument was frequently cited in opposition to those who wanted to repeal the 55-mph limit after the easing of fuel shortages.

Driving more slowly surely does save lives, and through careful statistical analysis it may be possible to estimate how many lives are saved (but see footnote 8 below). But it also forces us to deive more slowly and therefore use up time which otherwise could be devoted to either leisure or work. To give us some feel for whether the 55-mph limit is an efficient way to save lives, we must compare the lives saved with the time used up. (After all, we could eliminate automobile deaths altogether by banning automobiles).

According to one study, saving one life via the 55-mph limit requires a total of 99 person years of additional driving time. (The estimate itself might be off; that is an issue beyond the scope of this book.) 99 person-years is more than a lifetime, of course. To see that the 55-mph limit is not an efficient way to save lives, all we have to do is perform the following mental experiment: Suppose there was a volunteer organization dedicated to saving lives, presumably by the most efficient means they could find. If this organization had access to 99 person-years of volunteer time, would they be able to save more than one life? If the answer is yes, then it is wasteful to ask Americans to spend an extra 99 years driving to work in order to save one life.

In talking about life-saving activities, we frequently hear public officials say something like, "If it saves even one life, it is worth the cost, whatever the cost." Yet the inescapable fact is that in our private lives we do not live by this maxim. Even when facing life-and-death decisions, there is no escaping the fundamental constraint imposed by scarcity. Since we cannot escape the fact of scarcity, we are left with the task of making difficult choices as efficiently as possible.

Conclusion

Almost all of modern economics rests on the foundation laid down by Adam Smith's monumental An Inquiry into the Nature and Causes of the Wealth of Nations, published in 1776.

---

[9]As an interesting aside, it is not clear that the reduction in highway deaths was actually caused by the reduced speed limit. First, the energy crisis itself reduced the volume of automobile travel. In addition, both cars and highways have been getting safer fairly continuously since World War II.

Fig 12.7

Cons/yr
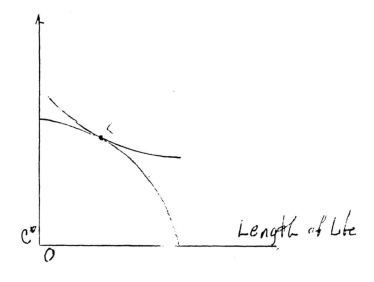

C^0

O   Length of Life

12.7a

Cons/yr
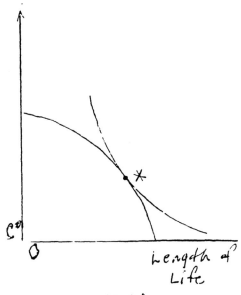

C^0

O

Length of
Life

12.7b

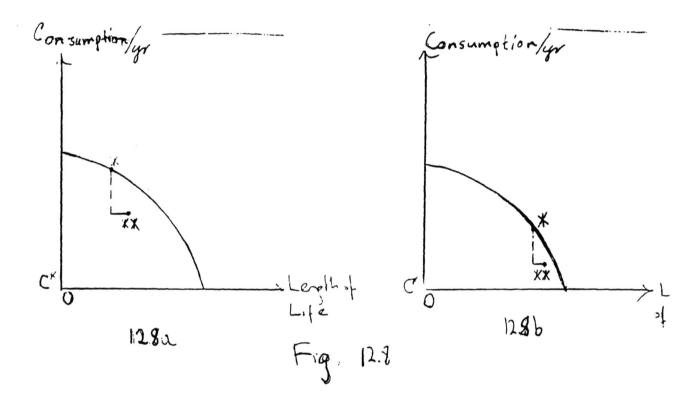

Fig. 12.8

Since Smith's time, economists have learned more and more about the nature of cost and scarcity, and about the ability of the price system to efficiently allocate prices. We have discovered that the price system is a wonderfully elegant and efficient mechanism for allocating resources, despite the fact that (as we have seen in the second half of this book) the price mechanism cannot lead us to economic efficiency in all circumstances.

But in one very important respect, modern economists have not advanced at all beyond the work of Adam Smith. More concisely and elegantly than anybody since his time, Smith compressed the essence of the workings of the price system into the following memorable paragraph:

A1

Appendix:
Budget Constraints, Indifference Curves, and Optimization

We will make heavy use of budget constraints, indifference curves, and tangencies between the two in this book. If you are not already comfortable with these concepts, you can learn about them in this Appendix. If you are familiar with them, you can begin the book in Chapter 1.

Throughout the book, and in the Appendix, we will discuss a world in which there are just two goods, and in the Appendix we will call the goods x_1 and x_2. Clearly there are a lot more than two goods in the world. But the value of discussing the 2-goods case is that we can use graphical analysis, with the y-axis representing x_1 and the x axis representing x_2. Everything we say about an economy with two goods carries over to an economy with many goods. But if we discussed the many-good economy (i.e., x_1, x_2, x_3, x_4, etc.) we would have to use complicated algebra rather than geometry.

Frequently it makes sense to think of x_1 as some specific good, such as food, and x_2 as a catchall good, "everything else."

The Budget Constraint

Figure A1 has x_1 and x_2, the two goods, on its axes. Any point in this graph represents a "bundle" of x_1 and x_2; for example, the point labelled α represents 3 units of x_1 and 2 of x_2.

The **budget constraint** shows which bundles of x_1 and x_2 a specific consumer can afford to buy. Of course, in order to know what our consumer can afford, we need additional information. We must know the consumer's income and we must know the prices of x_1 and x_2.

- Exercise A1: Suppose the price of x_1 is \$1.00 and the price of x_2 is \$2.00. And suppose that the consumer's income is \$20.00.
i. If the consumer buys no x_2 (spends all his income on x_1), how much x_1 can he afford?
ii. There is a general formula which gives the amount of x_1 that a consumer can afford if he spends nothing on the other good. The formula is

$$x_1(\text{max}) \quad = \quad \frac{Y}{p_1}$$

where Y stands for income and p_1 stands for the price of x_1. Does this formula give the same answer you got for this question? Do you see why it makes sense?

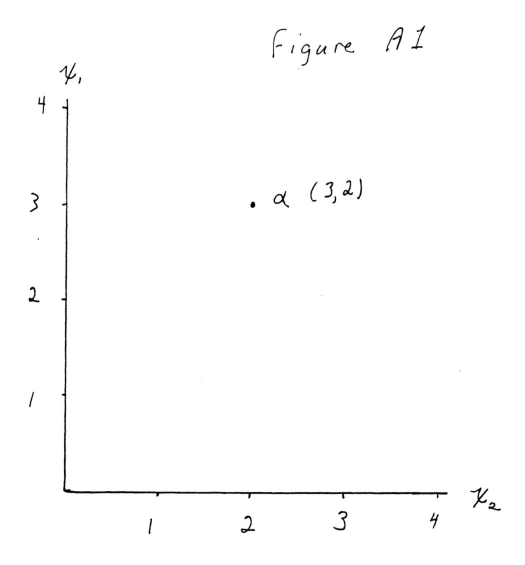

Figure A1

iii.   If the consumer buys no x_1 (spends all his income on x_2), how much x_2 can he afford? (Does the formula, properly modified, work right?)

iv.   Now suppose the consumer buys 2 units of x_1. Calculate how much x_2 he can afford and write the answer in the appropriate cell of Table A1 below.

v.   The budget constraint is found by repeatedly answering problems like the one posed in section iv above. Thus we could ask how much x_2 the consumer can afford if he buys 4, 6, 8 of x_1, and so on. Fill in Table A1 below and plot the results in Figure A1.

Table A1

x_1	0	2	4	6	8	10	12	14	16	18	20
x_2	10					5					0

vi.   Plot all of the x_1;x_2 combinations from Table A1 onto a graph like Figure A1 in the book, and draw a line connecting all of the points. Your graph should look like Figure A2, and the line represents all of the combinations of x_1 and x_2 that the consumer can afford. This line is referred to as the consumer's **budget onstraint**.

The budget constraint is a handy device because, once it is plotted in a graph, we can see at a glance what the consumer can afford. But it seems unhandy to have to fill out a table like Table A1 every time prices or income change. After all, the whole budget constraint changes if income changes or if either of the prices change. Fortunately, with a **little bit** of algebra, we don't have to construct buget constraints by laboriously filling out tables.

We'll refer to the price of x_1 as p_1, and the price of x_2 as p_2. Total expenditure on x_1 is equal to $p_1 \cdot x_1$, and total expenditure on x_2 is $p_2 \cdot x_2$. Now we write down the fact that total expensitue on x_1 plus total expenditure on x_2 must be equal to income[1]

$$p_1 \cdot x_1 + p_2 \cdot x_2 = y \tag{2}$$

This equation simply states that the consumer cannot spend more than his income. Notice that thclcft hand side is the consumer's total expenditure on the two goods, and the right hand side is income, the moe\ney he has to spend on the two goods.

Now, by fairly straightforward algebra, we can rewrite equation (2) as

---

[1]Clearly, total expenditure on x_1 plus x_2 could exceed or fall short of income if the consumer were borrowing or saving. We will deal with borrowing and saving in Chapter 7; for the moment, assume that our consumer spends all his income and no more.

$$x_1 = \frac{y}{p_1} - \frac{p_2}{p_1} \cdot x_2 \qquad\qquad (3)$$

An equation is a factual sentence, where "=" is the verb. Equation (3) is precisely the same sentence as equation (2); you should check to see that this is true. Here are two ways to do it:

- Exercise A2:
i.   Pick any (positive) numbers you want for p_1, p_2, and y. Make a table like Table A1 above, filling in the amount of x_2 the consumer can afford for various amounts of x_1 purchased.
ii.   Plug your values for p_1, p_2, and y into equation (2). Plug in one of your combinations of x_1 and x_2 (from the table you made in part i above) and see whether the equation is "true."
iii. Repeat your work from part ii, but using equation (3).
iv.   Repeat parts ii and iii for several other $(x_1;x_2)$ pairs from your table. Do the answers from the equations always agree with the table?

The reason we go from equation (2) to equation (3) is that equation (3) is particularly easy to plot on a graph like Figure A1.

First, we can see at a glance that if $x_2 = 0$ the consumer can afford y/p_1 of x_1 (if y = 20 and $p_1 = 2$, he can afford 10 units of x_1).[2] Thus, the **vertical-intercept** of the budget constraint is y/p_1. In other words, simply by glancing at the equation for the budget constraint, we can read off the vertical intercept for the graph of the budget constraint. And with not much more work, we can use the equation to tell us what the rest of the graph looks like.

If our consumer should decide to buy some x_2, he will have to cut down on x_1. By how much must he cut x_1 consumption per unit increase in x_2? The answer is given by the price ratio, $(- p_2/p_1)$. You can check this out by continuing with the example from above: $p_2 = 2$ and $p_1 = 1$. Our consumer must cut x_1 **expenditure** by $2 in order to buy one unit of x_2. So **quantity** of x_1 must fall by 2 every time the quantity of x_2 rises by 1.

Let's write this out in symbols. x_1 is going to have to decline by a specific amount; we'll call it Δx_1. And x_2 can rise, by an amount we'll call Δx_2. In the example above, $\Delta x_1 = -2$ when $\Delta x_2 = 1$ (the only way to buy 1 extra unit of x_2 is to reduce x_1 by 2). The ratio, $\Delta x_1/\Delta x_2$, tells us the amount by which x_1 must fall **per unit** increase in x_2.

---

[2]You worked with this formula in Exercise A1.

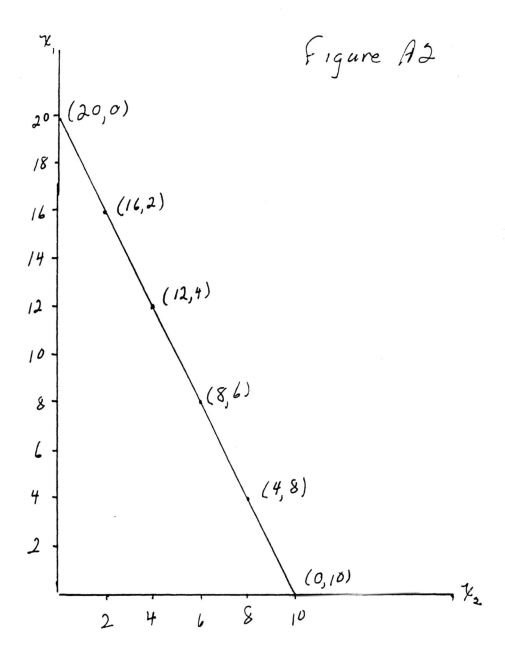

Figure A2

If x_1 were expensive, our consumer wouldn't have to cut consumption of x_1 by very much in order to buy one more unit of x_2.

Now we can put all of this together: The consumer cuts x_1 which frees up some income, which is in turn spent on x_2. First, let's write down the amount of income freed up by cutting x_1:

$$freed\ up\ income\ =\ -\Delta x_1 \cdot p_1 \tag{4}$$

And of course this freed up income can be spent on extra x_2:

$$freed\ up\ income\ =\ \Delta x_2 \cdot p_2 \tag{5}$$

Expression (4) tells the consumer how much extra income he can have by cutting x_1; expression (5) tells him how much extra x_2 he can afford as a result of getting the freed up income.

Now we can simply put the two halves together:

$$-\Delta x_1 \cdot p_1\ =\ \Delta x_2 \cdot p_2 \tag{6}$$

Notice that expression (6) makes perfectly good sense; if the consumer cuts expenditure on x_1 by $-\Delta x_1 \cdot p_1$, he can afford precisely $\Delta x_2 \cdot p_2$ of extra x_2.

Now perform two pieces of algebra: First, divide both sides of expression (6) by Δx_2:

$$\frac{-\Delta x_1 \cdot p_1}{\Delta x_2}\ =\ p_2 \tag{7}$$

Expression (7) is just a synonym for (6); we changed both sides of (6) by the same proportion. Now we're going to do it again; we'll divide both sides of (7) by p_1:

$$\frac{\Delta x_1}{\Delta x_2}\ =\ -\frac{p_2}{p_1}$$

Now after all of this, look again at equation (3). $(-p_2/p_1)$ is the item that gets multiplied by x_2 in the expression.

And this, at last, tells us what we want to know. The left-hand side of (8) is a way of writing the slope of a line (and the line we're working with is the budget constraint). So equation (8) tells us that the slope of the consumer's budget constraint is given by $(-p_2/p_1)$.

This means that we can write a budget constraint in the "form" of equation (3) as soon as we know the consumer's income and the prices of the goods he buys, and immediately see how to plot it in a graph. y/p_1 is the vertical intercept, and $(-p_2/p_1)$ is the slope.

Many students will recognize equation (3) as the equation of a straight line, and indeed the budget constraint is a straight line. Since it is a straight line, we know everything about the budget constraint once we know its vertical intercept and its slope. And we know the vertical intercept and the slope once we know p_1, p_2, and y. In the exercises below we will make up numbers for p_1, p_2, and y, and then plot the resulting budget constraints.

Now that we have the system down, we can plot budget constraints quickly and easily.

- ☆[3]Exercise A3: Suppose Y = 50, p_1 = 5, and p_2 = 2.
i. Make a table like Table A1, and plot the resulting combinations of x_1 and x_2 on a graph like Figure A2. Do you get a straight line? What are the slope and the vertical intercept?
ii. Plug the numbers from this exercise (income and prices) into Equation 3. According to the equation, what is the slope, and what is the intercept, of the consumer's budget constraint?
iii. When you determine the slope and intercept of the budget constraint from the equation, do you get the same answer as you do from the table?

Now that we have developed the budget constraint from both the perspective of algebra and geometry, it is time to back off and remember what the budget constraint is designed to depict. **The budget constraint shows all of the combinations of x_1 and x_2 that the consumer can afford.** And what the consumer can afford changes as income and prices change.

- Exercise A4: Make up whatever values you want for y, p_1 and p_2, and pick an arbitrary combination of goods (x_1 and x_2).
i. Calculate the total cost of your chosen x_1 and your chosen x_2, and check to see whether the consumer can afford the bundle.
ii. Using equation A3, plot the budget constraint on graph paper, and also plot your x_1;x_2 combination from the beginning of this exercise. Is your x_1;x_2 combination inside or outside the budget constraint? Is your answer consistent with what you learned in part i above?
iii. If your consumer **can** afford the bundle (it depends on the values you picked at the beginning of the exercise), calculate how much his income would have to fall in order to

---

[3]As in the main body of the book, a ☆ at the beginning of an exercise means that you might find it easier to do it using a spreadsheet program. But the program is not necessary; all exercises can be done with just a pencil and paper.

make the bundle too expensive for him. Do this both using the "total expenditure" method of part i and the equation you employed in part ii.

iv.   If your consumer **cannot** the bundle you picked above, calculate how much extra income you must give him in order to make it possible for him to buy the bundle.

● Exercise A5: Begin with y = $20, p_1 $1, and p_2 = $2, as in Exercise a1.

i.   Plot the budget constraint. (The easiest way, assuming you have been doing the exercises, is to retrieve your answer from Exercise A1.)

ii.   On the same graph paper, redraw the budget constraint, now assuming that p_2 = $1. The new budget constraint should show that the consumer can afford more goods now that p_2 has fallen; did you get it right?

iii. Leave p_2 $1 and cut income to $10. Plot the new budget constraint, and verify that it makes sense.

iv.   Leave p_2 = $1 and y = $10 (as in part iii above), and now cut p_1 to $0.50. Draw the new budget constraint. (You should have gotten back to the same budget constraint you got in Exercise A1; did you?)

v.   Why does it "make sense" that the answers to Exercise A1v and A5iv are the same?

Indifference curves

A budget constraint enables us to depict the combinations of goods that a consumer can afford. Our next task is to come up with a way to describe what combinations of goods a consumer likes. The device we use to depict an individual's likes and dislikes is the **indifference curve**.

Indifference curves are reflections of consumers' preferences. As with budget constraints, we draw a graph whose axes are x_1 and x_2. Suppose that our consumer currently owns (and plans to consume) the bundle represented by point β in Figure A3. There are likely to be other bundles of x_1 and x_2 which leave the consumer feeling precisely as good as the original bundle β. Suppose for example that an experimenter takes away a certain amount of x_1 (depicted as Δx_1 in figure A3. The experimenter then gives the consumer little increments of x_2 and stops when the consumer says he is as happy with the new bundle as the original, β.[4] The new bundle, call it γ, is on the same **indifference curve** as the original bundle. A patient interviewer could plot out out all of the bundles which leave the consumer as happy as the original bundle β. To sum up, then, an indifference curve shows all of the combinations of x_1 and x_2 which leave the consumer equally happy. Suppose, for example, that a consumer's indifference curve through the bundle β is the curve II in Figure A3. If the consumer were offered any point he wanted, so long as it is on the curve II, he would say, "I don't care which one I get." He is indifferent among all the points on II; that's why we call it an indifference curve.

---

[4]Of course, a smart consumer would lie to the experimenter. But we do not need to concern ourselves with this problem.

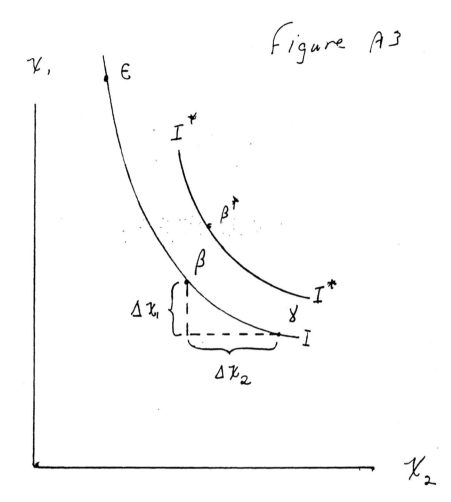

Figure A3

Notice that we built up a consumer's indifference by supposing at the outset that he has bundle β. We might equally well have supposed that he has bundle $\beta*$. By the same method we described above, we can construct (or at least imagine) an indifference curve through point $\beta*$. This curve represents all of the combinations of x_1 and x_2 that leave the consumer as happy as $\beta*$. Let's suppose that for our hypothetical consumer this curve looks like I*I*. Whereas our consumer is indifferent among all points on II, and indifferent among all points on I*I*, it is reasonable to assume that he would rather be at a point (any point) on I*I* than at a point (any point) on II.

If we can draw an indifference curve through β, and another through $\beta*$, then (in principle, if we are patient enough) we should be able to draw an indifference curve through **any** point in Figure A3.

Properties of Indifference Curves

1. **Different people have different indifference curves**. An indifference curve is a description of a person's preferences. The fact that I am indifferent between combinations β and γ in Figure A3 does not mean that you too should be indifferent; we are different people with different personalities and different tastes. Thus the shapes of indifference curves are reflections of individual personalities, and vary from person to person.

Despite the fact that indifference curves are reflections of individual personalities, it is reasonable to expect all consumers' indifference curves to have certain basic properties. We discuss these below.

2. **Indifference curves slope downward**. What would it mean if indifference curves sloped upward, as in Figure A4? It would mean that our consumer is indifferent between bundles like δ and $\delta*$. But this is not very plausible; $\delta*$ represents more of both x_1 and x_2 than δ. So an upward sloping indifference would describe a consumer who is indifferent between a lot of both goods and a little of both goods.[5] For this reason we will assume that all consumers' indifference curves slope downward.

3. **Indifference curves are bowed in toward the origin**. We assume that indifference curves are generally shaped as we have drawn them in Figure A3. Here's the rationale for this assumption: Let's start at a point like β in Figure 3; the consumer has "reasonable" amounts of both x_1 and x_2. If we take away some x_1, we must give back some x_2 to leave the consumer as happy as before. But what happens if we are not at β but at some point like ε. The consumer at ε

---

[5]Such a circumstance might arise; suppose that δ represents all of the x_1 and x_2 I can use; more of both does me no good. In economics we are generally interested in the world of **scarcity**, in which there are not enough goods to fully satisfy our wants. Once we get to the point where indifference curves no longer slope downward, we get to a situation in which scarcity no longer prevails. Such a possibility is beyond the scope of this book.

has a lot of x_1 and hardly any x_2. The thought of losing still more x_2 is very distressing, and the consumer is unwilling to do it unless compensated with a lot of additional x_1. If consumers are more willing to give up goods which they hold in relative abundance, then indifference curves must be bowed in, as in Figure A3. We'll explore this more in Exercise A4.

- Exercise A4: Draw a graph with x_1 and x_2 on the axes, and plot a point like β of Figure A3 (that is, a point which gives the consumer a "reasonable" amount of each good). But don't draw any indifference curves.
  i. Experimentally take away some x_2 from this consumer and give him some x_1, and we will suppose that the Δx_2 and Δx_1 you chose are just enough to leave the consumer as happy as he was at β. So the new point (call it γ) is on the same indifference curve as β.
  ii. Now we'll do it again, only starting at γ: Take away the same amount of x_2 as you did in part i. But now the only way to make the consumer as happy as before is to give him a larger increment of x_1 than you gave him the first time. Why must you give him more x_1 when moving from γ than when moving from β?
  iii. Repeat part ii a few more times, repeatedly taking away equal-sized Δx_2's, and giving ever larger Δx_1's.
  iv. Connect the dots you constructed from this exercise. Did you get an indifference curve roughly the shape of Figure A3?

4. **With x_1 on the vertical axis and x_2 on the horizontal, a relatively steep indifference curve depicts a relatively strong desire for x_2** (the good on the horizontal axis), **and a relatively flat** indifference curve depicts a relatively strong desire for x_1 (the good on the vertical axis).

- Exercise A5: Draw another graph like the one from Exercise A4, with only a point like β. We're now going to plot **two different consumers' indifference curves on the same graph**. It might be easier if you draw them in different colors; we'll call them consumers R (for red) and B (for blue).
  i. Take away some amount Δx_2 from consumer R, just like you did in the beginning of Exercise A4. Consumer R really likes x_1 relative to x_2. How much x_1 must you give R in order to compensate for the loss of Δx_2? Draw in Δx_1 and Δx_2 for Consumer R, and label her point γ.
  ii. Now repeat part i for consumer B. Again begin at β, and take away the same amount, Δx_2 from B as you took from R. But B, unlike R, is an x_2 lover. Draw in the Δx_1 which is necessary to compensate Consumer B for his loss of x_2.
  iii. For both consumer R and consumer B, sketch out the shape of the indifference curve through point β.[6]

In Exercise A5, you should have gotten a graph that looks approximately like Figure A5.

---

[6]You do not know enough about these consumers to know precisely their values of Δx_1, their values of γ, or the shapes of their indifference curves. But you should be able to show how they look **relative to one another**.

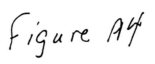

Figure A4

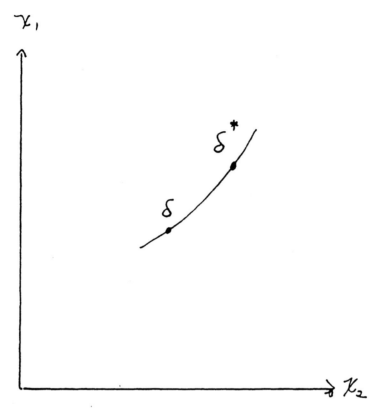

Figure A5

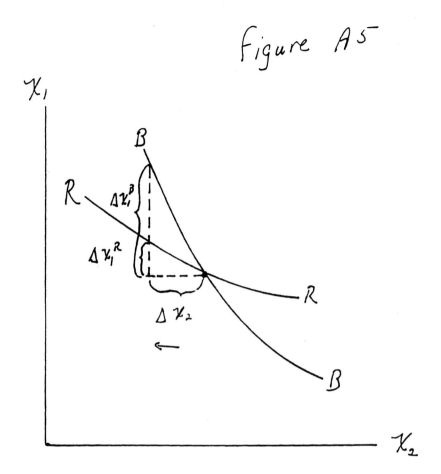

Note: Curve RR should be red;
BB should be blue.

Since B is an x_2 lover, his indifference curve through β is steeper than R's. And for both R and B, their indifference curves get steeper as they move toward the x_1 axis. As they move toward the x_1 axis they become more x_2-deprived; they value x_2 more highly, and their indifference curves become steeper.

5. Each individual consumer has a whole family of indifference curves. For a given consumer, no two indifference curves cross one another.

Remember, indifference curves are depictions of consumers' preferences. We saw above, for example, that a consumer who strongly prefers x_1 has different indifference curves from a consumer who has a strong preference for x_2. We assume that an individual consumer's indifference curves do not cross one another for a simple reason: A consumer whose indifference curves did cross one another would be a very strange person. To see this, look at Figure A6, which purports to show two indifference curves for a given individual.

- Exercise A6: Looking at Figure A6, you can see that point δ represents more of both x_1 and x_2 than does point γ.
 i. So any reasonable consumer prefers point δ to point γ. Doesn't this make sense?
 ii. Now, looking at indifference curve II, which point does our consumer prefer, point δ or point β?
 iii. Shifting your attention to indifference curve I*I*, which point does our consumer prefer, point γ or β?
 iv. Describe the logical contradiction among the answers to parts i, ii, and iii.

As we will see throughout the book, indifference curves are a very useful concept for economists. The reason is as follows: If a consumer prefers to be on a higher, rather than a lower, indifference curve, we can easily describe and analyze a consumer's economic agenda:

- **Each consumer goes to the highest indifference curve he or she can afford; that is, the highest indifference curve that is not beyond the reach of the budget constraint.**

Utility Maximization

Almost all of us wish we could afford more goods and services, but because of our limited incomes, we must make difficult choices among many desirable products. Budget constraints characterize the limits we face, and indifference curves depict our preferences among various consumption bundles.

Figure A7 depicts a consumer who can afford any combination of x_1 and x_2 which is on or below the line BB (the budget constraint). Now look at the indifference curve labelled II. Our consumer cannot afford to buy the bundle labelled * on this indifference curve. But that's OK; he can afford point # (it's inside the budget constraint), and since it's on the same indifference curve it makes him just as happy as *.

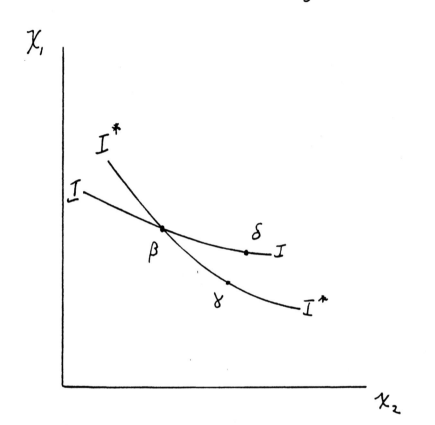

Figure A6

Our consumer can afford to get to indifference curve II. But you can see that there is a higher indifference curve within reach. If he chooses his bundle very carefully he can reach indifference curve I'I', by selecting point ☺. This point is the consumer's best choice; there is no other point which he both prefers and can afford.

Different consumers have different budget constraints (some are rich; some are poor) and different maps of indifference curves (some like x_1; some like x_2). But all consumers will end up at points that look basically like ☺ in Figure A7.

The fundamental feature of point ☺ is that the indifference curve is **tangent** to the budget constraint. If you look at the graph, you can see that this tangency ensures that there is no higher indifference curve which touches the budget constraint. In other words, once we have found a tangency between a budget constraint and an indifference curve, we have found the consumer's optimal choice of goods.

Of course, if the indifference curve and the budget constraint are tangent to one another, then at that point of tangency they have the same slope. And it is useful to write this fact down as an equation:

$$\frac{\Delta x_1}{\Delta x_2} = -\frac{p_2}{p_1} \tag{9}$$

(*slopeofindifferencecurve*) = (*slopeofbudgetconstraint*)

The left-hand side, $\Delta x_1/\Delta x_2$, is just an expression for the slope of an indifference curve (the rise over the run). The right hand side, $-p_2/p_1$, is the slope of the budget constraint (see equation A3 and the discussion that follows it). We will make frequent use of equation (9) in the text; it turns out to be an extremely informative way to describe the behavior of consumers.

Demand Curves

Look at Figure A8. It shows the quantity of x_1 (on the x axis) that a consumer will purchase at various levels of the price of the good, p_1 (shown on the y axis). The curve shows that the lower is the price, the more x_1 the consumer chooses to buy. This relationship is called a **demand curve**.

Now look again at Figure A7. This graph already shows us how much x_1 (and how much x_2) the consumer will buy for a given value of p_1 (and a given value of p_2 and y). In other words, the question answered in the demand curve is already answered in the tangency between a consumer's budget constraint and indifference curve. The demand curve is just a handy way of summarizing the information contained in the budget constraint/indifference graph.

Figure A7

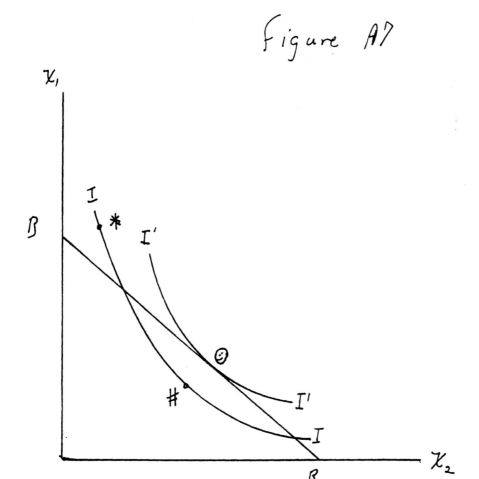

Figure A8

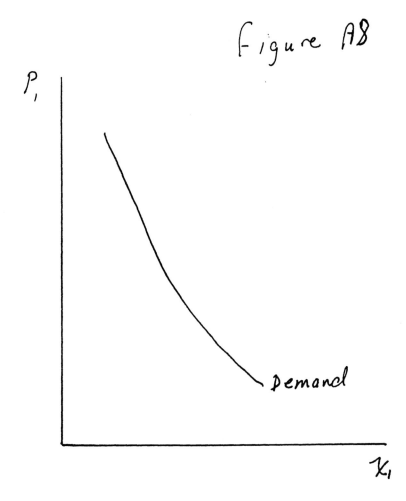

P_1

Demand

x_1

- Exercise A7: On a piece of graph paper, draw a budget constraint for the following values: $p_1 = \$1$; $p_2 = \$1$; $y = \$20$. Draw your graph big enough that you will be able to depict $x_1 = 40$ and $x_2 = 20$.
i. Draw an indifference curve tangent to this budget constraint, and indicate the utility-maximizing values of x_1 and x_2.
ii. Draw a new graph with p_1 on the vertical axis and x_1 on the horizontal. (draw the axes such that p_1 can range from 0 to 2, and x_1 from 0 to 20). On this graph, plot the point $\{p_1 = 1; x_1 = $ whatever you got in part i above$\}$. This is one point on your consumer's demand curve.
iii. Now let p_1 fall to $\$0.50$ (leaving p_2 and y at their original levels), and draw the new budget constraint in your original graph.
iv. Now draw an indifference curve tangent to this new budget constraint, taking care to obey all of the rules of indifference curves (in particular, don't let this indifference curve touch or cross the first one).
    a. Back when p_1 was $\$1$, could the consumer afford this higher indifference curve?
    b. Can he afford it now that $p_1 = \$0.50$?
    c. Is this new indifference curve the highest one he can afford (at $p_1 = \$0.50$)?
v. Draw the combination of x_1 and x_2 that the consumer buys now that p_1 has fallen to $\$0.50$.
vi. On your second graph (the one with p_1 and x_1 on the axes) draw the point $\{p_1 = \$0.50; x_1 = $ whatever you found in part v$\}$. This is another point on the consumer's demand curve; do you see why?
vii. Now plot the point on the demand curve corresponding to $p_1 = \$2$. As above, you will have to work first with the budget-constraint/indifference-curve graph and then the demand-curve graph.

- Exercise A8. Redo all of Exercise A7, but this time set $y = \$10$. Do you get the same demand curve? Why or why not?

- Exercise A9: Once again redo Exercise A7, with $y = \$20$, but with $p_2 = \$2$. Do you get the same demand curve as in either Exercise A7 or A8? Why or why not?

In Exercises A7-A9 you should have seen the following:

1. A demand curve presents the same information as appears in a budget-constraint/indifference-curve graph; however the demand curve emphasizes the relationship between the demand for a good and the price of that good.

2. The shape of a demand curve depends on a consumer's preferences; if you had drawn the indifference curves differently in Exercise A7 (but still consistent with the rules) you would have gotten a different demand curve. Thus different consumers have different demand curves.

3. The demand curve for x_1 (or for any good) changes whenever the consumer's income changes, and also whenever the prices of other goods change.

Figure A8

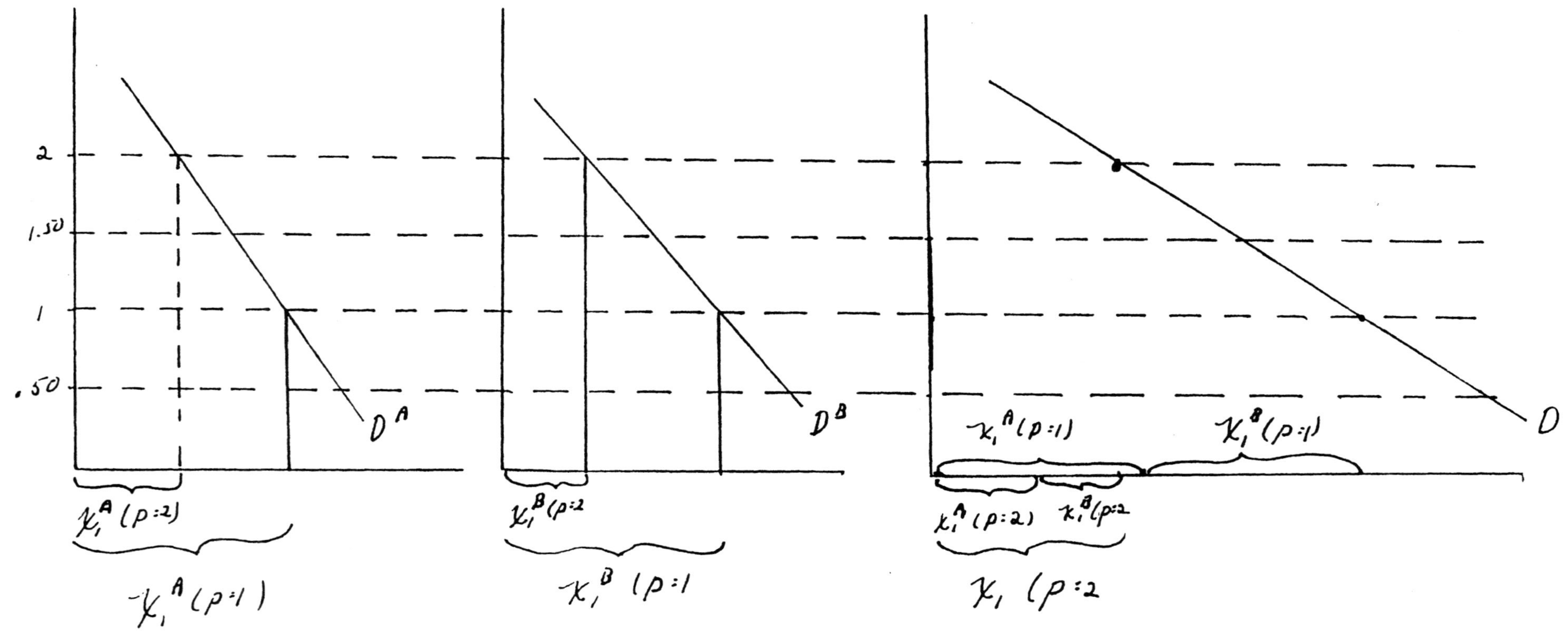

2
1.50
1
.50
D^A
D^B
D
χ1^A (p=2)
χ1^A (p=1)
χ1^B (p=2
χ1^B (p=1
χ1^A (p=1)
χ1^B (p=1)
χ1^A (p=2)
χ1^B (p=2
χ1 (p=2

4. **Almost**[7] inevitably, demand curves slope downward, reflecting the fact that consumers buy more of a good when its price is low than when it is high.

Market Demand Curves

In Exercises A7-A9 you took basic information about **an individual** consumer (budget constraints and indifference curves) and generated demand curves **for that consumer**. But many times in economics we don't care about the shape of an individual consumer's demand curve; we want to know the relationship between the price of a good and the total quantity demanded by all consumers in the economy. Manufacturers, for example, are much more interested in the effect of a price cut on total sales than the effect of the same price cut on sales to an individual consumer.

Fortunately, the link between individual consumers' demand curves (like the ones you derived in Exercises A7-A9) and market demand curves is very straightforward: Once we have individual demand curves, we can simply add them up to get market demand curves. We'll do that in Exercise A10:

- Exercise A10: Begin with three pairs of axes on graph paper; for each the vertical axis is p_1 and the horizontal is x_1. The units should be the same size on all three graphs, and the x axis should be approximately twice as long on the third as on the first two. On each vertical axis indicate p_1 running from 0 to about 3.
i. On each of the frist two graphs draw a downward-sloping demand curve. They need not be the same as one another. Label these Demand Curve A (for Consumer A) and Demand Curve B (for Consumer B) respectively.
ii. If $p_1 = 2$, show the amount of x_1 that consumer A will buy (on your first graph) and the amount of x_1 that consumer B will buy, on your second graph. On the third graph plot the total amount of x_1 that **both** consumers will buy, if $p_1 = 2$.
iii. Now repeat step ii under the new assumption that $p_1 = 1.50$.
iv. Repeat step ii once again, under the assumption that $p_1 = 1$.
v. In steps 2, 3, and 4 you should have plotted three points on the market demand curve (assuming there are only two consumers in the market).

Your answers to Exercise A10 should look something like Figure A9; each point on your market demand curve is the sum of the amounts demanded by the two consumers. Obviously, if the market has more than two consumers, we simply add up more than two demand curves to get the market demand curve.

---

[7]It is possible to draw a set of indifference curves (consistent with the rules of indifference curves) which will generate an upward-sloping demand curve, but it is quite implausible. And in reality economists have found no credible evidence that upward sloping demand curves really exist. If you want, you can return to Exercise A7 and try to draw indifference curves which cause demand for x_1 to rise when p_1 rises. You should be able to do it. But you should also see that you have to draw rather strange-looking (though still within the rules) indifference curves.